The Politics of Migration
and Immigration in Europe

Sage Politics Texts

Series Editor
IAN HOLLIDAY
City University of Hong Kong

SAGE Politics Texts offer authoritative and accessible analyses of core issues in contemporary political science and international relations. Each text combines a comprehensive overview of key debates and concepts with fresh and original insights. By extending across all main areas of the discipline, SAGE Politics Texts constitute a comprehensive body of contemporary analysis. They are ideal for use on advanced courses and in research.

The Politics of Migration and Immigration in Europe

Andrew Geddes

SAGE Publications
London • Thousand Oaks • New Delhi

First published 2003

 SAGE Publications Ltd
6 Bonhill Street
London EC2A 4PU

SAGE Publications Inc.
2455 Teller Road
Thousand Oaks, California 91320

SAGE Publications India Pvt Ltd
B-42, Panchsheel Enclave
Post Box 4109
New Delhi 110 017

British Library Cataloguing in Publication data

A catalogue record for this book is available
from the British Library

ISBN 978-0-7619-5669-3

Library of Congress Control Number: 2002107096

Typeset by C&M Digitals (P) Ltd., Chennai, India

Summary of Contents

Contents

List of Tables

Figure

Acknowledgements

A number of debts have been incurred while writing this book. The first is to the Robert Schuman Centre for Advanced Studies at the European University Institute in Florence, Italy, where I spent 1997–98 as a Jean Monnet fellow in the European Forum on international migration. The book was then completed during a second stay as a Schuman Centre Visiting Fellow between July 2001 and January 2002. I am very grateful to Professors Yves Mény, Helen Wallace, Christian Joppke and René Leboutte for these opportunities. Professors Stephen Padgett and John Corner in the School of Politics and Communication Studies at Liverpool University offered invaluable support for which I am very appreciative. Special words of thanks are due to Adrian Favell, Richard Gillespie, Heather Grabbe, Virginie Guiraudon, Sandra Lavenex, and Maarten Vink who took the time to read parts of the manuscript. I'd also like to thank Maria Baganha, Roland Bank, Michael Bommes, John Crowley, Romain Garbaye, Robert Geyer, Elspeth Guild, James Hollifield, Dora Kostakopoulou, Marco Martiniello, David Richards, Shamit Saggar, Michael Samers, Yasemin Soysal, Paul Statham, Emek Uçarer and Joanne Van Selm. Any errors, oversights or omissions are, of course, my responsibility. I am grateful to the series editor, Ian Holliday and to Lucy Robinson at Sage for bearing with this seemingly never-ending project. As always, I am thankful for the support offered by my family. My greatest debt is to Federica, to whom this book is dedicated with love.

1

Analysing the Politics of Migration and Immigration in Europe

In one week in March 2002 international migration in its various forms once again hit the headlines across Europe. To give some examples: the Italian government was considering declaring a state of emergency in response to the arrival at the Sicilian port of Catania of a boat with 928 Kurds on board amidst concerns that more people could soon arrive on Italian territory. Lebanon, Syria and Turkey were identified as being at the centre of human trafficking networks sending people to European countries with calls from EU member states for stricter controls in these countries. Meanwhile, the leading German political parties at federal and regional level were engaged in discussions about new legislation that would for the first time put a regulated immigration system in place in that country to attract and integrate skilled workers in the belief that this would help the German economy to remain competitive. In Central and South America, tens of thousands of people of Spanish origin were reported to be mobilising via the internet in a campaign to be granted the citizenship of the country of their ancestors. At the same time, a report in the Netherlands on Muslim schools claimed that 5 of the 32 state sponsored Muslim schools were funded by Islamic fundamentalist organisations, although the claim was rejected by the schools and by the government minister responsible for immigrant integration as anti-Muslim hysteria. In southern Europe, the new Portuguese coalition government pledged more restrictive immigration policies. While in northern Europe, the company responsible for the channel tunnel between Britain and France demanded written confirmation from the French train operator, SNCF, that every train had been checked for asylum seekers following countless incidents of asylum seekers being discovered on trucks and trains going to the UK. Finally, in the UK the chief executive of the UK Commission for Racial Equality was reported as calling for stronger efforts to ensure that people from different ethnic groups lived alongside each other in northern English towns that had become divided on ethnic grounds and where there had been civil unrest in the summer of 2001. The UK government was also pushing ahead with the recruitment of high skilled migrants while discussing reforms of citizenship legislation that could include loyalty oaths for immigrant newcomers.

These examples provide a snapshot of what can be called the conceptual and geo-political widening of the migration issue in contemporary Europe. In conceptual terms, there are new types of migration and new forms of state and international response to this movement. In geo-political terms, the impact of international migration has widened from western Europe to include newer immigration countries in southern, central and eastern Europe. International migration is also part of the relations between European countries and surrounding states and regions.

This book analyses this migration and responses to it. What is the basis for this analysis? The focus could be placed on the ways in which international migration 'challenges' these nation states. In these terms, international migration in its various forms challenges organisational and conceptual boundaries, borders, important forms of social organisation, such as the welfare state, as well as ways of thinking about 'us' and 'them'. International migration is then understood as an independent variable that can help explain various social and political changes in European countries.

Is this an entirely satisfactory way to approach the issues? This book argues that it can be equally – if not more – useful to reverse the analytical focus and explore the ways in which institutions and organisations within European countries, as well as changed relations between European states, play a key role in producing and shaping understandings of international migration. For instance, whether international migration in its various forms is seen as 'good' in the sense that it offers economic benefits or as 'bad' as a drain on resources is very dependent on the view of international migration taken by organisations in receiving societies. In such terms, these views are more to do with decisions made within organisations than they are a result of the personality or character of individual migrants. By reversing the analytical focus in this way, we can account for the ways in which the world-views of institutions and organisations shape perceptions of international migration and migrants. International migration can thus be understood as a dependent variable the understanding of which is shaped to a considerable extent by institutions and organisations in receiving states, as well as by relations between these states.

The role of welfare states and the relationship of migrants to these welfare states in European countries helps illustrate this point. Welfare states play an important part in mediating the relationship between individuals and society and generating inclusion and exclusion. This has been particularly so in the longer-standing immigration countries of western Europe. Welfare state pressures, changes in welfare state organisation and changed welfare state ideologies have had important effects on the categorisation of migrants. For instance, as the numbers of asylum seekers grew in the 1990s there was pressure to place asylum applicants outside of what can be called the community of legitimate receivers of welfare state benefits because of the view that many of the claims were unfounded (Bommes and Geddes, 2000). In this case, it's not so much the personality or character of asylum seekers that matters, but rather the ways in which they are viewed by institutions and organisations in the countries to which they move. The EU's role provides a further illustration of the ways in which changes in the institutions and organisations of European countries shape perceptions of international migration. European integration is state sovereignty-altering mainly through the market integration that it seeks to promote and a device for the attainment of immigration and asylum policy objectives by its member states. European integration has important effects on the production of 'good' and 'bad' types of international migration – to be encouraged or restricted – that have less to do with the character of migrants than with the ways in which international migration is viewed by state and supranational decision-makers.

By developing the analysis in this way responses to international migration can be linked to more general changes in European nation states and relations between them with these changes then helping to shape understandings at elite and popular level of the various forms of international migration. On this basis, it is possible to develop a sociologically richer analysis of international migration if we analyse the role that organisations and institutions in European countries and at supranational level play in structuring perceptions of international migration. As such, international migration can be explored as one factor that impinges upon the political sociology of the nation state in an integrating Europe. But just because immigration is the subject of this book does not mean that it is the only factor that has these effects. Rather, analysis of the politics of migration and immigration in Europe needs to be placed in the context of more general changes affecting European nation states both internally – welfare state and labour market changes, for instance – and resulting from international engagements such as European integration.

Analytical themes

While the history of European countries is entwined with the history of the movement of people within, from and between them, this migration history has not become part of national self-understanding for European countries in the way that it was for settler societies such as Australia and the United States. European countries have tended to view international migration rather nervously as challenging their territorial, organisational and conceptual boundaries; to their ways of thinking about themselves and others. This introductory chapter introduces three themes that help develop these points and that will then be the basis for the comparative analysis in the chapters that follow: immigration policies, immigrant policies (see also Hammar, 1985), and the impact of European integration.

Immigration policies are analysed in relation to types of migration rather than to an undifferentiated notion of 'immigration'. Some forms of international migration such as by high skilled workers are often encouraged and facilitated. European countries have shown an increased interest in labour migration since the late 1990s in a bid to overcome skills shortages and counter the effects of an ageing population. Other forms, such as asylum-seeking migration and migration defined by state policies as illegal, have become increasingly unwanted and the subject of restrictive policies. These categorisations highlight the capacity of states to categorise migrants, on this basis to then attempt to regulate international migration, as well as to develop international co-operation that can facilitate the attainment of these tasks.

The EU's developing migration policy role is particularly significant in an international context. But this role should not be exaggerated as, for instance, somehow signifying the redundancy of European states. European co-operation and integration on immigration and asylum have facilitated the attainment of restrictive immigration policies rather than necessarily signifying a loss of control. Although the nature of relations between them has been changed in important ways by supranational European integration these European nation states display considerable resilience.

The chapter then addresses immigrant policies. These concern themselves with the ways in which European countries respond to immigration-related diversity. Immigrant policies mark some attempt to reframe the conceptual and organisational boundaries of a given community with the capacity then to include or exclude newcomers. If we understand these societies as both structures and actors then as structures we are interested in their organisational characteristics while as actors we pay attention to the ideas that animate these practices. The ways in which these organisations view the world plays an important part in the production of migrant categories and thus shapes responses to international migration in its various forms. Organisational practices are typically concerned with procedures governing legal residence and the rights associated with this status; naturalisation and nationality laws; access to the labour market and welfare state (health care, education etc.); political rights; anti-discrimination laws; and policies that can seek to promote, preserve or protect aspects of immigrants' cultural identity. In turn, these are informed by and generate ideas about membership and belonging. If a central aspect of political activity is the attempt to control shared meaning, then debates about immigration's effects on European countries are good examples of conflict over the concepts used in framing political judgements on social problems and public policies (Edelman, 1988).

The term 'immigrant integration' is widely employed to refer to the desired end-state of these policies. The term is problematic because it raises the rather obvious questions of 'from what?', 'into what?', and 'by whom?'. An air of compulsion and forced adaptation hangs over this process, although conservatives would tend to require adaptation to host society norms by immigrant newcomers. For this reason and others the term has been described as a 'treacherous metaphor' because it rests on an allusion to the mathematical process of building a whole number without being clear about the components of the whole into which newcomers are supposed to 'integrate' (Banton, 2001).

Despite this, there has been a reassertion of policies that emphasise socio-economic integration that place more onus on immigrants to adapt. Sweden and the Netherlands, for instance, moved since the 1980s from their own versions of identity-affirming multicultural policies to approaches that emphasised language training and education as ways of encouraging fuller participation by immigrants in these societies. The UK government's 2002 White Paper on migration and citizenship spoke of 'integration with diversity' and sought to re-open a debate about the importance of common values, the need for newcomers to speak English and allegiance oaths for new citizens (Home Office, 2002).

Changes in background institutional conditions are highly relevant. The assertion of nationalistic or communitarian values can lead to an emphasis on protecting a given community in either ethno-cultural or welfarist terms. This can then justify the exclusion of newcomers if they are viewed as in some way 'bogus' or 'abusive'. This is far less likely to be linked to some personality flaw in these people than to the ways in which they are viewed by the organisations of the receiving country. If these organisations are under more general pressures then this can lead to demands to demarcate a boundary that excludes immigrant newcomers. This then requires a rationale for exclusion. That these people are abusing the system is just such a rationale.

A recurring theme throughout the book will be the ways in which welfare state pressures and changed welfare state ideologies have affected the perception of migrants and their descendants in European countries, both in relation to those forms of migration that are supported – skilled labour migration that could help save the welfare state, apparently – and those that are rejected – asylum seeking migration that is portrayed as a drain on resources. On the former point, new immigration has been highlighted as necessary to overcome the effects of Europe's ageing population. On the latter, forms of welfare state chauvinism with regards to unwanted migrants have become a feature of anti-immigration politics in Europe. This can lead to pressures to defend the borders of the national welfare state.

The policy reference to 'integration' and the attempt to establish shared meaning and frame political judgements in these terms also applies to newer immigration countries too, as marked, for instance, in the reports by the Italian government's commission on immigration integration (Zincone, 2000, 2001). As the EU expands to include central and eastern European countries then minority rights also become a salient concern. There are between 8 and 10 million Roma in central and eastern European countries who have encountered systematic discrimination dating back for centuries. The protection of minority rights is a political pre-condition for EU membership while the EU has introduced anti-discrimination legislation applying to race, ethnicity and religion that must become part of the law of all member states by 2003 and be included into national law by any country that wishes to be an EU member.

The third of this chapter's themes is European integration. European integration could be seen as in some sense eroding these national societies. This book will test the extent to which the politics of migration and immigration in Europe have been influenced in shape, form and content by European integration. Is it possible to identify a distinct *European* politics of migration and immigration influenced by supranational law and politics?

On the face of it, this does not appear to be too extravagant a claim given that 15 European countries have voluntarily pooled their sovereignty (soon likely to expand to include as many as 28 countries), that the free movement of people has been one of the EU's central aspirations, that this has immigration and asylum implications, and that a form of EU citizenship has been created. In such a situation it would appear misguided to characterise European migration politics as the juxtaposition of diverse and/or competing national exceptionalisms.

It would, however, be equally misguided to blithely assume that the EU is locked into a path heading inexorably towards some kind of United States of Europe with common migration policies in a post-national, Euro-federal polity. For one thing, national modes of immigration politics are well entrenched. For another, European integration is far more contingent than teleological, federalising perspectives would suggest. And for another, member states have so far held the upper hand in matters relating to immigration and asylum. It can be more useful to conceptualise the EU as a regional bloc of rather resilient nation states that have moved towards a highly developed form of market integration that extends a (limited) package of rights to their citizens under the banner of EU citizenship while also building barriers between themselves and surrounding states and regions.

The EU's supranationality is its key and defining feature. Supranational institutions independent of the member states have been created with the capacity to make and implement laws that bind participating states. At the same time, the EU is essentially hybrid in the sense that it rests on a balance between intergovernmentalism expressed through the Council of Ministers and European Council and supranationalism in the forms of the Commission, European Court of Justice and European Parliament.

The effects of European integration on the member states also need to be explored, as well as the reasons for the shift to European co-operation and integration. We can thus distinguish between the *institutionalisation of Europe* and the *Europeanisation of institutions*. This Europeanisation of institutions is more marked in some areas than others. European integration has proceeded with most vigour in areas linked to single market integration. Key in this respect has been provision for free movement for EU citizens within the single market (intra-EU migration). It has proceeded more cautiously in those areas closely linked to state sovereignty such as immigration and asylum (extra-EU migration). The effects of European integration are then likely to be variable in relation to (i) those areas that have become EU competencies and (ii) the relation between these competencies and laws, policies, politics and collective identities in member states, as well as in surrounding states and regions that can also be affected (Lavenex and Uçarer, 2002).

Before embarking on these considerations of immigration and immigrant policies we first step back to investigate the object and subjects of this book more closely: international migration and migrants. Why do people move? How has this movement of people between states become embedded in migration systems? How have European states categorised migrants and what effects do these categorisations have on distinctions between 'wanted' and 'unwanted' forms of international migration?

Why do people move? Explaining mobility and immobility

The term international migration might seem relatively straightforward: movement by people across state borders that leads to permanent settlement. This movement is then viewed by receiving states as immigration. It is in these terms – as immigration and permanent settlement in a political universe of nation states – that the politicisation of these issues has occurred across Europe. But it is not as straightforward as this. There are, in fact, many types of movement by people that cross state frontiers and each are 'capable of metamorphosing into something else through a set of processes which are increasingly institutionally driven. What we then choose to define as migration is an arbitrary decision, and may be time-specific' (Dobson et al., 2001: 25). Migration can be short-term or long-term. Migrants could live in one country and work in another. There can also be movement back and forth between sending and receiving countries. The categorisations of migrants by state policies plays a key role in defining those forms of migration that become viewed as policy problems.

Given its many and diverse forms, migration experts highlight the difficulty of specifying what actually is meant by the term international migration. While at a basic level, international migration can be defined as permanent or semi-permanent movement by people across state borders, the growth of short-term, rotation or contract migration shows how the distinction between permanent and temporary becomes blurred. So too does the distinction between economic migration (presumed voluntary) and asylum (presumed involuntary). The categories 'voluntary labour migrant' and 'forced refugee' are defined from the vantage point of receiving states and can be redefined by these states. Are people who leave countries because of unemployment and poverty voluntary or forced migrants? Voluntarism would be the supposition in receiving countries. This legitimates restriction on this migration viewed as a disguised form of economic migration. Faist (2000: 23) argues that if we change the perspective and try to think from the point of view of the migrant then the voluntary/involuntary distinction is better viewed as a continuum reflective of the varying degrees of choice or freedom available.

If the term international migration is unclear then there are likely to be some difficulties putting in place policies to establish authoritative capacity to manage and regulate it. Governments make claims to be able to plan, regulate and even control international migration. It is politically important that they do this because these issues relate very strongly to their ability to regulate access to the national territory and thus to an important aspect of their sovereign authority. But by doing so, governments assume that the phenomena associated with international migration are relatively knowable, to some extent predictable and thus manageable. The assumption appears to be that the policy environment is relatively stable and that states possess the policy tools that enable them to manage and regulate this migration. Yet, more often than not, migration policy can seem more like muddling along in the face of unpredictable migration pressures within institutional settings that do not always facilitate the translation of policy objectives into policy outcomes (Sciortino, 2000).

Words such as flooding, swamping and invasion can enter the anti-immigration vernacular, frame debates about international migration, and prompt the perception of international migration as a threat to security, welfare or internal social cohesion (Huysmans, 2000). Tables 1.1, 1.2 and 1.3

TABLE 1.1 Inflows of foreign populations into selected European countries, 1990–99 (thousands)

	1990	1991	1992	1993	1994	1995	1996	1997	1998	1999
Belgium	50.5	54.1	55.1	53.0	56.0	53.1	51.9	49.2	50.7	57.8
Denmark	15.1	17.5	16.9	15.4	15.6	33.0	24.7	20.4	21.3	–
Finland	6.5	12.4	10.4	10.9	7.6	7.3	7.5	8.1	8.3	7.9
France	102.4	109.9	116.6	99.2	91.5	77.0	75.5	102.4	138.1	104.4
Germany	824.4	920.5	1207.6	986.9	774.0	788.3	708.0	615.3	605.5	673.9
Greece	–	–	–	–	–	–	–	–	38.2	
Hungary	37.2	23.0	15.1	16.4	12.8	13.2	12.8	12.2	12.3	15.0
Ireland	–	–	–	–	13.3	13.6	21.5	23.5	20.8	21.6
Italy	–	–	–	–	–	–	–	–	111.0	268.0
Luxembourg	9.3	10.0	9.8	9.2	9.2	9.6	9.2	9.4	10.6	11.8
Netherlands	81.3	84.3	83.0	87.6	68.4	67.0	77.2	76.7	81.7	78.4
Norway	15.7	16.1	17.2	22.3	17.9	16.5	17.2	22.0	26.7	32.2
Portugal	–	–	13.7	9.9	5.7	5.0	3.6	3.3	6.5	10.5
Sweden	53.2	43.9	39.5	54.8	74.7	36.1	29.3	33.4	35.7	34.6
United Kingdom	–	–	203.9	190.3	193.6	206.3	216.4	236.9	258.0	276.9

Source: OECD SOPEMI Report 2001: 278

TABLE 1.2 Inflows of Asylum seekers into selected European countries, 1991–2000 (thousands)

	1991	1992	1993	1994	1995	1996	1997	1998	1999	2000
Austria	27.3	16.2	4.7	5.1	5.9	7.0	6.7	13.8	20.1	18.3
Belgium	15.4	17.6	26.5	14.7	11.7	12.4	11.8	22.1	35.8	42.7
Bulgaria	–	–	–	–	–	–	–	–	1.3	1.8
Czech Republic	2.0	0.9	2.2	1.2	1.4	2.2	2.1	4.1	7.2	8.8
Denmark	4.6	13.9	14.3	6.7	5.1	5.9	5.1	5.7	6.5	10.1
Finland	2.1	3.6	2.0	0.8	0.8	0.7	1.0	1.3	3.1	3.2
France	47.4	28.9	27.6	26.0	20.4	17.4	21.4	22.4	30.9	38.6
Germany	256.1	438.2	322.6	127.2	127.9	116.4	104.4	98.6	95.1	78.6
Greece	2.7	2.0	0.8	1.3	1.4	1.6	4.4	2.6	1.5	3.1
Hungary	–	–	–	–	–	–	1.1	7.4	11.5	7.8
Ireland	–	–	0.1	0.4	0.4	1.2	3.9	4.6	7.7	10.9
Italy	26.5	6.0	1.6	1.8	1.7	0.7	1.9	11.1	33.4	18.0

(Continued)

TABLE 1.2 Continued

	1991	1992	1993	1994	1995	1996	1997	1998	1999	2000
Luxembourg	0.2	0.1	0.2	0.2	0.2	0.3	0.4	1.6	2.9	0.6
Netherlands	21.6	20.3	35.4	52.6	29.3	22.9	34.4	45.2	42.7	43.9
Norway	4.6	5.2	12.9	3.4	1.5	1.8	2.3	8.5	10.2	10.8
Poland	–	–	–	0.6	0.8	3.2	3.5	3.4	3.0	4.4
Portugal	0.2	0.5	1.7	0.6	0.3	0.2	0.3	0.3	0.3	0.2
Romania	–	–	–	–	–	–	–	–	1.7	1.4
Slovak Republic	–	–	–	–	–	–	–	–	0.9	1.5
Spain	8.1	11.7	12.6	12.0	5.7	4.7	5.0	6.8	8.4	7.2
Sweden	27.4	84.0	37.6	18.6	9.0	5.8	9.6	12.5	11.2	16.3
United Kingdom	73.4	32.3	28.0	42.2	55.0	37.0	41.5	58.0	91.2	97.9

Source: OECD SOPEMI Report 2001: 280

TABLE 1.3 Stocks of foreign population in selected European countries (thousands and percentages)

	1990	1991	1992	1993	1994	1995	1996	1997	1998	1999
Austria	456.1	532.7	623.0	689.6	713.5	723.5	728.2	732.7	737.3	748.2
% of total population	5.9	6.8	7.9	8.6	8.9	9.0	9.0	9.1	9.1	9.2
Belgium	904.5	922.5	909.3	920.6	922.3	909.8	911.9	903.2	892.0	897.1
% of total population	9.1	9.2	9.0	9.1	9.1	9.0	9.0	8.9	8.7	8.8
Denmark	160.6	169.5	180.1	189.0	196.7	222.7	237.7	249.6	256.3	259.4
% of total population	3.1	3.3	3.5	3.6	3.8	4.2	4.7	4.7	4.8	4.9
Finland	26.3	37.6	46.3	55.6	62.0	68.6	73.8	80.6	85.1	87.7
% of total population	0.5	0.8	0.9	1.1	1.2	1.3	1.4	1.6	1.6	1.7
France	2596.6	–	–	–	–	–	–	–	–	3263.2
% of total population	6.3									5.6
Germany	5342.5	5882.3	6495.8	6878.1	6990.5	7173.9	7314.0	7365.8	7319.5	7343.6
% of total population	8.4	7.3	8.0	8.5	8.6	8.8	8.9	9.0	8.9	8.9
Hungary	–	–	–	–	137.9	139.9	142.2	143.8	–	127.0
% of total population	–	–	–	–	1.3	1.4	1.4	1.4	–	1.3
Ireland	80.0	87.0	94.9	89.9	91.1	96.1	118.0	114.4	111.0	117.8
% of total population	2.3	2.5	2.7	2.7	2.7	2.7	3.2	3.1	3.0	3.1

(Continued)

TABLE 1.3 Continued

	1990	1991	1992	1993	1994	1995	1996	1997	1998	1999
Italy	781.1	863.0	925.2	987.4	922.7	991.4	1095.6	1240.7	1250.2	1252.0
% of total population	1.4	1.5	1.6	1.7	1.6	1.7	2.0	2.1	2.1	2.2
Netherlands	692.4	732.9	757.4	779.8	757.1	725.4	679.9	678.1	662.4	651.5
% of total population	4.6	4.8	5.0	5.1	5.0	4.7	4.4	4.3	4.2	4.1
Norway	143.3	147.8	154.0	162.3	164.0	160.8	157.5	158.0	155.9	178.7
% of total population	3.4	3.5	3.6	3.8	3.8	3.7	3.6	3.6	3.7	4.0
Portugal	107.8	114.0	123.6	131.6	157.1	168.3	172.9	175.3	177.8	190.9
% of total population	1.1	1.2	1.3	1.3	1.6	1.7	1.7	1.8	1.8	1.9
Slovak Republic	–	–	–	11.0	16.9	21.9	24.1	24.8	27.4	29.5
% of total population	–	–	–	0.2	0.3	0.4	0.5	0.5	0.5	0.5
Spain	278.7	360.7	393.1	430.4	461.4	409.8	539.9	609.8	719.6	801.3
% of total population	0.7	0.9	1.1	1.1	1.2	1.3	1.4	1.6	1.8	2.0
Sweden	483.7	493.8	499.1	507.5	537.4	531.8	526.6	522.0	409.9	487.2
% of total population	5.6	5.7	5.7	5.8	6.1	5.2	6.0	6.0	5.6	5.5
United Kingdom	1723	1750	1985	2001	2032	1948	1934	2066	2207	2208
% of total population	3.2	3.1	3.5	3.5	3.6	3.4	3.4	3.6	3.8	3.8

Source: OECD SOPEMI Report 2001 : 282

provide a statistical overview of immigration into European countries, the numbers of asylum seekers and the stocks of foreign-born populations.

These figures show particularly large-scale migration in the early 1990s, with a focus on Germany as the main country of destination. Yet it is also worth bearing in mind that international migration is at a lower level in the era of 'globalisation' than in the late nineteenth and early twentieth centuries when millions of Europeans left for the US or moved from colonising to colonised parts of the world (Moch, 1992). The International Organisation for Migration's *World Migration Report* (IOM, 2000) esti-mated that there were around 150 million international migrants living outside the country of their nationality in 2000 (around 2.5 per cent of the world's population). Of these, 52.5 per cent were men and 47.5 per cent were women. Fewer than 10 per cent of the world's international migrants lived in EU member states (around 15 million people out of an EU population of 370 million). This is a considerable number of people, with important implications for relations between states and for politics within them, but the scale should not be exaggerated. Human mobility is not the default setting. The vast majority of the world's population are born, live and die within a relatively small geographical area within one state. Human immobility is actually more common despite the vast dis-parities in wealth between poor and rich countries that could be assumed as factors that would impel movement (Hammar et al., 1997).

Of the ten per cent of the world's international migrants that do move to Europe, most originate from certain countries and even from towns and villages in those countries. Faist (2000: 1) calls this a 'baffling puzzle'. Why so few migrants from so many places, yet so many migrants from so few places? When addressing this puzzle it is too simplistic to imagine that international migration results from a person's decision to move from one state because of economic hardship or political instability (a push factor) to another with relative stability or prosperity (a pull factor). The key questions of why migration networks linking particular countries (and particular parts of these countries) with others are sustained with some regularity over time are central aspects of the study of international migration (Portes, 1995).

Post-war migration to western Europe was structured by links between sending and receiving countries and by the development of the European economy that generated demand for migrant workers. The post-war eco-nomic boom in western Europe was sustained by migrants from other European countries and beyond. Much of this movement was based either on colonial ties or resulted from labour recruitment agreements between states. Those migrants that settled then increased their level of engagement with the institutions of the host societies, particularly the labour market, welfare state and political system.

Migration networks linked sending and receiving countries. Communication and the transmission of images within these networks have been important. For instance, research into contemporary southern

European migration has shown that migrants can be attracted to these countries because they have found out that there are more chances for finding informal or irregular employment and less chance of being observed by the state authorities (Reyneri, 1998, Baganha, 2000).

The result is that push and pull factors have been located within the context of links between sending and receiving countries with the resultant development and consolidation of migrant networks. Paths are established between countries, which can become highways as others take the same route (Messina, 1996). This movement was not necessarily a one-way ticket. Links between sending and receiving countries could be maintained and developed with the emergence of transnational communities linking sending and receiving countries (Vertovec, 1999; Faist, 2000; Kivisto, 2001).

The guests that stayed

Immigration into western societies since the 1950s was central to the economic reconstruction of these countries. There was, however, a lurking assumption that this labour migration was temporary and that migrants would return to their countries of origin when economic conditions changed. This assumption was misplaced: the guests stayed (Rogers, 1985). By the late 1970s it was clear that supposed temporary migration had turned into permanent settlement. The immigrant-origin communities changed in profile to include more women, younger and older people with increased engagement with key social institutions, particularly welfare states. There was also scope for a backlash from anti-immigration and nationalistic political forces that could claim that immigration had occurred by stealth and not been subjected to open political debate.

How did European countries respond to permanent settlement? Again, we need to pay attention to the various types of international migration and not just refer to 'immigration'. There was a closing of the door to large-scale labour migration, but migration by family members continued. Most labour migrants in the 1950s and 1960s were men, although there were also women labour migrants (Phizacklea, 1983). Family reunion led to a further feminisation of international migration, as well as bringing more younger and older people. The origins of migrants also differed. Some migrants arrived from former colonies, holding the passport and nationality of the country to which they moved, and thus with the same formal rights as other citizens (France, the UK and the Netherlands all stand out in this respect). Meanwhile, non-national migrants such as guestworkers in Germany were granted legal rights and welfare state membership in accordance with what Hammar (1990) calls 'denizenship'. This status can be understood as legal and social rights linked to legal residence falling short of full citizenship. The transformation of the incomplete membership status of denizenship into full citizenship would then depend upon naturalisation laws. As Chapters 3 and 4 on France and Germany demonstrate – and from very different starting points – issues of nationality, membership and belonging came to dominate the discussion of immigration.

There is another point here too. France, the UK and the Netherlands experienced significant post-colonial migration by people who arrived with the same rights as other French, Dutch or British citizens. Yet the formal extension of rights should not be confused with the ability to utilise these rights. Problems of adaptation, racism and discrimination have hindered the effective utilisation of legal, social and political rights (Wrench and Solomos, 1992). There has also been the development of new forms of political action by migrants attempting to play some part in shaping their own chances for inclusion. Mark Miller (1981) described migrant workers as an emerging political force in Europe, although even in 2002 there still seemed to be quite a lot of emerging to do.

So far the discussion has tended to focus on 'older' immigration countries in western Europe. What effects have the conceptual and geo-political widening of migration had on newer immigration countries in southern, central and eastern Europe? Countries in southern, central and eastern Europe for which these are relatively new issues experience migration that is less structured by the political and historical factors that linked older immigration countries to their former colonies. In southern Europe there are different labour market and welfare state contexts with higher levels of economic informality and irregular immigration. The debate about the widening of the EU to include new member states in central and eastern Europe has also been heavily influenced by concerns that these countries are more open to international migration. Fears of large-scale migration across 'soft borders' have contributed to the politicisation of east-west migration as a security concern. The requirement for applicant states in central and eastern Europe to adopt stringent immigration and asylum measures has been a key feature of the accession debate, as too has a lack of mutual trust and reciprocity on these security-related issues and the suspicion that the EU is establishing new boundaries and borders on its southern and eastern borders that could confound other objectives such as liberalisation and democratisation (Lavenex and Uçarer, 2002).

These preliminary reflections suggest that terms that we could take for granted such as 'international migration' and 'migrants' need to be explored in some depth if the diversity of forms and types of movement and their relation to policies are to be explored. It is also important to think about the ways in which policies categorise migrants and the effects that these categorisations have on understandings of migration and migrants. It is to these categorisations that we now turn. Or, put another way, when assessing the politics of migration and immigration in Europe then 'it is necessary to account for the wall they [the developed states] have erected as well as for the small doors they have provided in it' (Zolberg, 1989: 408).

Trends in post-war migration

It is helpful to make a distinction between three periods of migration to western Europe since the Second World War.

- Primary labour migration between the 1950s and 1973–4 driven in large part by the exigencies of west European economic reconstruction (Piore, 1979). Large-scale labour migration was at its peak in the 1960s and ended with the recruitment-stop following economic slowdown and the oil price rises of 1973–4. Most labour migrants were men, although some of the 'birds of passage' that Piore (1979) refers to in his study of immigration during the *trente glorieuses* of the post-war economic boom were also female (Moroksavic, 1984). A distinction between male–dominated primary, labour migration and feminised secondary migration does not hold. If we accept that women migrants were present in this first stage as either labour migrants or family members and that as such they played a role in the workplace and in household decision-making then this helps disabuse us of the idea that men were always the pioneers and women the followers and dependants.

- Secondary/family migration accelerated in the mid-1970s, after the cessation of labour recruitment, as migration for purposes of family reunion became the main form of immigration to Europe. The term family reunion applies both to immediate family members (spouses and children) and to new family creation when settled migrants bring in a marriage partner. The numbers of women migrants rose as family migration became the predominant form of migration into many European countries from the 1970s onwards with a consequent femi-nisation of migration (Castles and Miller, 1998). The numbers of children also increased with the emergence of a second generation often caught between the home country affiliations of their parents and the need to build lives for themselves. A key point to bear in mind in rela-tion to the discussion of secondary migration is that the decision to restrict labour migration did not lead to the end of immigration. It did not even lead to the end of labour migration. Rather, the labour migra-tion channel was narrowed to allow mainly high-skilled immigrants to enter while there was still scope for family migration. Much of the political debate about immigration in the 1970s and 1980s centred on family migration and the implications of permanent settlement.

- The 'third wave' of migration developed in the aftermath of the end of the Cold War in 1989–90 with a particularly noticeable increase in asylum seeking migration and migration defined by state policies as illegal. This has contributed both to a diversification in terms of the countries of origin of international migrants and the numbers of European countries affected by international migration.

This third wave of migration deserves closer attention because it has become so central to the politicisation of migration since the 1990s. An international legal framework covering the rights of asylum seekers and refugees developed after World War Two, the Geneva Convention of 1951 protected the rights of people who feared persecution on grounds of race, religion, nationality or membership of a particular social group or political opinion (Goodwin-Gill, 1996). Asylum seeking is assumed to be involuntary while immigration is assumed to be voluntary, although this distinction is problematic, as discussed above.

Attitudes towards asylum-seekers have become more negative since the end of the Cold War. Before this the development of refugee flows was linked to decolonisation and to US and Soviet intervention in the developing world (Zolberg et al., 1989). Refugees in western Europe fleeing Soviet bloc countries were welcomed because of the implicit vindication of west European liberal democracy that their movement provided. While these people were seen as escaping totalitarianism there were also very few of them. Their presence was hardly likely to be a political concern or to be perceived as a threat and elicit a security-oriented response.

The refugee regime enshrined in international law after the Second World War was underpinned by ideas about human rights and the universal applicability of such rights, but the system also provided vindication for western liberal values in the face of their socialist competitor. When both the scale and the national origins of asylum-seeking migrants increased and widened in the 1980s and 1990s states sought to restrict inflows that they viewed with suspicion. Many of these asylum-seekers were viewed as 'bogus' in the sense that they were seen as economic migrants seeking to avoid dodging controls on labour migration by using the asylum channel. The category of the 'bogus asylum seeker' was thus substantially defined by continued migration pressure, conflicts in various parts of the world, and the narrowing of the channel for labour migration in receiving countries. The idea of moral equality between individuals that was the philosophical basis of the liberal, universalistic international asylum and refugee system has been questioned by those who assert the moral relevance of communities and the ability of community members to regulate access to their territory (Boswell, 1999).

There is also a gendered element to this discussion of asylum seeking. Most asylum seekers are men. It has been far more difficult for women to seek asylum because they find it less easy to flee their country while gender-specific reasons for an asylum claim, such as rape, forced marriage, genital mutilation and opposition to moral codes that oppress women are not always recognised as forms of persecution (Kofman, 1999).

The growth in asylum-seeking needs to be linked to both the continuation of migration pressures and the reduction of the scope for legal migration. So too can the rise in migration be defined by state policies as illegal, when people:

- Enter legally – on a tourist visa, for example – and overstay;
- Cross state borders without appropriate authorisation and documentation;
- Are legally resident, but find employment in the underground/informal economy (they live 'legally' but work 'illegally');
- When administrative acts or bureaucratic procedures consign people to 'illegality'. For instance, tightened immigration regulations in France in the early 1970s led many people who had entered France in search of work to fall foul of the new system.

Illegal or irregular immigration is particularly evident in southern, central and eastern Europe. Chapters 7 and 8 demonstrate how these forms of migration need to be linked to prevailing economic informality – the underground economy in other words – that create social and economic spaces for irregular migration. The persistence of economic informality and irregular migration points towards much more general issues associated with state-society relations and social control. This re-emphasises the point that the institutions and organisations of the countries to which people move play a key role in shaping understandings of international migration. It is not that the people who move to southern, central and eastern Europe are themselves 'illegal', but that their movement falls into the category of illegality even though there are spaces for such movement.

The distinction between primary (mainly labour), secondary (mainly family) and the 'third wave' (asylum, refugees and irregular migration) gives some chronological and organisational structure to migration flows. The next section analyses attempts to manage and regulate international migration in its various forms and then discusses state responses.

Immigration policies

The parameters of the debate about the regulation of international migration need to be established. International migration in its many and various forms is a fact of life for liberal states. Movement of people from, within and between states is part of the mode of operation of these states in a liberal international trading order. In 2000, for instance, 89 million people arrived at UK points of entry of which 29 million were not British. Most of course were passing through or were tourists. Others had the right to enter as family members of British citizens, as EU free movers, as citizens of other countries covered by agreements that give them the right to enter, or as workers with skills prized by the receiving society. Britain and other EU member states are open and have, in fact, become increasingly open to movement of goods, capital, services and money, but at the same time make quite stringent efforts to filter the movement of people and to distinguish between wanted and unwanted forms of migration. This has been called the 'liberal paradox' of open markets and relatively closed states (Hollifield, 2000a).

The other side of the 'openness' coin can be the argument that European countries are being over-run or are in danger of being 'flooded' by migrants, but this rests on a global demand for admission that is over-stated. The idea that European countries are in some sense losing control of immigration is unlikely to be the perception of would-be immigrants from the poorest or most politically unstable parts of the world that seek to enter prosperous European countries. The fact that in March 2002 more than 900 Kurds risked their lives by crossing the Mediterranean in a rust-ing old boat in an attempt to enter Italy is not a sign of lax policies or uncontrolled migration, but of restrictive policies and the high costs of entry into EU member states (it was reported that each migrant paid $4000 to the gang of smugglers).

While immigration has continued, European states still possess a formi-dable regulatory capacity. In fact, it could be argued that European countries have actually increased both their capacity and willingness to control immi-gration, especially migration flows defined by state policies as unwanted, such as asylum seekers and migrants defined by state policies as illegal. As Brubaker (1994: 230) argues: 'True, states are open at the margins to citizens of other states, but only at the margins. Seen from outside, the prosperous and peaceful states of the world remain powerfully exclusionary'.

As part of the attempt to regulate international migration the borders of Europe have 'moved' in the sense that efforts have shifted beyond receiv-ing countries (Guild, 2001). For instance, a would-be migrant is likely to encounter the immigration control authorities of the destination country while making a visa application or at an airport in the country of origin. New control strategies have also developed. 'Non state actors' such as air-lines, truck drivers and ferry companies have been co-opted as agents of the immigration control authorities and can face 'carrier sanctions' that run into thousands of Euros if they carry unauthorised immigrants (Guiraudon and Lahav, 1999). Controls have been 'externalised' in the sense that EU co-operation and integration have involved the incorporation of central and eastern European states as a 'buffer zone' (Lavenex, 1999). European states have also established complex webs of re-admission agreements with neighbouring states to return unwanted immigrants with migration thus acquiring a foreign policy dimension.

This still leaves us with the puzzle referred to earlier. European coun-tries continued to accept immigrants even after politically declaring them-selves to be non-immigration countries. How can this be explained, if we reject the argument that states are being over-run or have lost control of international migration? To this puzzle we can add that public opinion has not usually been very supportive of immigration or immigrants.

To address this we need to analyse the *form* that immigration politics takes and the institutional venues where decisions were made. Gary Freeman (1995) has argued that immigration policies in liberal states are inherently – not intermittently or contingently – expansive. His work draws from studies of the politics of regulation which identifies the role that small groups with high stakes in a given policy area can play when trying to maximise the political benefits from a particular policy (Stigler, 1971; Wilson, 1981). Freeman thus analyses the form of immigration politics that arises as a result of the distribution of costs and benefits to argue that the concentrated beneficiaries (business and pro-migrant groups) have a greater incentive to organise than the diffuse bearers of costs (the general public). The result he argues is 'client politics' and expansive immigration policies that reflect business and pro-migrant NGO interests.

This claim seems unlikely to accord with a general perception of restrictive policies in so-called 'fortress Europe'. A case can be made that immigration into European countries during the post-war economic boom until the mid-1970s was underpinned by the pro-immigration attitudes of business, which were often the main recruiters, although much of this recruitment was relatively disorganised rather than the result of structured relations between government and business interests. From the mid-1970s until the late-1990s it is difficult to identify a pro-immigration business lobby in Europe. Nor for that matter have their been powerful pro-immigration/immigrant NGOs and civil rights groups with the ear of government. Pro-migrant NGOs seem more likely to rail against marginalisation or acquire only limited opportunities for influence. Freeman's insights are, though, important, because they encourage analysis of the form taken by immigration politics within states and the arenas within which policy is made.

Those contending that the role of courts as guarantors of the rights of nationals and non-nationals in liberal states needs to be considered have taken this point forward. Over the last 30 years or so, courts have offered protection to immigrant newcomers with the effect that the liberalness of liberal states constrains the restrictive urges of politicians (Hollifield, 1992; Guiraudon, 1998; Joppke, 1998, 1999). Brian Barry (1996: 538) writes that 'the basic idea of liberalism is to create a set of rights under which people are treated equally in certain respects, and then leave them to deploy these rights (alone or in association with others) in pursuit of their own ends. In the past two hundred years, western societies have been transformed in accordance with the precept of equal treatment'. The generality of liberal institutions with courts as defenders of rights has been seen as leading to the development of 'rights-based politics' linked to what Ruggie (1983) characterised as the 'embedded liberalism' of the post-war order. In the words of the most notable exponent of this position, James Hollifield (1992), this has helped open 'social and political spaces' for migrants and their descendants in European states with courts, for instance, defending the right to family life for national and non-national migrants in accord with national and international laws.

This presents a quite rosy picture of expansive policies and immigrant inclusion based on a universalistic ethic of inclusion that over-rides communitarian or nationalistic ethics of closure. Yet, communitarian and nationalistic values can justify the exclusion of immigrants on the grounds that the moral relevance of community membership supersedes the openness of liberal universalism (Boswell, 1999, 2000). This can justify exclusion on the basis of ethno-cultural identity and/or welfare state chauvinism. There was also a 'dark side' to the foundation of many European states based on ethno-cultural nationalism rather than liberal universalism (Mann, 1995, 1999).

While not arguing that courts have always and at all times been progressive bastions of migrants' rights, the point to take forward is that judicial cool heads have tempered restrictive policies that contravened legal or constitutional provisions. Courts, for instance, protected the right to family reunification, but the definition of the family, for instance, has tended to be traditional in the sense that it has not always been well-suited to changes such as increased levels of divorce with parental and child custody issues, more co-habitation, as well as claims for recognition by same sex partners (Ellman, 2001). The social construction of migrants' identities within the legal and judicial system can also lead to harsh and discriminatory treatment (Quassoli, 2002). Moreover, while courts address formal access to rights, there are inequalities, racism and the structural weaknesses of Europe's immigrant and ethnic minority populations that play major roles in hindering the effective utilisation of rights. Anti-discrimination laws in many member states are often weak with limited scope for redress (European Parliament, 1998).

It is not only the role of courts that is relevant. So too is the function of welfare states as key arenas within which inclusion and exclusion are mediated. The organisation of these welfare states differs between European countries (Esping-Andersen, 1990; Ferrera, 1996; Bommes and Geddes, 2000). Legally resident non-nationals immigrants – the denizens that Hammar (1990) wrote about – have been included in welfare states because welfare states function on the basis of contribution rather than nationality. In countries with highly developed social democratic welfare states such as Denmark and Sweden, there has been some welfare state chauvinism and pressure to reinforce the borders of the national welfare state against new and unwanted immigration, with immigrants portrayed as a drain on welfare state resources. In the November 2001 elections the extreme right-wing Danish Peoples' Party got 12 per cent of the vote with calls for a 7-year transition period for newcomers during which time they would be excluded from full access to welfare state benefits. This would roll back denizenship and lead to a welfare state marginalisation of those deemed undeserving of welfare state benefits.

Immigrant policies

If international migration is a fact of life for liberal states then how should European countries respond to immigration-related diversity? Immigrant policies mark an attempt to re-organise and re-imagine the organisational and conceptual boundaries of a given community in response to immigration such that capacity to include or exclude newcomers is generated. The organisations of European countries (their political system, the distribution of power and authority within them, the organisation of the welfare state and labour market etc.) and the ideas that animate these practices (about the nation and about membership of the imagined national community) are of central importance.

This suggests strong associations between immigrant policies in European countries of immigration and European nation states as political authorities regulating entry to the territory (sovereignty) and membership of the community (citizenship). This also means that the vocabulary of integration becomes heavily imprinted with historical, political and social processes associated with the nation state and national self-understanding. Put another way, these national organisational contexts and self-understandings – while obviously not static and unchanging – affect the perceptions of immigrant 'others' and thus the chances for their 'integration'.

The term 'integration' looms large in this debate, but it needs to be borne in mind that there is a social expectation of integration that affects everyone and the costs of failure – social exclusion – are high for the individual and society. Integration in these terms can be linked to core nation state principles and associated with the ideas of T.H. Marshall (1964) who saw modern citizenship as a vehicle for the building of a national community based on the extension of legal, political and social rights (in that order). Marshall wrote before the arrival of large numbers of immigrants. Responses to immigration upset Marshall's categorisation in the sense that non-citizen immigrants accessed legal and social rights but often did not get political rights. Hammar (1990) then understood the status of non-national immigrants as denizenship – legal and social rights falling short of full citizenship because of the absence of political rights.

Three points arise from this. First, we usually recognise integration only in its absence as social exclusion or disintegration rather than being able to specify what is meant by an integrated society. It's likely that in any room full of co-nationals there would be strong disagreement about what exactly are the requirements for community membership. Second, the integration of immigrants is often linked to discussion of the supposed racial, ethnic or cultural differences of immigrants as though these militate against inclusion or are vehicles for creation of a more progressive multicultural society. Clearly, the absence of knowledge about the society to which a person moves – such as the inability to speak the language – can militate against inclusion; but to emphasise supposed racial, ethnic and cultural differences can reify these differences and create social chasms between newcomers and their new country. Third, citizens tend to look to the state to guarantee the expectation of integration, i.e., not that this will necessarily be attained given that it's difficult to say what it would mean, but that governments are at least expected to show that they care. Social exclusion or disintegration is then accompanied by the social and political expectation that it is the responsibility of the state to address these worrying phenomena. If they won't or can't then this can swiftly become a legitimacy problem for governments. While debates about the 'integration' or lack of it of immigrants often focus on supposed racial, ethnic or cultural traits of newcomers, this can miss an important point. These debates are also, if not more, about the capacity of European countries to secure social inclusion or social integration in the face of factors such as welfare state and labour market changes that affect the capacity of states to perform this role.

There's another point here too. If we focus entirely on national differences between countries and on the particularities of debates within these countries then this could lead to the conclusion that national particularities are the key element of immigrant policies in Europe. This would diminish the possibility for comparison. Yet, we are, after all, analysing responses in liberal states in an integrating Europe to ostensibly similar phenomena associated with international migration. European countries of immigration have sought in some form or other to adopt immigrant policies that are often linked to ideas about the social utility of integration. Patterns of inclusion and exclusion are mediated in arenas – nationality laws, welfare states, labour markets – that display some broad similarities in both their structure and recent pressures. While there are clear national particularities, there are also cross-cutting factors presenting similar dilemmas to European countries of immigration.

A state-centred emphasis on national cases and national political processes has also come under fire from those who argue that rights and identities as rights have become decoupled and that post-national membership changes the position of migrants and their descendants in European countries. Yasemin Soysal (1994) argues that a universalised discourse of entitlement derived from international human rights standards underpins claims for social and political inclusion made by immigrants and their descendants. Thus the incomplete membership status of denizenship is recast as a progressive model for new forms of post-national belonging that no longer take the nation state as their frame of reference. The EU could be construed as a significant 'post-national' development. Yet, as currently constituted the EU does defy a narrow state-centrism, but also tempers post-national claims because it retains a strong state-centred focus, offers limited rights and entitlements to EU citizens, excludes non-EU nationals from EU-level rights, and seeks to build barriers between itself and neighbouring states and regions to the east and south that may be sources of unwanted immigration.

The widening of migration

A drawback with analyses of European immigration politics can be that they largely centre on the experiences of older immigration countries in north western Europe and pay little attention to the experiences of newer immigration countries in central, eastern and southern Europe. Immigration is a relatively new issue for these countries and their capacity to regulate international migration may be less developed. At the same time migratory pressures may be greater because of proximity to emigration regions. The development of policy co-operation and integration within the EU has also had significant effects on policy development. Older countries of immigration may seek to export their policy ideas and practices to newer immigration countries. Southern European immigration policies have been heavily influenced by EU commitments while it is also the case that central and eastern European countries must adhere to the immigration, asylum and internal security pre-requisites of the EU's *acquis communautaire* if they are to be admitted to the club.

To make a formal policy commitment does not mean that this commitment will be fulfilled if legal, bureaucratic and administrative resources are lacking. In the case of restrictive immigration policies we have already seen that in older immigration countries there has been continued immigration despite restrictive policies. Constraints may arise because of implementation dilemmas such as the costs of control and the lack of well-developed bureaucratic or administrative resources. Control capacity can also be hindered if policy is not based on a valid theory of cause and effect. For example, if there is a continued demand for migrant labour in some economic sectors and well-entrenched economic informality that provides a context for the economic insertion of irregular migrants then the discussion of internal controls and the regulatory capacity of states is also important as will be shown in Chapters 7 and 8 (Geddes, 2000a: 24–6).

Immigration has become politicised across the EU both at state level and in the form of collective EU responses. The move towards restriction since the 1970s coupled with continued migration pressure has helped create increased numbers of people who fall into categories of immigrants defined by state policies as unwanted or bogus. National governments were instrumental in stoking up this pressure through policies that sought ever-tighter restriction, which had the simultaneous effects of raising the rhetorical stakes while also questioning the presence of immigrants already resident in European countries.

At the same time, immigration controls are 'gappy' in the sense that immigration has continued with new rules often producing their own evasions. Restrictive immigration policies have not meant the end of immigration, rather they have co-existed with continued immigration. Also, despite facing many obstacles, immigrants and their descendants have been able to build new lives for themselves in European countries.

European integration

'Europe' can lurk in the background of analyses of European immigration politics either as the repressive 'fortress Europe' or as a potentially progressive source of post-national rights. Both these perspectives pay too little attention to the form and content of EU migration policy. The basic analytical problem is that while it is clear that the EU's importance has grown, it's not always clear how and why this has been the case and what European integration's effects on immigration and immigrant policies are (Favell and Geddes, 2000). The EU is not a nation state and there is no reason to assume that European integration can be likened to a nation-state building process. In fact, there are probably more reasons to suggest the opposite, which means that we need to think about the type of organisation that the EU is. This requires analysis of power and authority in a distinct non-national setting, as well as an appreciation of what can be called the multi-levelling of European politics with some power-sharing between sub-national, national and supranational unit levels.

There are three main elements of EU migration policy, these will be analysed more closely in Chapter 6.

- Free movement laws for (mainly) EU citizens within the single market. The EU has extended rights of free movement to its citizens and sought to create a single market defined as an area without internal frontiers, which means the removal of national frontier controls.

- Immigration and asylum provisions that have developed since the mid-1980s and are related to a number of factors such as the implications of single market integration for immigration and asylum coupled with the growing awareness of domestic legal and political constraints on immigration control.

- Immigrant policies that offer some legal, social and political rights to EU citizens who exercise their right to move freely, but these are not extended to non-nationals (third country nationals). The EU did, however, in the 1997 Treaty of Amsterdam, introduce a Treaty commitment to the combating of discrimination based on race, ethnicity and religion that applies to EU citizens and third country nationals.

Later discussion will focus on two key issues, which can be introduced here. Why have states ceded some authority over migration issues to supranational institutions? This implies some loss of control because of the empowerment of supranational institutions above the nation state. Yet, it could also be the case that this shift to EU level co-operation and integration does not render the nation state redundant. Rather, EU co-operation and integration since the 1980s could allow states to attain domestic policy objectives.

What impact do these competencies have on member states? The EU is more than an external venue to which member states 'escape' in order to attain their policy objectives. We also need to account for the impact that EU migration policy competencies can have on these member states. If the impact on laws, institutions, policies and collective identities is to be explored then we could hypothesise that newer immigration countries in southern, central and eastern Europe will be more open to EU influence on national policies. If this is the case, then we also need to explore the national contexts in these southern European countries more carefully to examine basic questions of institutional compatibility between the EU policy frame and national policies.

These questions are analysed more carefully in Chapter 6. At this stage, we can note that the unevenness of integration across policy sectors – some sectors are more integrated than others – and the unevenness of effects – some member states are more affected than others – means that we need to assess both the reasons for the shift to Europe and the effects on member states and on surrounding states and regions. We should also avoid ascribing political and institutional changes to the impact of the EU without first being sure that it was actually the EU that drove these changes rather than domestic or other international factors. The congruence of EU developments does not make the EU a cause of all change in the member states. It is easy to over-state the EU's influence, but at the same time, the sources of legal, material and symbolic power associated with this supranational context needs to be carefully analysed.

Plan of the book

The three themes introduced in this chapter are now used to structure each of the chapters that follow. The chapters take as their themes immigration policies, immigrant policies and the development of EU co-operation and integration.

This book's analysis of European migration politics is organised at two repetition levels.

- A horizontal dimension compares responses in European countries. To what extent is European immigration politics characterised by distinct national responses to international migration? How have national responses changed over time and what factors have underpinned these changes? Where are the points of convergence and the points of divergence between European countries? If there is convergence then what causes this?

- A vertical dimension analyses the impact of European integration. We can assess both the institutionalisation of Europe (the development of common institutions and policies) and the Europeanisation of institutions (the impact on member states of EU integration).

These two dimensions can then be connected to explore the extent to which it makes sense to talk of a politics of migration and immigration in Europe with linkages at both horizontal and vertical level.

The horizontal and vertical analytical dimensions are analysed in relation to the two themes discussed in this introductory chapter.

- Immigration policies to regulate and manage international migration.

- Immigrant policies that centre on the development of a social and political response to the presence of immigrant newcomers and their descendants.

We now take these ideas forward and apply them in Britain (Chapter 2), France (Chapter 3), Germany (Chapter 4), the Netherlands and Sweden (Chapter 5). Chapter 6 examines the development of EU responsibilities. This is followed by consideration of the politics of migration in southern (Chapter 7) and Central/Eastern Europe (Chapter 8) where EU obligations have been an important part of the debate about migration policy and where European policy ideas and practices have had important effects on the development of national policy frames in these countries. The EU chapter is pivotal to the analysis rather than being an add-on. The aim is to explore the development and impact of European co-operation and integration.

The cases selected for analysis focus on developments in around fifteen European countries. The selected countries provide heuristic case studies that allow the development of a good understanding of responses to immigration in older and newer immigration countries, as well as analysis of the EU's impact. In order to facilitate comparison the chapters that follow draw from the themes established in this introduction to consider immigration and immigrant policies. The aim is then to highlight divergence and convergence, while seeking explanations for these when and where they arise. The book aims to show both the conceptual (new types of migration and new types of response) and geo-political (more countries) widening of the migration issue in contemporary European politics.

2

Maintaining 'Fortress Britain'?

CONTENTS

Analysing developments in British immigration policy and politics gives a robust test to some of the ideas outlined in the introductory chapter. What could *European* migration and immigration politics mean for a country that has enacted strict controls on immigration, opted out of key EU developments, and looked to North America rather than Europe for policy lessons when developing its immigrant policies? The particularity of the British national response seemed to be reaffirmed when in 2001 and 2002 – in response to urban unrest in some English towns and then after the September 11 attacks on New York – there was a renewed debate about the meaning of national citizenship, as well as the importance of ties binding British citizens and newcomers based on shared understanding of what were called 'norms of acceptability' and the importance of learning the English language. At the same time, these signify a shift in emphasis that borrows from the communitarian values of New Labour with emphasis placed on the responsibilities of individuals rather than the rights of groups.

This chapter analyses these developments and this apparent national particularism, but argues that Britain has not escaped quite so comprehensively from a European politics of migration and immigration as might at first seem. The chapter focuses on the immigration policy implications of Britain's post-imperial downsizing, UK immigration control capacity, race relations policies, debates about new migration (particularly asylum), and finally, the sceptical attitude of successive British governments towards common EU immigration and asylum policies. The aim is to outline distinct aspects of British policy and politics while also locating British developments in relation to debates in other European immigration countries.

To develop a point already made in the introduction, the *form* taken by UK immigration politics and the *locations* where key decisions have been made, particularly the dominance of the executive branch of government, has facilitated the introduction of strict immigration controls since 1962. Executive dominance also helps explain the reluctance of British governments to cede power to supranational EU institutions. The executive in Britain has acquired substantial powers to restrict immigration through both 'primary legislation' that is debated in Parliament as well as the discretionary powers afforded by barely scrutinised 'secondary legislation'. Britain's position as an island on the northern edge of Europe also gives natural advantages to a regime of control based on external frontier controls with the absence of identity cards signifying a weaker internal control regime. Even so, British controls have been 'gappy' in the sense that there has been continued immigration by labour migrants, family members and, more recently, asylum-seekers. Yet, this gap has not been filled by growth in support for extreme right wing parties. The first-past-the-post UK electoral system has made it difficult for extreme right-wing parties to make an impact, although the 2001 election saw relatively minor but much publicised 'successes' for the extreme right-wing British National Party. The extreme right was also identified as a contributing factor in the civil unrest in northern English cities in the summer of 2001.

Disquiet about the BNP became even more noticeable when they won 6 seats in the Lancashire towns of Burnley and Oldham in the May 2002 local elections. This is a tiny number when it is borne in mind that more than 6,000 seats were contested; but at a time when the extreme right was making inroads across Europe there was some concern about the implications for UK immigration and race relations policies.

When immigrant policies are considered, the key point is the centrality of ideas about race and supposed racial differences. British 'race relations' policy has been centred on the strict control of immigration defined as unwanted (from African, Asian and Caribbean people in the 1960s and 1970s and by asylum seekers, more recently) coupled with anti-discrimination laws that tackle both direct and indirect discrimination and allow for positive action to tackle inequalities. The effect has been that ideas about 'race' and ethnic difference matter in British social and political debate about immigration and its sequels to an extent that they do not in many other European countries. Discussions of in the UK are almost always tied to a discussion of good or better 'race relations'. Even though there is no credible evidence to suggest that 'races' exist or that we can meaningfully analyse society in terms of such categories the point is that ideas about race and racial difference have acquired social and political meaning in the UK. Policy responses to issues understood in terms of 'race', 'race relations', 'racism' and where the reference is to 'ethnic minorities' have become an everyday part of the discussion of immigration-related diversity in the UK.

Perhaps rather surprisingly, given its more general reluctance to move towards common EU immigration and asylum policies, the UK has been able to 'export' key elements of this approach to EU-level in the two directives on 'race equality' and workplace discrimination agreed by the Council of Ministers in June 2000. The export of one aspect of British policy should not disguise a more general scepticism about common EU immigration and asylum policies. The reasons for this are quite simple and can be linked to British immigration policy objectives (tight restrictions) and the measures chosen to attain these objectives (external frontier controls). Why jeopardise relatively successful controls for the EU's more uncertain environment? British governments have been convergent with other European states in terms of a restrictive policy orientation, but have consistently opposed common European policies that would empower supranational institutions such as the Commission and the European Court of Justice that could challenge the executive's tight grip on immigration policy. That said, it will be shown that it is not so easy to slip the net of European entanglements and that the UK has actually been quite favourable to key elements of the EU immigration and asylum *acquis* that try to secure Europe's external frontiers in a way, on paper at least, recognizsable in the context of a UK 'command and control' mentality.

Immigration policy

Britain has been called Europe's would-be zero immigration country (Layton-Henry, 1994). If we are to discuss the reasons for this and the origins and development of British immigration policy then we need to link this to Britain's post-imperial downsizing from a global, colonial to a regional, European power after the Second World War. This downsizing was evident in immigration and citizenship policies. From an expansive, imperial notion of citizenship that gave all subjects of the crown the right to enter Britain – formalised by the 1948 British Nationality Act – there was swift movement towards restriction. This was elaborated in three main pieces of legislation between 1962 and 1971 with the idea of citizenship downsized from the imperial understanding of the 1948 British Nationality Act to a more restricted ethnic understanding by the 1981 British Nationality Act (Layton-Henry, 1992; Saggar, 1992; Joppke, 1999; Hansen, 2000).

Post-imperial downsizing

Why did Britain retreat from the immigration and citizenship implications of its previous global role? One school of thought emphasises state racism and the 'whitewashing' of Britain to argue that racist hostility to black and Asian immigrants underpinned stringent immigration legislation (Paul, 1997). Such perspectives that emphasise a centrally-directed state racism have had a powerful grip on studies of British immigration policy and politics. A counter argument is put by Randall Hansen (2000) who argues that British immigration and citizenship policy can better be understood as public-driven rather than state-led racism: the advocates of strict controls were appeased while some space was created for the anti-discrimination legislation that laid the foundations for the British version of multiculturalism. This echoes the conclusions of Freeman (1994) who argued that British immigration policy can be understood as an example of 'responsible issue management' by government in the face of public hostility to immigrant newcomers. In these terms, public opinion has played an important part in shaping government responses to immigration. The counter-argument is that the shaping of the debate in which state actors play a key role has the effect of establishing the parameters of debate (Statham, 2001). To understand these developments and try to weigh the influences of state policy and public opinion on policy development we need to step back and explore British politics in the 1950s and 1960s when key decisions about immigration and race relations were made. Britain had effectively closed the door on large-scale labour migration with legislation between 1962 and 1971 before the economic downturn of 1973 prompted other European countries of immigration to do likewise.

Between 1948 and 1962 Britain had an open migration regime. The 1948 British Nationality Act formally gave all subjects of the Crown in Britain and its empire the right to move to Britain. People from the colonies and the commonwealth could state *civis Britannicus sum* (I am a British citizen) and access the same formal legal, social and political rights as other subjects of the crown. This created a potentially enormous pool of would-be migrants, although it would be a mistake to think that anything more than a small proportion of would-be post-imperial migrants would be actual migrants.

The British Nationality Act did not create post-war migration to Britain because when it was drafted such immigration could not have been foreseen. There were, however, strong pull factors at work in the 1950s with active recruitment of migrant workers for employment work in public transport, the newly created National Health Service, the textile industry, and the car industry. This also meant that the immigrant population was particularly concentrated in London, the industrial Midlands, parts of the north west and parts of Yorkshire where these occupations were located. The men and women who came took up key roles that played an important part in the development of the British welfare state. Britain was not flooded with immigrants. Yet through the 1950s there was growing concern in some quarters about the 'racial' aspects of 'coloured immigration' as it was called at the time.

Immigration in the 1950s was unplanned. There was no direct preference for black and Asian workers from former colonies. Indeed, their arrival was met in official circles with suspicion and sometimes with racist hostility. Even so, why did Britain maintain an open migration regime between 1948 and 1962? Arguments that centre on state-racism tend to stress the ways in which this policy of openness hung by a thread and was continually questioned on racist grounds at elite governmental level. Hansen (2000), on the other hand, demonstrates a debate in Whitehall about the desirability of continued immigration in which there were both pro- and anti-immigration voices. He goes on to link the continuation of immigration to a bi-partisan consensus between the Labour and Conservative parties coupled with an attachment to a post-imperial Commonwealth ideal. Within Whitehall, the Colonial Office was a parti- cularly ardent advocate of a continued open door policy. The Ministry of Labour pushed for controls because the kinds of migrant workers arriving were not always well attuned to the labour market gaps that existed.

Restrictions on black and Asian immigration came more squarely onto the political agenda in the late 1950s as a result of so-called 'race riots' – actually attacks on immigrants by white youths and neo-fascist organisa- tions – in the west London district of Notting Hill and the east Midlands town of Nottingham (Pilkington, 1988). These disturbances helped trans- form migration from a regional into a national issue (Hansen, 2000: 82). Paul Rich (1986) argues that this also coincided with the rise to prominence of a populist wing of the Conservative Party which became less upper class and paternalistic and more middle class and populist. Grassroots pressure from backbench MPs combined with anti-immigration groups outside the Party such as the Birmingham Immigration Control Association and the Southall Residents Association. Hansen (2000: 96) argues, however, that the key development was a Whitehall turf war between the anti-restriction Colonial Office and the pro-restriction Ministry of Labour, which the Ministry of Labour won as the Commonwealth ideal faded and limits to economic growth began to set in.

Racialised controls and the 'colour problem'

The rationale for the control legislation introduced by the Conservative government in 1961 was that Britain was a small island in danger of becoming overcrowded. This is a fairly familiar argument that is recycled in many European countries. In the UK in the early 1960s it rested on the exaggerated assumption that all those who could potentially move to Britain would actually do so. The Home Secretary of the time, R.A. Butler, claimed that around 800 million people were entitled to move to Britain. Although strictly true, this claim was ridiculous. The chances of 800 million people moving to the UK were about the same as the Conservative

TABLE 2.1   *The perverse effects of control? Net immigration from new Commonwealth countries to the UK, 1953–62*

Year	Net immigration from the New Commonwealth
1953	2000
1954	11,000
1955	42,500
1956	46,000
1957	42,400
1958	29,850
1959	21,600
1960	57,700
1961	136,400
1962*	94,900

*January–June 1962, prior to introduction of controls
Source: Layton Henry (1992: 13)

government of the day admitting the real reason for introducing the legislation: concerns about the 'racial' character of some immigrants.

The Labour Party denounced the legislation as a betrayal of the Commonwealth and as a concession to racism, although Labour's attitude swiftly changed when the electoral effects of anti-immigration sentiment became clear. The Labour Party's initial opposition to restriction faded when the electoral potency in key marginal constituencies of anti-immigration sentiment became clear. Indeed, even during the passage of the 1962 legislation Labour's oppositional ardour diminished (Hansen, 2000: 118–9). Labour's abandonment of opposition to controls can be linked rather straightforwardly to the effects of anti-immigration sentiment in marginal constituencies. Labour had opposed the 1962 Act, which its Home Affairs spokesman Patrick Gordon Walker described in the House of Commons as 'bare-faced, open race discrimination'. These words came back to haunt him at the 1964 general election when he lost his seat in the industrial West Midlands constituency of Smethwick to a Conservative candidate, Peter Griffiths, whose supporters used the racist slogan 'If you want a nigger for a neighbour vote Liberal or Labour'. Griffiths won Smethwick with a pro-Conservative swing against a more general pro-Labour swing at the 1964 general election (Deakin, 1964). Even though Prime Minister Wilson declared that Griffiths would be a parliamentary leper, the Labour leadership was also aware, as one

Cabinet minister put it, 'that immigration can be the greatest potential vote loser for the Labour party' (Crossman, 1977: 149–50).

One of the ironies of the discussion of control of Commonwealth immigration in the early 1960s was that it actually stimulated 'beat the ban' migration from people who feared that they might be affected by the restrictions and separated from their family members as a result (see Table 2.1). Restrictive legislation helped increase the numbers of immigrants and thus the perception of an immigration problem.

The 1962 Commonwealth Immigrants Act distinguished between citizens of the UK and its colonies and citizens of independent Commonwealth countries. The latter became subject to immigration controls via the issue of employment vouchers. The mechanism for control was fairly straightforward. In 1963, 30, 130 of these vouchers were issued. In 1972, only 2,290 were issued. Between 1963 and 1972, 20 per cent of these permits were issued to women, which reinforces the point made in the introduction that the 'birds of passage' were also female and that women did not simply follow the male migrants as their dependants (Bhabha and Shutter, 1994). In addition to this, the main migration flow into the UK has been from Ireland and women migrants have always been a fairly substantial component of this flow too. UK immigration laws were based on the assumption that men were the breadwinners and women were dependants who would follow their husbands. This was then the foundation for the British government's attempts to prevent women migrants from enjoying the same family reunification rights as men. When the European Court of Human Rights (ECHR) ruled against this discriminatory practice, the response of the UK government was to level down the regulations to hinder both male and female family reunion (Kofman, 1999: 276). New family migration was hindered both by the sexist regulations and by post ECHR judgement levelling down. In 1980 the Conservative government introduced the 'primary purpose' rule that gave the immigration authorities the power to probe the 'real' status and reasons for an application to enter the UK for purposes of marriage. The Labour government elected in 1997 fulfilled a pledge to their Asian supporters, who have backed Labour in large numbers since their arrival in the UK, and abolished this rule although restrictions remain tight.

The effectiveness of controls

How effective were the controls instigated by the 1962 legislation? They provided effective mechanisms to regulate primary, labour migration. Family migration of dependants such as wives, husbands, children and grandparents was protected by the legislation, but predicated on the assumption of male breadwinners and female dependants. As labour migration was restricted from the 1960s onwards then family migration became the main target for restriction from the mid-1960s. Those who argue that 'rights-based politics' have played an important part in opening social and political spaces for migrants in Europe (Hollifield, 1992) face some difficulties when applying their arguments to the UK. There was no constitutional protection of the rights of the family as there was in other European countries because there is not a formal, written UK constitution. Family migration was provided for by statute.

By the mid-1960s the outline of an immigration policy consensus can be seen resting on two pillars: tight restriction of black and Asian immigration coupled with anti-discrimination legislation introduced in three 'race relations' acts of 1965, 1968 and 1976. Labour politician Roy Hattersley summed up the resultant policy mix: 'Without integration limitation is inexcusable, without limitation integration is impossible' (Hansen, 2000: 26). Despite the ordering of Hattersley's maxim, the underlying logic flowed in the opposite direction: integration was predicated on the tight control of immigration. Indeed, integration would be jeopardised by large-scale immigration. This reasoning still underpins British immigration policy today and has been recycled more recently to cover asylum-seeking migration.

It is in these terms and as a set of 'common sense' assumptions about race and relations that the framing effects by state actors on debates about immigration and its sequels in Britain have been most evident. Responses to international migration in the UK have been heavily influenced by a framing of the migration issue – encapsulated by Hattersley's maxim – that was designed to take the heat out of the issue through strong controls and suspicion towards newcomers seen as bringing with them some potential to damage or threaten social cohesion. This does not mean that UK policy was simply – and simplistically – the outcome of a centrally directed state racism. Nor does it mean that politicians were not acutely aware of anti-immigration sentiment. What it does mean is that the argument that policy has been a responsible response to public racism does also require that the factors that shape public perceptions of immigration related issues also be explored. The framing by state actors of immigration and race related issues has been identified as particularly important both from the 'colour problem' of the late 1950s to the 'asylum crisis' of the late 1990s and early twenty first century (Statham, 2001; Geddes and Statham, 2002).

This means, for instance, that if we use the argument that there has been a 'gap' between the rhetoric of restriction and the reality of continued immigration (c.f. Cornelius, Martin and Hollifield, 1994) and that this 'gap' can be filled by racist and anti-immigration politics then we need also to analyse the ways in which the debate is framed and then how this structures perceptions of 'gaps' and of immigrants as a problem or threat on which anti-immigration politicians can build.

There were clearly concerns in the early- to mid-1960s that anti-immigration sentiment could damage the Labour Party. The Labour Party did not cause this hostility, but responded to it. Following its 1964 general election victory, the Labour government led by Harold Wilson feared being seen as soft on immigration. The Labour government reduced the number of work permits available under the 1962 Act. In 1968 a second Commonwealth Immigrants Bill was introduced. This removed the right to enter the UK from British citizens of Indian origin facing persecution as a result of Africanisation policies in Kenya and Uganda. The 1968 legislation was a kneejerk response to the sudden influx of 13,000 people of Asian origin fleeing 'Africanisation' policies in East Africa. Legislation rushed through Parliament in only three days made these East African Asians subject to immigration controls on the basis of a patriality rule stipulating that for anyone to enter the UK they needed to have one parent or grandparent born, adopted or naturalised as a British citizen.

The restrictive legislation culminated with the 1971 Immigration Act, introduced by Edward Heath's Conservative government. All preceding legislation was replaced by one statute that distinguished between citizens of the UK and its colonies who were patrial (essentially, the 'one grandparent' rule introduced by the 1968 Act) who could enter and settle in the UK and citizens of independent Commonwealth countries who could not. For non-patrials, work permits, to be renewed annually, replaced vouchers. The exceptions to this were nationals of EC member states. UK accession on January 1 1973 meant that nationals of other member states and their dependants could move to and reside in the UK.

The final piece of the jigsaw was the amendment of nationality law to reflect a post-imperial downsizing and the idea of patriality. Both reflected a shrinking of the UK's territorial and conceptual borders. The Labour government in 1977 had already proposed changes in a Green (discussion) Paper. Margaret Thatcher's first Conservative government developed these proposals to introduce the British Nationality Act (1981). This created three types of British citizen:

- Full British citizenship for those with close ties, i.e., that were patrial;

- British Dependent Territories Citizenship for people living in dependent territories i.e., Gibraltar, the Falkland Islands and Hong Kong.

- British Overseas Citizenship, a residual category to which almost no rights were attached. This category was designed to encourage East African Asians and Malaysians to acquire citizenship in their country of residence.

The effect was that millions of people found their citizenship status amended to deny them access to the country of which ostensibly they had been citizens. British governments had been able to implement tight controls and redefine national citizenship stripped of post-colonial implications. There were, however, limits to the populist pursuit of ever-tighter immigration controls and the rhetoric of zero immigration, with a resultant disjunction between zero immigration discourse and continued immigration. The more fervent imaginings of the anti-immigration lobby – repatriation and the dismantling of race relations legislation – never came to pass. This illustrates the point made by John Crowley (1999: 3) that the xenophobic right in British politics has been too powerful to ignore, but too weak to govern. He goes on to argue that it took British race relations sociology a long time to grasp that occasional Thatcherite lip-service to Powellism did not necessarily mean that the Thatcher governments would implement the Powellite agenda (repatriation and dismantlement of race relations legislation).

Playing the race card?

Immigration's political salience in the late 1960s and early 1970s meant that there was potential for the 'race card' to be played (Saggar, 2000). If the card is to be played successfully then it depends on issue saliency and whether the main parties can be distinguished on the issues. In the late 1960s, immigration was a salient concern but could Labour and the Conservatives be distinguished on the issue? Harold Wilson's Labour government between 1964 and 1970 did as much as they could to shut down the issue. Yet, at the 1970 general election immigration was the fourth most salient issue for voters and benefited the Conservatives (Studlar, 1974).

The main reason for this was the contribution to the negative politicisation of immigration made by Conservative politician Enoch Powell. Powell called for the repatriation of settled immigrants and the scrapping of the anti-discrimination legislation contained in the 1965 and 1968 Race Relations Acts. Powell displayed formidable rabble-rousing powers. Most famously in 1968 when he predicted 'rivers of blood' because of supposedly fundamental incompatibilities between immigrants understood as culturally distinct and therefore inassimilable to Powell's very particular notion of the 'English people'. Immigrants were portrayed as a fifth column who with a supporting hand from the Race Relations legislation would soon gain the upper hand over the 'white man'. Powell's public profile was raised enormously by his anti-immigration speeches, which tapped the strong anti-immigration sentiment among the general public; but he was sacked from the Conservative's shadow cabinet because his views ran counter to Party policy. That said, the Conservatives benefited indirectly at the 1970 general election through their association with Powell's hard line anti-immigration stance (Studlar, 1974).

The problem as defined by Powell and his supporters was that immigrants wanted to come to Britain and once they arrived, they wanted to stay. Powell's anti-immigration rhetoric led to the perception of immigrants as not being welcome in the UK. John Crowley (1999: 24) argues that saying immigrants were not welcome helped make this statement true with the result that 'such a discursive strategy in fact provided no way out, and indeed by poisoning the air without actually stimulating significant return migration aggravated the problems of social cohesion that Powell claimed to be concerned about ... Twenty years on the French *Front National* adopted similar tactics with similar results'.

In 1978 Prime Minister Thatcher resuscitated Powellite themes. As Conservative Party leader she was in a more powerful position than Powell, but was ultimately also more constrained by the realities of practical politics. In an interview given to the TV programme *World in Action* she stated that she could understand peoples' fears of being 'swamped' by what she called 'alien cultures'. She professed to be concerned that people might be attracted by the political message of the extreme right-wing National Front and that it was her duty to address the concerns of people attracted by right-wing extremism. This could be construed as an attempt to play the 'race card' at the 1979 general election. Yet, once the electoral victory had been secured there were constraints on the capacity to further restrict immigration. The 1971 Immigration Act and its forerunners had already tightly restricted labour migration and established a work permit system. Attempts by the Thatcher government to establish registers of dependants and thus clamp down on family migration failed because governments in sending countries refused to comply with measures they saw as discriminatory, and why should these countries be agents of the British immigration control authorities anyway? Tighter rules also meant that 'white' immigrants – ethnic belongers in the new era of patriality – fell foul of the tough regime, much to the chagrin of some Conservative MPs. Thatcher also encountered opposition from senior Conservative Party figures when expressing scepticism about the Commission for Racial Equality set up by the 1976 Race Relations Act. Despite rhetorical assaults on what was dubbed the 'race relations industry' the legislative and institutional framework introduced by the race relations acts of 1965, 1968 and 1976 remained largely intact, albeit hardly with the ear of government.

Extreme right parties did not fill the 'gap'. The National Front acquired some notoriety and a lot of publicity in the 1970s, but never won a seat on a local council never mind in the House of Commons. The UK's 'first past the post' electoral system played a key part in this. As too did Margaret Thatcher's harder line on immigration. These factors were compounded by the violence associated with the National Front and left-wing counter-mobilisations by the Anti-Nazi League and Rock Against Racism, which were particularly effective in their use of popular music to spread the anti-racist and anti-fascist message among young people.

After 1979, immigration declined as a political issue. The election of the Thatcher government effectively shut down debate on immigration because there was nowhere else for ostensibly liberal politicians to go and little scope for the racist extreme right to make a breakthrough. The tough talk of the first Thatcher government actually helped put pay to the immigration issue. Both the rhetorical and physical limits of control appeared to have been reached, at least in the face of secondary, family migration. Immigration faded as a political issue, although race relations concerns have frequently appeared on the political agenda, for instance, when urban disorder portrayed as 'race riots' broke out in major British cities in the early 1980s (Solomos, 1988) with recurrent outbreaks since, most recently in the summer of 2001 (Home Office, 2001).

Responses to asylum-seeking

Restrictive legislation does not mean that Britain has been invulnerable to the third wave of international migration. In the late 1990s there were increased numbers of asylum-seekers, although there were portrayals of floods and invasions that over-stated the scale (Kaye, 1999). The category 'bogus asylum seeker' has acquired particular resonance in British public debate. Kaye's (1999: 177–8) analysis of UK media coverage – particularly in newspapers – of the asylum issue saw the media as playing an intermediary role in 'an orchestrated government campaign to downgrade the public perception of refugees in 1990–1 and 1992–3 to control the numbers entering the UK'. We can also relate increased asylum seeking to changes in background institutional conditions under Conservative governments until 1997 and Labour governments after 1997. There had already been a shrinking of the conceptual boundaries of the British nation state by the 1981 British Nationality Act. In the 1990s, welfare state pressures and changed welfare state ideologies provided the backdrop for perceptions of asylum seeking migrants. Under New Labour, for instance, the influence of communitarian thinking has allowed greater emphasis on the moral relevance of communities and the rights and responsibilities of individuals within them – in comparison with the emphasis on moral equality that is the basis of the international refugee protection system. In such terms, a justification could be provided for the welfare state exclusion of asylum seekers on the basis that they were not legitimate members of the community of legitimate receivers of welfare state benefits.

Britain does not have dedicated asylum legislation. Indeed, between 1993 and 2002 there were four attempts to adapt the 1971 immigration legislation in response to asylum-seeking migration. Each piece of legislation sought to correct the errors of the previous legislation. In general terms, UK governments have (i) sought to impose tighter external frontier controls on asylum-seekers while (ii) using internal measures to control asylum applicants within the UK. The legislation also demonstrates the power of the executive branch of the UK government to develop controls through the extended discretionary powers granted by secondary legislation.

External controls have been expanded to include private actors such as airlines, ferry companies and truck drivers with fines for those who bring in people without the appropriate documentation. The UK government

TABLE 2.2 *Asylum applications in the UK 1990–2001*

Year	Number of asylum applications
1990	26,205
1991	44,845
1992	24,605
1993	22,370
1994	32,830
1995	43,695
1996	29,645
1997	32,505
1998	46,015
1999	71,155
2000	83,215
2001	71,700

Source: Home Office

TABLE 2.3 *Top ten applicant nationalities for asylum to the UK, September–December 2001*

Afghanistan	2,280
Iraq	1,835
Sri Lanka	1,425
Somalia	1,380
Turkey	830
China	805
Zimbabwe	775
Pakistan	695
Iran	690
Fed. Rep. of Yugoslavia	545
Other nationalities	6,735
Total	18,005

Source: Asylum Statistics, Fourth Quarter 2001, Home Office

was also a participant in intergovernmental EU co-operation on immigration and asylum after the Single European Act until the Amsterdam Treaty in 1997. Rules were introduced to cover 'manifestly unfounded applications', the automatic rejection of applications from countries deemed safe, visa requirements and carrier sanctions. This toughening of external controls temporarily stemmed the number of asylum applicants in 1992 and 1993, but from 1994 until the end of the 1990s applications rose, as Table 2.2 shows. Table 2.3 shows the ten leading countries from which asylum applicants in the UK originated at the end of 2001.

External controls were brought into focus by the events at the Red Cross's reception centre at Sangatte near Calais, in northern France. A regional decree in 1999 opened the shelter in order to get migrants off the streets of French port cities. Many of the migrants then left the camp and tried to board the channel tunnel trains bound for the UK. Those who failed were returned to the camp, from where they could try again. In September 2001, British Home Secretary David Blunkett asked the French government to shut down Sangatte while Eurotunnel sued the French government to achieve the same result. However, a French court refused to shut down the Sangatte camp, which is operated by the Red Cross. The reasons for the Sangatte problems were more difficult to discern. The UK is an attractive destination for these asylum seekers, but this does not mean that the UK is a soft touch. Perhaps Britain is out of step in some way with Europe? There are some legislative differences between Britain and France. The UK recognises non-state persecution while France does not. Even so, research has shown that the main reasons that asylum-seekers might choose to make an application in a particular country are the presence of co-nationals (Böcker and Havinga, 1998). In addition to this, cultural and historical ties between countries are also important factors (Joly, 1997).

The situation at Sangatte worsened in late 2001 and early 2002. In January 2001 Eurotunnel filed a new court action in France in an attempt to close the camp after some 500 refugees breached security and entered the Eurotunnel terminal at Coquelles on Christmas night 2001. Of these around 130 managed to enter the tunnel. By January 2002, the Sangatte camp was holding more than 1,500 asylum seekers (it was built for around 650), mainly from Iraq, Iran and Afghanistan. What is interesting here is the involvement of private actors – ferry companies, train operators, truck drivers – as agents of the immigration control authorities.

As well as this border control issue, there is also a developing internal dimension to asylum policy. Access to welfare state benefits was the target of legislation introduced by the Conservative and Labour governments in the 1990s. The first main piece of legislation was the Conservative government's 1996 Asylum and Immigration Act. The legislation removed access to welfare benefits for 'in-country' asylum applicants, as opposed to applications made at the point of entry such as an air- or seaport. The effect was the risk of destitution for thousands of in-country applicants whose access to welfare state benefits would be removed. The courts intervened to determine that destitution for in-country applicants could lead to homeless and hungry asylum-seekers, that such an outcome would be barbaric and that it could not have been the legislation's intention. It was ruled that asylum seekers were the responsibility of local authorities under the terms of the 1948 National Assistance Act. The Court of Appeal upheld this decision in February 1997.

The effects of legislation were that the costs of caring for asylum seekers fell on a relatively small number of local authorities, such as London boroughs or seaside resorts with plenty of accommodation that housed the majority of asylum seekers. The expenditure on asylum seekers of around £400 million in 1997–98 fell unevenly on local authorities in London and the south east of England. In the seaside towns of southern England resentment among some local people to asylum seeking migration was most evident. The local newspaper in the coastal town of Dover ran a front page editorial in December 1998 that claimed that 'Illegal immigrants, asylum seekers, bootleggers and scum of the earth drug smugglers have targeted our beloved coastline. We are left with the back draft of a nation's human sewage and no cash to wash it down the drain' (Geddes, 2001a).

While in opposition prior to their 1997 election landslide, the Labour Party had opposed the Conservative government's toughening of asylum legislation. In government, Labour pursued with equal if not greater vigour measures designed to reduce the numbers of asylum seekers entering the UK. The 1999 Immigration and Asylum Act had two core elements (i) the introduction of vouchers for asylum seekers in place of cash paid welfare benefits and (ii) a national dispersal system to reduce the concentration of asylum seekers in London and the south east. The murder in summer 2001 of an asylum-seeker dispersed to a Glasgow housing estate was seen as an indictment of a dispersal policy that was ill conceived and hurriedly implemented with little consideration for the effects it was likely to have on either asylum seekers or on those who lived on the housing estates to which they were dispersed. Vouchers were criticised for being more expensive than the cash system that they replaced, while also stigmatising asylum seekers when they used vouchers. A government White Paper in October 2001 proposed a combination of induction, accommodation and detention centres for asylum seekers and the abolition of vouchers. Instead, asylum seekers would be issued with 'ID smart cards' in an attempt to reduce fraud in the system. The network of induction, accommodation and removal centres was designed to ensure swifter processing and tracking of claims.

New openings to labour migration

The UK government has also sought to create some new routes for labour migration in an attempt to re-establish a labour recruitment policy – or positive immigration policy. The difference this time is that the British government intends to plan the migration and link it to labour market needs. Indeed, the new policy has developed in response to labour shortages in key sectors such as health care and information and communication technologies (ICT). Before the 2001 general election, the Education Department's overseas labour division began advertising a fast-track entry to Britain for people with ICT and other specialist skills while immigration rules for other occupations such as nursing and teaching were also relaxed because of chronic shortages of labour in these areas. In January 2002, the government announced a Highly Skilled Migrant Programme (HSMP) based on a Canadian-style points system for would-be migrants.

The UK has thus been forced to reflect on its immigration and immi-grant policies because of the exigencies of economic change and its open-ness to international migration. It has begun to recast its immigration policies in a bid to attract more labour migrants and also had to consider how its immigrant policies match up to the diversity of migrant groups and origins in the wake of new forms of migration, particularly asylum seeking. It is to these immigrant integration policies that we now turn.

Immigrant policy

Britain looked to North America for a policy model in response to post-war immigration. The 1965, 1968 and 1976 Race Relations Acts put a policy frame in place. They sought to combat discrimination based on racial and ethnic origin and establish institutions to monitor compliance, particularly in the work place. The UK legislation of the 1960s reflected the US debates on civil rights, while in the 1970s there was more influence from ideas of race consciousness that had become prevalent in the US (Bleich, 2001). In 2001 new legislation extended the scope of race relations legislation to cover the police force in the aftermath of the Macpherson report's criticisms of the police's investigation of the racist murder of Stephen Lawrence while also imposing tougher equality obligations on employers.

The origins of race relations policy

UK policy has rested on a notion of multiculturalism defined by the Home Secretary of the time, Roy Jenkins, as 'not a flattening process of assimilation', but 'equal opportunity accompanied by cultural diversity'. The result, as Adrian Favell (1998a) put it has been 'multiculturalism on one island' with immigrant and ethnic minorities 'nationalised' in relation to British social and political institutions and in a way that is distinct in both practical and conceptual terms from responses in many other European countries. The continued resonance of the national point of reference is also evident in the report produced by the Commission on the Future of Multi-Ethnic Britain (Parekh, 1999), which was established after Labour's 1997 election victory and in its conclusions spoke of a vision of the UK as a 'community of communities'. The report highlighted the accumulation of pressure from Britain's ethnic minorities for greater social inclusion with calls for employers to be required to produce employment equity plans. The report makes scant reference to developments in the rest of Europe. The implicit assumption is that the UK policy frame is more advanced and that there is little to learn from the rest of Europe. Whether or not this is true, it could be argued that the establishment of EU level anti-discrimination legislation – which does actually reflect UK provision – also means that UK debates are now likely to acquire a European frame.

If we trace the origins of the UK response then we can see the links between immigration and immigrant policies: tight controls lead to better race relations or so the policy logic goes. The Home Secretary responsible for introducing the 1965 legislation, Frank Soskice, argued in a letter to Prime Minister Harold Wilson that control and integration should be seen as part of a 'package deal' with the government introducing measures not only 'to make controls effective, but to integrate the coloured immigrants into the community as first and not second class citizens' (cited in Hansen, 2000: 139). The first Race Relations Act in 1965 made discrimination on grounds of race, ethnicity, colour and national origin illegal, but was toothless because it only applied to public places such as cinemas and restaurants, but not to areas where discrimination was rife, such as education, employment and housing. The legislation also made such discrimination a criminal rather than civil offence, which meant that the burden of proof was high. In fact, the burden was so high that no prosecutions were brought. The emphasis was placed on conciliation through the newly created Race Relations Board.

A 1967 report by the organisation Political and Economic Planning revealed continued widespread racial discrimination (PEP, 1967). The Home Secretary of the time, Roy Jenkins, was prepared to act against it, although the draconian 1968 Commonwealth Immigrants Act overshadowed the measures. The 1968 Race Relations Act extended the provisions of the 1965 legislation to cover education, housing and employment, as well as the provision of goods, facilities and services to the public. The police were, however, excluded from the provisions of the legislation. It wasn't until 2001 that the police force was brought within the remit of race relations legislation. The most notable current exemption is the immigration service, which actually uses ethnic and national origins to identify potential unwanted immigrants.

The main weakness of the 1965 and 1968 Acts were that they were centred on direct discrimination and that they relied on conciliation rather than legal redress. The institutional architecture of race relations was also interesting. Responsibility was devolved to local institutions. The Community Relations Commission set up in 1968 sponsored local Community Relations Councils whose task was the promotion of good race relations. These committees were often composed of the local 'great and good', rather then by immigrants themselves. The good intentions of such organisations may have been overshadowed by their objectification of the immigrant presence: immigrants were a 'problem' to be solved rather than actors with some capacity to shape their own chances for social and political inclusion (Crowley, 1993). The transition from object to actor since the 1960s has been problematic, imbued with the assumptions of race relations, and emblematic of the difference between the formal extension of rights of citizenship and the effective utilisation of these rights.

The third piece of race relations introduced in 1976 sought to redress the deficiencies of the 1965 and 1968 legislation by introducing the concept of 'indirect discrimination' where treatment is formally equal, but the actual effect is to discriminate against a group defined in racial or ethnic terms. The allocation of public sector housing, for instance, could be formally equal, but the requirement for certain duration of residence could effectively exclude newly arrived immigrants and thus constitute indirect discrimination. The 1976 Act also allowed for 'positive action', a weak form of US-style affirmative action and established the Commission for Racial Equality (CRE) to monitor compliance with the power to initiate civil proceedings in cases of contravention. Erik Bleich (2001) has assessed the origins of the 1976 Race Relations legislation and highlighted the importance of North American influences. In particular, he argues that US policy was a continuous frame of reference and thus as ideas changed in the US – particularly heightened 'race consciousness' in the 1970s – then so too did the influences on British policy. UK policy changes arose because of the continuity imparted by the US frame of reference and the ways in which changes in the UK affected UK policy-makers.

The pathologies of a progressive idiom

Debates in the UK highlight the distinction between formal access to rights and effective utilisation of rights. There remains widespread and deep-seated discrimination against Britain's ethnic minorities while public opinion seems to be unsupportive of either immigration or immigrants. In surveys on British public attitudes towards ethnic minorities common responses were that there were too many black/Asian people and that black/Asian people get too much help. Older, poorer, less educated people or those living in the north of England were found to be more hostile to ethnic minority groups. There was also evidence of ignorance of the true size of the ethnic minority population, a MORI poll in 2000 for the *Readers Digest* found that on average respondents estimated the size of the ethnic minority population to be 26 per cent when the real figure was 7.1 per cent. Respondents thought that on average 20 per cent of the population were immigrants. The real figure was 4 per cent.

We also need to bear in mind that the term 'ethnic minorities' is a broad-brush characterisation of diverse population groups and that patterns of inclusion within and between ethnic minority groups are uneven

(Modood and Berthoud, 1997). For instance within the broadly defined Asian population, there is evidence of an 'Asian middle class' with higher levels of educational attainment and occupational and social mobility compared to people from Bangladesh and Pakistan. There are also important differences between men and women in the labour market and education system, for instance.

An area in which the formal extension of rights has not been matched by their effective utilisation is political representation. There are increasing numbers of local councillors and MPs of ethnic minority origin, but their numbers remain low. At the 2001 general election there were 57 ethnic minority candidates for Parliament, a record number of which 12 were elected (only one woman), all representing the Labour Party. A key feature of these patterns of representation is that 10 of the 12 represent areas with relatively large ethnic minority populations. It has been argued that this consigns ethnic minority representation to those areas where race is deemed to matter and away from those where it does not (Saggar, 1999; Geddes, 2001b). The implication is that ethnic minorities are best represented by people from the same ethnic group. If so, then the corollary is that white people are best represented by other white people. This form of race related politics imposes conceptual and practical constraints on increased representation. The Parekh report (1999) appeared to follow the political logic of race related politics when arguing that the main political parties should seek to select ethnic minority candidates in seats where more than 25 per cent of the population are from ethnic minorities. Such ideas highlight the underlying power of institutions and ideas associated with race related politics, which have meant that the representation of ethnic minorities has tended to be seen as concern for the ethnic minority population rather than a more general representational dilemma – as a minority rather than a mainstream issue.

These pathologies, of a progressive idiom, as Favell (1998b) calls them, were thrown into stark relief by urban disorder in the northern English towns of Bradford, Burnley and Oldham in the summer of 2001. Activity by the extreme right-wing British National Party contributed to the tensions. In effect, these had become near-segregated towns in which young white people and young Muslims scarcely mixed with each other. The clashes were portrayed as between the local white population and Muslim youths in towns that had become highly segregated between these population groups. The official Home Office report into this disorder brought forward 67 recommendations that sought to address the root causes of this segregation. The underlying poverty, unemployment and lack of opportunities were also a key factor uniting both sides of what had become an ethnic divide in these towns. Social deprivation had become fertile ground for the re-invention of social and economic issues as 'racial' and 'cultural' problems.

Interestingly, these pathologies of race relations policies arose – with associated agonising about the necessary response – at a time when the

UK government could congratulate itself on 'exporting' key elements of the UK policy approach to EU level in the form of the EU directives on 'race equality' and anti-discrimination in the workplace agreed by the Council of Ministers in June 2000. It is to these EU developments that we now turn.

European integration

UK responses to immigration appear to have been driven by domestic concerns. There was an international dimension in the sense that colonial ties structured movement to Britain and that post-war British immigration politics can be understood as part of a retreat from empire. But whether Britain's new role would be as a leading player in the EU has remained a vexed and, as yet, unresolved issue. While successive British governments have agonised about relations with the developing supranational structures on its doorstep, there have been significant EU migration policy developments with important effects for how we think about British immigration politics.

In this section of the chapter, UK policy towards the EU is explored. Various metaphors have been deployed to characterise this relationship: awkwardness, semi-detachment and reluctance to name three. But these metaphors describe rather than explain relations. How can the fact that British governments have exhibited a marked preference for intergovernmental co-operation on immigration and asylum be explained? Why have British governments opposed the extension of powers to supranational institutions? Why did the Labour government opt-out of the Amsterdam Treaty's Title IV, which brought free movement, immigration and asylum together within the 'Community' method of decision-making, as opposed to the intergovernmental Justice and Home Affairs pillar where they previously resided and with which the UK has been more comfortable? Is it the type of EU policy that causes difficulties with fear of a 'European model' that could be imposed on all member states? Are there fundamental institutional incompatibilities that divide British policy responses from those in other European countries? Is there some kind of mismatch in both the organisational practices and ideas associated with British race relations and the evolving EU migration policy framework?

Britain is subject to Community laws guaranteeing free movement for EU citizens within the single market, it never joined Schengen and opted out of the free movement, immigration and asylum provisions in Title IV of the Amsterdam Treaty. UK governments were enthusiastic participants in the intergovernmental co-operation at EU level that occurred from the mid-1980s until the Amsterdam Treaty came into effect, both in their 'informal' guise prior to the SEA and the more 'formal' co-operation in Maastricht's 'third pillar', from 1993 until 1999. The opt-out from

Amsterdam does not preclude UK participation in Title IV measures. The UK government has opted into the EU directives on temporary protection for refugees, the European Refugee Fund and the Eurodac database. It has opted out of the draft directives on family reunion and long term residents. UK governments have seen the 'security' aspects of European integration as a benefit that the UK electorate will accept.

The UK's establishment of external frontier controls at its main air and sea ports and a central command structure and mentality within which the role of the executive has been unquestioned can explain these policy preferences. Increased powers for the European Commission and European Court of Justice would threaten this. Why change a system that has by and large attained restrictive objectives? As outlined in the introductory chapter, European governments may well choose European co-operation and integration because they face domestic legal and judicial constraints. But why should British governments 'escape to Europe' when they face only limited constraints and, moreover, do not trust other states to implement strict controls as rigorously as the British authorities have?

Has the EU also had any effect on the 'race related' approach to immigrant integration pursued in the UK? The US reference has led to a detachment. The exponents of British race relations were able to pat themselves on the back in the belief that Britain had a more advanced policy frame, with anti-discrimination legislation in the civil code focused on employment issues and the Commission for Racial Equality monitoring compliance. There was a lack of interest in European developments and a belief that Britain had little to learn (Favell, 1998b). Perhaps most significantly, it was also feared that EU competencies could water down the British policy framework.

This changed after 1997. The election of a Labour government that was prepared to accept anti-discrimination provisions in the EU Treaty coincided with increased EU attention to problems of racism and xenophobia. More specifically, the entry of Haider's extreme right-wing Freedom Party into the Austrian coalition government in February 2000 created an intergovernmental impetus for anti-discrimination legislation. The policy frame adopted by the Commission drew heavily from that provided by pro-migrant lobby groups at EU level who had been strongly influenced by UK ideas on direct and indirect discrimination. When the member states decided that 'something needed to be done' there were already a set of ideas in circulation at European level advanced by pro-migrant groups (the Starting Line Group, in particular) that proposed anti-discrimination laws that drew from ideas and practices (such as indirect discrimination) that were a feature of UK policy. The development of EU anti-discrimination legislation indicates some potential for 'levelling up' rather than 'watering down' in the EU's Council of Ministers when certain conjunctural factors (the election of Haider) coincide with the prior existence of policy ideas on anti-discrimination and allow the acceptance of legislation that either exceeds that already in place in most member states, or in the case of France, does not fit with key ideas that have informed policy development (as we see in the next chapter).

Conclusion

It's tempting to argue that the main concerns of British immigration policy and politics have been to maintain 'fortress Britain' on the edge of 'fortress Europe' probably because of the view that 'fortress Europe' doesn't exist, but that 'fortress Britain' can. Britain can thus be detached from the effects of European integration, while benefiting from restrictive policies, and maintaining it's own distinct form of 'race related' immigrant integration policy. Almost immediately, the idea of a European politics of migration convergent in either horizontal or vertical terms is severely dented, if we follow this line.

It's not as simple as this, however. If we focus on the 'fortress Britain' side of things, we can see that controls in the UK have been 'gappy' and that anti-immigration rhetoric has not been matched by an ability to attain restrictive targets. This is a commonality with other European countries of immigration. At the same time, we can see that the UK has exerted powerfully exclusionary controls. Any openness to international migration is at the margins. The UK has not been a soft touch for immigrants. Rather, it has faced constraints on its control capacity similar to those faced by other European countries and there are also some points of convergence in the range of measures adopted to deal with international migration defined as unwanted. Moreover, in common with other European countries, institutional and organisational changes play an important part in shaping perceptions of migration and migrants. Post-imperial downsizing loosened any sense of obligation to people from former colonies while economic crises in the 1970s and 1980s and welfare state pressures and changed welfare state ideologies since the 1990s have structured perceptions of those migrants deemed as abusive or bogus. This has been particularly the case in relation to asylum-seeking migration. The point is that this has less to do with the personality or character of the individuals falling into the category of asylum-seeker than it does with the ways in which institutions and organisations view this form of migration and categorise those men, women and children that fall into it.

The UK has also possessed the capacity to re-imagine its conceptual and organisational borders to integrate people from former colonies but has done so in relation to a national model of 'multiculturalism in one country' that 'nationalised' the immigrant and ethnic minority population. This national approach has been receptive to external influences, although in the UK case these came mainly from the US. This nationalisation of immigrant and ethnic minorities could be seen as a pan-European commonality. The connection between European countries is that they have all developed nationally particular responses to the objectively similar phenomena associated with international migration. It has been in these national terms that the renewed debate about multiculturalism and citizenship in the UK has been cast with emphasis on language training and what are called 'norms of acceptability' for immigrant newcomers. That said, the recent introduction of EU anti-discrimination with key elements of British provision within it does mark a potentially interesting re-framing in a European direction of the traditional way of thinking about these issues in the UK.

When we probe recent UK policy developments in more detail we see evidence of convergence on restriction and a readiness to accept some aspects of the post-Amsterdam EU (including both immigration and immigrant policies). Some resistance to the effects of European integration has been combined with unavoidable entanglements and some new opportunities. The central issue, however, is that the distinct form of immigration politics in the UK has meant that successive UK governments have not looked to the EU as a means to 'escape' domestic constraints on control capacity. Indeed, Britain's relations with the EU remain one of the most troubling immigration policy issues and one that will be hard to resolve so long as Britain insists on maintaining its external frontier controls while these are dismantled across 'Schengenland'.

The distinctness of the British response becomes more apparent when we make the geographically short but conceptually longer journey to look at developments in France. Yet, at the same time, when some of the rhetoric is stripped away, some points of convergence in terms of both the immigration and immigrant policy also become evident.

3

France: Still the One and Indivisible Republic?

That France is a long-standing country of immigration but has not defined itself as a nation of immigrants is not unusual in itself. Other European countries have not understood themselves as immigration countries either. This chapter focuses on national particularities, points to some convergence with other European countries and explores European integration's impact. The chapter shows that debates in France about immigration were actually debates about nationality and citizenship. They were shaped by responses to movement to France by Muslims from France's former Maghrebi colonies, but also by a perceived 'crisis of integration' that had much deeper roots in French society. The ensuing debates about nationality and citizenship demonstrate how national citizenship evokes both a formal, legal membership *and* political, cultural and social membership. This chapter examines the extent to which these debates were grounded in domestic political factors within France and to what extent they were influenced by developments outside France, such as social and political processes common to liberal states. It also probes the impact of European integration. It is argued that debates in the 1980s and 1990s were largely driven by domestic political factors, but that the EU's role grew in the 1990s with implications for immigration and – more recently – immigrant policies.

Immigration policy

Rather than seeking to 'control' immigration, France has a long history of positively encouraging it because of concerns dating back to the nineteenth century about low levels of population growth (Noiriel, 1996). Migrants came from neighbouring or nearby countries such as Italy, Poland, Portugal and Spain. By the 1980s, 25 per cent of people living in France were either immigrants or had at least one immigrant relative (Tribalat, 1995).

Post-war expansiveness

A post-war debate between 'economists', who favoured bringing in workers to fill labour market gaps and 'demographers', who favoured families coming to France for longer-term settlement with an emphasis on their ability to assimilate, was won by the economists, in the sense that French policies remained expansive with no explicit ethnic hierarchy. Weil (1991) does, though, identify *de facto* ethnic selectivity marked by a decline in North African immigration while immigration from Italy, Portugal and Spain increased. A government ordinance of November 2, 1945 separated work and residence permits, which meant that the right to live in France was not dependent on the possession of a work permit. The 1945 ordinance also created the *Office national d'immigration* (ONI) followed in 1952 by the *Office français de protection des réfugiés et des apatrides* (OFPRA, French Office for the Protection of Refugees and Stateless Persons).

Labour migration to France until the 1970s was organised by the private sector with foreign workers recruited to fill labour market gaps and was thus largely uncontrolled by state authorities. (Hollifield, 1994: 146). Many migrant workers entered France during the 1950s and 1960s without the appropriate papers and regularised their status after settling. This was tolerated because, as the Minister of State for Social Affairs, Jean Marie Jeanneney, put it in 1966: 'Illegal immigration has its uses, for if we rigidly adhere to the regulations and international agreements we would perhaps be short of labour' (cited in Hargreaves, 1995: 178-9). By the late 1960s, 90 per cent of immigration was processed inside France.

The French government also signed labour recruitment agreements with 16 European and non-European countries. These reflected rather than created migration flows while extending legal and social rights to these labour migrants as denizens. The route to repairing this incomplete membership status was naturalisation. French nationality law was open and expansive and provided a relatively straightforward route for foreigners to become French.

Decolonisation in the 1950s and 1960s was the backdrop for debates about immigration and nationality in France. Between 1946 and 1990 the proportion of Europeans as a share of the foreign population fell from

TABLE 3.1 *Total French population by nationality, 1982–99*

	1982	1990	1999
Total population	54,295,612	56,651,955	58,520,688
French by birth	49,159,844	51,275,074	52,902,209
Acquired French nationality	1,421,568	1,780,279	2,355,293
Foreigners	3,714,200	3,596,602	3,263,186
	6.8%	6.3%	5.6%
Spanish	327,156	216,047	161,762
Italian	340,308	252,759	201,670
Portuguese	767,304	649,714	553,663
Algerian	805,116	614,207	477,482
Moroccan	441,308	572,652	504,096
Tunisian	190,800	206,336	154,356
Others	842,208	1,084,887	1,210,157

Source: INSEE

89 per cent to 41 per cent with strong growth in the numbers of people from the Maghreb. Until 1956 Morocco and Tunisia had been French protectorates. Until independence in 1962, Algeria was regarded as part of France. Under the terms of provisions made in 1947, Algerians had the right to freely enter France. In 1946 there were 22,000 Algerians in France, by 1982 there were 805,000 (see Table 3.1).

Ending immigration?

Economic recession led the French government to suspend labour and family migration in 1974 through two circulars. The Council of State overturned the suspension of family migration in 1978 because it contravened the constitutional right to family life. This is a point much emphasised by those who identify the role of courts and rights-based politics in opening social and political spaces for migrants and their descendants in Europe (Hollifield, 1992). The suspension also didn't apply to EC nationals moving for purposes of work who could freely enter France, asylum seekers who were covered by separate laws, and high skilled migrants who could still secure access to the French labour market.

The circulars had the unintended effect of creating 'illegal immigration' because previous irregular immigrants who had faced little difficulty regularising their status now faced major problems. The suspension also encouraged permanent settlement and helped change the composition of the French immigrant-origin population with:

- more women migrants;

- more younger and older people. In time, there was to be a second generation of Franco-Maghrebi youth oriented towards French society and making political claims on those terms;

- reduced economic participation because of the broader age distribution, but at the same time, increased engagement with the French welfare state, particularly the education and housing systems;

- increased unemployment resulting from discrimination and effects of the restructuring of the French economy;

- increased service sector employment that reflected more general economic shifts and feminisation of the immigrant-origin workforce;

- increased small business employment with the growth of ethnic entrepreneurialism. (Tapinos, 1994)

Did the continuation of immigration signify a loss of control? This would be an exaggeration. It makes more sense to argue that French control capacity was constrained in relation to particular types of migration linked to the legacy of French colonialism and recruitment agreements. The French courts also played a part in offering some guarantees for migrants' rights.

There was not during the 1970s a broader politicisation of migration. The 1974 suspension of labour migration and permanent settlement did not mean that immigration became subject to more open public debate. The circulars were bureaucratic devices and not widely discussed. The reliance on government circulars and bureaucratic discretion also helped create a tangled web of regulations that gave significant discretion to the executive in pursuit of restrictions aimed in particular at non-European immigrants. A 1968 report by the Economic and Social Council had characterised non-European immigrants as an 'inassimilable island' (cited in Schain, 1999: 207). A distinction between 'good' and 'bad' immigrants centred on the question of perceived assimilability. Europeans, particularly Catholics, were seen as more assimilable than non-Europeans, particularly Muslims. In turn, this led to a 'juridical balkanisation' (Miller, 1981) with a tougher regime against non-Europeans. The Badinter Law of June 1983, for instance, gave the police powers to use a person's hair and skin colour when deciding which people to stop for ID checks. This feature was again discussed in 1993, during the debate on the Pasqua law, with an article that stipulated that ID checks should not be based on racial or national origin.

In France, as in the UK, there was some talk of repatriation. Between 1977 and 1981 the minister of state for immigrant workers, Lionel Stoléru, provided repatriation assistance (*l'aide au retour*), but this was mainly taken up by Spanish and Portuguese people rather than by the intended Maghrebi immigrants. The Bonnet Law of 1980 tightened entry and residence rules, although plans for forcible deportations drawn up by Stoléru and the interior minister Christian Bonnet were rejected by Parliament in 1980. Many parts of the French administration including the ministries of Social Affairs and Foreign Affairs, as well as INSEE, the statistical institute, were against these measures and contacted members of the Council of State and MPs to lobby against them (Weil 1991).

The politicisation of immigration and nationality since the 1980s

During the 1980s immigration and nationality rose up the political agenda, with greater open public debate on the issues that divided the main political parties, providing fertile ground for the extreme right-wing *Front National*. Many immigrants had actually greeted the 1981 presidential election victory of the Socialist François Mitterrand with optimism. Immigration had not been a salient concern during the campaign. Indeed, Mitterrand and his opponent, Valéry Giscard d'Estaing, had agreed not to mention the issue during their televised debates. The Socialist government's first step was to address the irregular status of many immigrants caused by the 1974 immigration-stop. The Socialist government declared an amnesty for immigrants who had entered before January 1 1981. They would be allowed a 3-month permit, which would give them time to fill in the necessary forms to regularise their status. During the winter of 1981–2, 123,000 people had their status regularised. In 1984 the Socialist government gave more secure residency rights to foreigners via an automatically renewable 10-year combined work and residency permit. When the right regained a majority in the National Assembly in 1986 they restricted access to the permit with the effect that it didn't offer the security initially envisaged. The Socialists also continued with the repatriation assistance policy pursued by the right during the 1970s, although it was renamed *aide de reinsertion*.

In the 1980s, the relation between immigration, nationality and citizenship came to the fore in response to a perceived 'crisis of integration' (Wieviorka, 1991). This has largely been seen as a response to movement to France by people from the Maghreb, most of whom were Muslims. Yet, it needs also to be linked to deeper economic, social and political changes hitting France in the 1970s and 1980s that led to perceptions of a 'crisis of integration'. It would be a mistake to assume that it was the culture or identity of immigrants that induced this crisis. After all, there has been a longstanding tradition in France – and other European countries, for that matter – to view as problematic the cultural or ethnic identity of new migrants (Noiriel, 1996). There's little to suggest that Muslim immigrants were any more or less assimilable, but in the context of economic, social and political crises, it was not too difficult for links to be made between these problems and the presence of immigrant newcomers. In these terms, rather than in the debate about nationality and citizenship being linked to

the character of migrants, it can be connected to institutional and organisational pressures and changed understandings of the social and political
world by these organisations.

The political-cultural foundations of French perceptions of nationhood
and citizenship provided a backdrop for debate, although central tenets of
this 'tradition' were malleable and could be used by those opposed to and
those in favour of changes to nationality laws. French perceptions of
nationality and citizenship also are a distinct aspect of national particularity that stand in marked contrast to many other European countries.
Rogers Brubaker (1992: 1) sums up the distinct French position as follows:
'French nationhood is constituted by political unity, it is centrally
expressed in the striving for cultural unity'. Political inclusion within the
French nation state has meant the socio-cultural assimilation of both
indigenous (Bretons, Basques, Corsicans and the like) and immigrant-
origin minorities. A French republican model of national integration with
a strong assimilatory emphasis 'combines universalist and assimilationist
state strategies with the fusion of political and cultural ideologies of
membership' (Feldblum, 1999: 177). Republican ideas rest on:

- Universalism as enshrined in the Rights of Man of 1789;

- Unitarism in *la république une et indivisible*;

- The separation of church and state (*laïcité*);

- Assimilation with an onus on foreigners to become French and on
French institutions to facilitate this process.

In the nineteenth century expansive nationality laws had allowed France
to turn its substantial foreign-born population into French citizens. The
1889 nationality law automatically gave French citizenship at the age of
majority to all children born to foreign parents in France without any act
of affirmation, such as an oath of loyalty. In 1927, first generation foreigners were given easier access to French nationality via liberalisation of
naturalisation laws. In 1945 a reformed nationality law code annulled the
racist legislation of the Vichy regime that had removed citizenship rights
from Jewish people. After 1945 the nineteenth century nationality law
with birth and residence as the basis for the acquisition of French nationality was reaffirmed leading to a relatively open system combining *jus soli*
(birth on the territory) and *jus sanguinis* ('blood'/ethnic descent). To be
specific, Article 44 of the nationality code gave the right to automatic
acquisition of French nationality at the age of majority 'without formality'
to children born in France to non-French parents who had lived in France
for five continuous years. Automacity was the key part of debates in the
1980s and 1990s, but was less likely to apply to people from former French
colonies than to the children born in France of Italian, Portuguese or
Spanish immigrants.

If the aim was to restrict access to nationality for post-colonial migrants then Article 23 of the nationality code was actually the more relevant provision because it made people born in Algeria before 1962 legally French, as were their children. This was extended in 1973 to cover Moroccans and Tunisians. In 1973 the Gaullist deputy Pierre Mazeaud said that 'France, which is known for all time to be a land of immigration, affirming her character in the search for foreigners to espouse our nationality, must follow in the same spirit of generosity of complete assimilation' (cited in Hargreaves, 1995: 75). By the 1980s, Mazeaud would be a leading advocate of restricting access to French nationality.

The rich but malleable French republican tradition provides a backdrop to debate. It has been argued that these ideas underpin expansiveness and inclusion (Hollifield, 1992). Others identify a tension between the commitment to political universalism and egalitarianism and cultural particularism and intolerance towards 'others' deemed culturally distinct. Silverman (1992) links the move towards restrictions on access to nationality in the 1980s and 1990s with a 'racialisation' of French politics and the attempt to exclude those non-Europeans deemed to be racially distinct on the grounds of physical or cultural differences.

There are some other problems with using the 'republican model' as an overarching explanatory device. First, the 'republican tradition' is a moveable feast. Left and right-wing politicians espouse republican values to justify expansive and restrictive nationality laws. The term seems to have political rather than analytical usage with the model functioning on a rhetorical level rather than as a practical programme of action (Feldblum, 1993; Schain, 1999).

The rise of the Front National

The first round of presidential elections in May 2002 sent shockwaves through the French political establishment when the leader of the extreme right-wing *Front National* (FN), Jean Marie Le Pen, took 17 per cent of the vote in the first round. This pushed the Socialist candidate, Lionel Jospin, into third place. Le Pen then entered the second round to contest the Presidency with the incumbent, Jacques Chirac. Le Pen emphasised crime and feelings of insecurity and linked these to France's immigrant and immigrant-origin population. He was also aided by allegations of corruption against Chirac, 'the super-liar' as Le Pen dubbed him. In the second round, Chirac portrayed the election as democracy versus extremism and picked up support from both left and right to secure 82 per cent of the vote. Nevertheless, Le Pen secured around 18 per cent of the vote and the support of 5.5 million French people.

The FN has, though, been a presence in French politics for nearly 20 years. In this section we can attempt to disentangle two issues. Why did immigration and nationality become more salient since the 1980s? And what role did Europe's most successful extreme right party, the *Front National*, play in this salience?

The FN rose to prominence when it won control of the town of Dreux near Paris in the 1983 municipal elections (Gaspard, 1995). A run of electoral successes in the 1980s and 1990s followed with the FN picking up between 10 and 15 per cent of the vote. One result of the FN's prominence and its hard-line anti-immigration and extreme nationalist stance has been that 'Le Pen has at times been given nearly sole credit for imposing the tone and themes of the political debate, politicising citizenship and generating the rise of racial politics' (Feldblum, 1999: 32).

But were other factors at work too? Was the FN a symptom rather than a cause of the politicisation of immigration and nationality? Feldblum (1999) argues that a broader 'new nationalist politics of citizenship' stretched across the political spectrum to include mainstream political opinion and provided a backdrop against which citizenship and membership of the French national community could be re-envisioned. Four factors contributed to this.

First, it was clear by the 1980s that non-European immigrants were permanently settled in France. The ensuing debate in the 1980s and 1990s about national identity became a reformulation of a longer-standing debate about assimilation within the French national community that dates back to at least the nineteenth century. This debate was exacerbated by economic recession and increased unemployment.

Second, the stirrings can be detected in the 1960s and 1970s of a debate about pluralism in France encompassing both national and immigrant minorities (Safran, 1985). Mitterrand's Socialist government appeared more receptive to ethno-cultural diversity. For instance, at a 1981 presidential campaign rally in Brittany, Mitterrand said that 'we proclaim the right to difference'. In the first year of the Socialist government the Ministry of Culture produced a report entitled *Cultural Democracy and the Right to Difference* applicable to all minority cultures. A denunciation of the left's flirtation with multiculturalism then became a key aspect of the right's critique of the Socialist government. The FN even took the 'right to difference' and used it in an anti-immigrant 'right to be French' argument (Taguieff, 1991).

Third, the Muslim population in France were represented in ways that directly contributed to the perception of an inassimilable Muslim population and, more extremely, as some kind of subversive fifth column. This portrayal helped consolidate the idea of a 'crisis of integration' that defied the capacity of French institutions to rectify. Renan's (1882) classic nineteenth century formulation of French nationhood identified the church, army and schools as key agents of socialisation into the French national community. In the 1980s, the 'republican' institutions that many young North African origin youth were most likely to encounter were the housing authorities, criminal justice system and social workers with which relations were often conflictual (Schnapper, 1991). This represented an institutional crisis in its broadest terms involving both the nationality code as well as the ideas that underpinned French institutions.

Fourth, the media played a part in the politicisation of immigration, nationality and citizenship. In October 1985, for instance, the right-wing magazine, *Figaro*, published a special edition enquiring in apocalyptic language redolent of Powellism in Britain whether 'Will we be French in thirty years?'. The magazine also purported to reveal the 'secret numbers' that 'put in peril our national identity and determine the destiny of our civilisation' (Hargreaves, 1995). *Figaro* managed to combine the whiff of conspiracy and sell-out by the political elite that underpinned much of the FN's populist rhetoric with apocalyptic forecasts about the longer-term consequences of supposedly inassimilable non-European immigration.

At stake appeared to be the core institutions of French society in the face of immigration. This tended to depend on the perception of these immigrants as somehow less assimilable than earlier immigrants. This is a questionable assertion. The history of immigration in France suggests that new immigrant groups were likely to encounter hostility and that their presence was likely to be accompanied by some agonising about what immigration meant for society. In these terms the response was familiar. What had changed, however, was the confidence in the ability of key social and political institutions to perform an integrating role. This reaffirms the point made in this book's introduction: we can understand immigration as a challenge to the nation state, but changes in these nation states have important effects on our understanding of immigration and immigrants. The 'crisis of integration' in France was far more than a debate about immigration and nationality, but immigrants could be identified rather simplistically as the challenge when in reality the causes were more deep seated.

Guiraudon (2000a) develops these points about the rising salience of immigration, but locates them in relation to specific features of the French political system. She argues that although there was hostility towards immigrants in other European countries and negative portrayals of them by the media, the level of politicisation in France was heightened by features of the French political system. First, there were numerous national electoral campaigns because of the dual executive system (presidential and parliamentary elections). Second, the left-right cleavage was displaced after 1983 away from macroeconomic issues towards societal issues including immigration. Third, there were extra-institutional protests that were much more developed than in other European countries and that this mobilisation by pro-migrant social movements created a backlash. Fourth, there were flirtations with the *Front National* by both the left and right. President Mitterrand risked increased support for the *Front National* with his introduction of proportional representation for National Assembly elections in 1985 (in an attempt to weaken the mainstream right). The Socialist Prime Minister Laurent Fabius went so far as to state the FN were asking the right questions. The mainstream right adopted FN themes on immigration and insecurity.

The conditions were thus created for the debate about nationality and citizenship to be contested on a 'national terrain' (Feldblum, 1999). Articles 23 and 44 were the focus of attention. Article 23 had already provoked hostility and resentment among some Algerians born before 1962 because even after independence their children were still claimed by France. In the 1970s the left had called for a voluntarist revision of the nationality code that would remove this problem. Article 23 also became the target for the right's critique of the nationality code, or as a book arguing for more restrictive nationality laws put it, 'to be French you have to deserve it'.

There were three main arguments for more restrictive nationality legislation (Brubaker, 1992). Voluntarist arguments stressed the need for an act of affirmation. Statist arguments focused on the ways that expansive laws allowed some foreigners to evade immigration controls. Nationalist arguments centred on a suspicion that some people were *français des papiers* (French by document) rather than *français de coeur* (French in the heart).

Resistance to change in 1986

The joint manifesto of the centre-right RPR/UDF parties for the 1986 legislative elections stated that individuals must accept French nationality through an act of affirmation. In the run-up to the legislative elections President Mitterrand altered the electoral system to proportional representation in a bid to split the right-wing vote and minimise Socialist losses. To some extent this was accomplished, although the right still triumphed while the FN secured 35 seats in the National Assembly and became a more credible political force because of the legitimacy bestowed by parliamentary representation.

The new right-wing government of Prime Minister Chirac adopted a more restrictive immigration policy with extended deportation powers and restricted access to the 10-year residence permits introduced by the Socialists only two years earlier. Chirac's government did, though, face major problems with the proposed alterations to the nationality code. Article 23 was a difficult target because it was the most straightforward way for *all* French people to prove that they were French. In addition, altering Article 23 to exclude people born in Algeria would be tantamount to a denial of France's imperial past. The Bureau of Nationality (BoN) within the Ministry of Justice highlighted the technical difficulties, although it favoured removing the 1973 alterations to the nationality code that had extended Article 23's coverage to include Moroccans and Tunisians (Feldblum, 1999: 78-85). Attention turned to Article 44. It was proposed that an oath of allegiance be introduced and formal assimilation conditions be prescribed, including knowledge of the French language and an enlarged list of offences that disqualified individuals.

Opposition to the proposed changes was strong. President Mitterrand made it clear that the philosophy underpinning the legislation was one that he did not share. Presidential disdain combined with the right's precarious parliamentary majority and the legal and technical difficulties identified by the BoN to weaken the legislation. There was also strong extra-parliamentary opposition with protesters against higher education legislation teaming up with protesters against the nationality legislation (Wayland, 1993). The legislation failed because the burden of proof lay with the restrictionists who found themselves exposed on a number of issues while resting on a small parliamentary majority. This imposed political and institutional constraints at a time when 'the rhetorical playing field was not a level one. Opponents of the reform could and did mobilise the rich symbolic and rhetorical resources associated with the French assimilationist tradition' (Brubaker, 1992: 159).

In an attempt to defuse the issue a *Commission des Sages* (Commission of Experts) was appointed to examine French nationality law. The final report emphasised the correlation between nationality law and national identity with nationality law seen as promoting the integration of immigrants. The result was the maintenance of existing practices with relatively open naturalisation (Long, 1988).

The left's victory in the 1988 parliamentary elections put the nationality issue on the backburner. The Socialist government adopted an immigration policy with three main elements: labour market regulation; restrictions on undocumented migration, and; integration of settled immigrants. In addition, the *Haut Conseil à l'intégration* (the High Council for Integration) was created (discussed more fully later). In 1989 the Joxe laws toughened immigration controls, although this was counterbalanced with extended anti-discrimination provisions contained in July 1990 legislation. In contrast with British race relations laws that looked to the US and imported ideas about civil rights and anti-discrimination, the reference point for French legislation was the racist Vichy regime. Yet, French legislation was based in the criminal code where sanctions were severe, but where the burden of proof was also high. This becomes interesting when the impact of EU anti-discrimination legislation is considered later in this chapter.

The right's victory in the 1993 legislative elections prompted further swift commitment to tighter immigration controls and a restrictive amendment of the nationality code. The policies were designed to counter the FN, but also heightened the air of crisis and further increased the heat of debates about immigration, nationality and citizenship. The second Pasqua law of 1994 required foreign workers and students to wait two years rather than one before family members could join them, and prohibited the regularisation of status for undocumented migrants who married French citizens. Mayors were given the power to annul suspected marriages of convenience (*mariage blanc*). Any person expelled from France was denied access to French territory for a year. The Pasqua law also denied welfare benefits to illegal migrants except for obligatory schooling (a duty not a right) and emergency health care.

Externalising controls

It has already been suggested that the EU can provide new opportunities for its member states to pursue restrictive policies. An additional advantage is that EU co-operation is shielded from legislative or judicial scrutiny. The French government had encountered domestic constraints such as the Council of State's 1978 decision on the right to family reunification. Could co-operation at European level provide a new venue for the development of restrictive policies where legal and parliamentary constraints would be minimal? James Hollifield (2000b) has argued that French governments have sought to externalise controls via bilateral and multilateral agreements such as the EU and the Schengen arrangements where legal and political constraints are less onerous. Indeed, in response to the second Pasqua Law, the Council of State warned that measures on family reunification and asylum were likely to be unconstitutional. In August 1993 the highest constitutional authority, the Constitutional Council, deemed the one-year exclusion from French territory for people who had been deported, restrictions on family reunification, marriage restrictions, and EU asylum co-operation to be unconstitutional. Pasqua was not prepared to accept 'government by judges' and pushed the issue to a constitutional amendment passed by a specially convened joint session of the National Assembly and Senate held at Versailles in November 1993.

Participation in EU structures helped the French government to restrict the ability of unwanted immigrants such as asylum-seekers to enter French territory. The Constitutional Council's concerns arose because the French constitution guarantees that people who are persecuted because of their actions in favour of freedom have the right to asylum on the territory of the French republic. This created a territorial right to asylum independent of the granting of refugee status (Wihtol de Wenden, 1994: 87). The number of asylum requests made in France between the mid-1970s and mid-1980s had risen with more asylum seekers coming from countries such as Vietnam, Turkey and Sri Lanka. The externalisation of controls through European integration was part of the response.

Changed nationality law in 1993

Nationality and citizenship came back onto the political agenda following the right's 1993 legislative election victory. In order to achieve a more restrictive CNF the Méhaignerie law resurrected the core aspects of the failed 1986 legislation. The advantage this time was that the proposed

TABLE 3.2   *Naturalisations in France by decree and declaration 1984–95*

Year	Decree (a)	Declaration (b)	Total (a+b)	Ratio (a/b)
1984	20,056	15,517	35,573	1.3
1985	41,588	19,089	60,677	2.2
1986	33,402	22,566	55,968	1.5
1987	25,702	16,052	41,754	1.6
1988	26,961	27,338	54,299	1.1
1989	33,040	26,468	59,508	1.2
1990	34,899	30,077	64,976	1.2
1991	39,455	32,768	72,213	1.2
1992	39,346	32,249	71,595	1.2
1993	40,739	32,425	73,164	1.3
1994	49,449	43,035	92,484	1.1
1995	40,867	18,121	58,988	2.3

Source: Hollifield, 1999: 71

measures faced an entirely different political context to that encountered at the time of the 1986 legislation. The right held 80 per cent of the seats in the chamber of deputies, which ensured a smooth passage for the legislation.

The nationality legislation was steered through the National Assembly by Deputy Mazeaud, a Gaullist who had advocated expansive policies in the 1970s. Mazeaud's u-turn on this issue appears to have been motivated in part by concerns about the religious affiliations of North African immigrants. In an interview with *Le Monde* Mazeaud stated that: 'The role of Islam stands out more and more – Islam and particularly the fundamentalist threat, which refuses all adherence to our society' (cited in Hargreaves, 1995: 174).

The Méhaignerie law proposed changes to Article 44 so that children born in France of foreign parents would have to file a formal request for French nationality between the ages of 16 and 21 and have to 'manifest their wish' to be French. The law also rescinded the 1973 expansive amendment of the CNF that had included Moroccans and Tunisians and tightened provisions relating to Algerians by introducing an extended period of residence for the parents of children born in France before their children could acquire French nationality. The legislation meant that *jus soli* continued to exist but in a reduced form with a move towards voluntarism rather than automacity. Naturalisations increased in the aftermath of the legislation, as Table 3.2 shows.

Efforts to restrict immigration continued. The Debré law of 1997 was a reaction to the issue of immigrants *sans papiers* (without papers) who were of mainly west African origin and had been in France for many years, but because of tightened regulations had not been able to regularise their status. The Debré law specified that to renew a residence permit individuals needed to prove that they were not a threat to public order. In effect this required people to prove that they were innocent and was struck down for this reason by the Constitutional Council. The bill also stipulated that children under the age of 16 would need to prove 10 years of residence before they could become French nationals and that foreign spouses would need to be married for two years before they would be eligible for a residence permit. Most controversially, the legislation proposed that French citizens notify the authorities whenever they received a non-EU citizen as a guest. The local mayor would be given powers to ensure that the person had actually left. Nationals of 30 countries were exempted from this measure and the list that remained made it clear that 'unwanted' immigrants from African countries were the main targets. The initial proposals met with strong opposition and were of dubious constitutionality. In the final version of the law the obligation fell on non-EU foreigners to report their movements, but even so were portrayed by opponents as redolent of Vichy restrictions.

The Socialists and the 'new Republican pact'

President Chirac's political risk of calling early parliamentary elections in May-June 1997 backfired when the left emerged victorious and a third period of co-habitation began with the executive split between the Gaullist President Chirac and the Socialist Prime Minister Jospin. The FN also polled well in the 1997 elections with 15 per cent of the vote. In 70 seats the FN candidate got more than 12.5 per cent of the votes in the first round and was entitled to contest the second round, which led to triangular contests that split the right-wing vote and contributed to the scale of the left's victory.

In June 1997 Prime Minister Jospin's first speech to the National Assembly spoke of a 'new republican pact', a 'return to the roots of the republic' and stated that birthright citizenship was inseparable from the French nation and that his government would restore this right (Hollifield, 2000b). His speech outlined four main aspects of the socialist government's policies on immigration, nationality and citizenship: control efforts directed towards undocumented migration; co-operation with sending states; a review of immigration and nationality law; and a resolution of the *sans papiers* problem.

A June 1997 amnesty sought to address the *sans papiers* issue. By December 1998 143,000 applications had been received and 80,000 residence permits granted. Jospin also announced a review of immigration and nationality legislation (Weil, 1997). The report published on August 1 1997 contained 120 propositions for modifying immigration and nationality law. It was argued that the most contestable aspect of the 1993 legislation was its revision of Article 44, although it was accepted that people should not become French without their knowledge. The key proposal, therefore, was to reverse the 1993 changes so that anyone born in France with French parents could acquire French nationality at the age of 18 so long as they could show continuous or discontinuous residence in France for at least five years after the age of 11. The report also proposed the creation of 'republican identity cards' for minors born in France to legally resident foreign parents that would guarantee readmission to French territory and free movement within the Schengen area. These changes were included within legislation presented to the National Assembly in December 1997.

At the same time, the interior minister, Jean Pierre Chevènement, amended rather than repealed the Debré legislation. The May 1998 legislation abolished the requirement for accommodation certificates introduced by the Debré law. These were replaced by a declaration signed by the French host that the foreigners accommodation needs would be met. In fact the change of name (*attestation d'accueil*) disguises the fact that the procedure remains pretty much the same: the mayor's signature is still necessary. The legislation also amended the asylum laws of July 1952 in order to extend the possibility of refusing admission to applicants from 'safe' countries. Two new forms of protection were also created: 'constitutional' asylum could be granted to people persecuted because of attempts to promote freedom, and 'territorial' asylum was open to those who could show that their life or freedom was threatened or that they were liable to inhuman or degrading treatment.

Restrictive immigration policies, battles over nationality, and alterations to the CNF were combined with attempts to 'integrate' settled immigrants and their descendants within the territorial, organisational and conceptual boundaries of the French nation state and changes in understanding of these boundaries.

Immigrant policies

French 'national integration' rests on the idea that as immigrants become 'integrated' then they disappear as a distinct component of French society as they are emancipated from the 'status of minorities as collectivities or communities' (Gallisot, 1989: 27; see also Weil and Crowley, 1994; Favell, 1998b). An effect of this is that the concept of minority is absent from French law with policy-makers finding it very difficult to think about the notion of minority groups (Lochak, 1989). Individualism and assimilationism were central to the mode of national integration without intermediary bodies expressing particular group identities based on ethnic background (Feldblum, 1999: 132). French *égalité, homogénéité* and *unité* contrasts with the opening towards ethnic pluralism and multiculturalism of British race relations.

Localisation and ethnicisation

There is also a strong local policy dimension. The main actors in France are associations, financed either through a national agency with regional offices (the *Fonds d'Action Sociale*, FAS) or through municipalities. Policy has not targeted immigrants and ethnic minorities *per se* so much as neighbourhoods as part of the *politique de la ville* (urban policy). That said, the contracts signed between the central state and the local authorities mention the immigrant population and integration issues. Measures tend to focus on this local level with, for instance, tax free zones in deprived areas to encourage business start-ups and the targeting of money in Education Priority Zones. There can also be markedly different responses in relatively small geographical areas as Garbaye's (2000) study of Lille and Roubaix in the north east of France demonstrates.

Despite the formal disavowal of ethnicity and ethnic minorities, Hargreaves (1995: 36) argues that there has actually been an 'ethnicisation' of French politics with 'political behaviour conditioned to a significant degree by consciousness of ethnic difference'. Lochak (1989) argues that the French authorities position moved since the 1970s from a toleration of difference to the institutionalisation and management of difference. In a similar vein, Ireland (1994: 31, emphasis in original) argues that France *created* an ethnic minorities problem with far reaching effects on its political system'. Schain (1999) explains this apparent opening to ethnic-based difference as the result of a gap between official rhetoric and actual practices. French republicanism, he argues, has been mediated on the ground by the state's interest in controlling and integrating its immigrant population and that this leads to *de facto* multiculturalism. Schain calls this 'the recognition of ethnicity in practice if not in theory' (p. 199) and an example of the ways that 'the best Jacobin traditions of French governments are tempered by emerging realities' (p. 214).

This development rests uneasily with a 'French model' and with state policies that formally do not take into account the ethnic background of immigrant groups. This is illustrated by the controversy surrounding demographic research conducted in the early 1990s. French official statistics have tended not to systematically analyse the immigrant and immigrant-origin population in the kinds of ways that would be familiar in the UK and the Netherlands. Indeed, this opposition to ethnic data was a specific French reservation when the June 2000 EU anti-discrimination directives were agreed (Geddes and Guiraudon, 2002). An exception to this was the report by Tribalat (1995), which asked questions about ethnic origin and language that had not been asked before. Tribalat's study focused on adults born in Algeria, Morocco, Portugal, Spain, Turkey and in certain

African and South Asian countries and interviews with people born in France (mostly with people between the ages of 20–29) where the head of household was not born in France. The data derived from the interviews was then compared with a control group of the indigenous population. The Tribalat report was oriented to French debates about assimilation, but was controversial because it collected data that highlighted differences between French people (Banton, 2001).

The local recognition of ethnic difference

The local roots of a *de facto* recognition of ethnic difference can be traced to the early 1970s, during which time key issues were housing inequalities and discrimination experienced by immigrants and their families. The status of immigrants as guests and the ban on foreign associations dating back to 1939 meant that foreign workers could make no formal claims on French politics. Rather, their political activity was supposed to remain directed towards the politics of their country of origin (Schmitter-Heisler, 1986). In 1979, the Minister of State for Immigrant Workers, Lionel Stoléru, spoke of *le droit à la différence* in the context of policies that sought to maintain links with countries of origin and was thus 'the antithesis of integration' (Hargreaves, 1995: 194).

A side-effect of the *laissez-faire* approach to immigration of the 1950s and 1960s was widespread discrimination, poor housing and local *seuils de tolérance* (thresholds of tolerance) although the policies and non-policies of the government had contributed directly to the high concentrations of immigrants in certain parts of towns and cities (Weil, 1991). Housing was a particularly thorny issue because of poor provision with many immigrants having no choice but to live in *bidonvilles* (shanty towns). In 1974, the post of Minister of State for Immigrant Workers was created. In 1975, 20 per cent of the payroll tax, which amounted to 1 per cent of the total salary bill for companies employing more than 10 workers, was directed towards immigrants' housing.

Amongst immigrant communities there were signs during the 1970s of mobilisation through housing associations. State institutions began to deal with immigrants in terms of their ethnic collective identities, which signified both a measure of toleration, but also a desire to control and channel these new and potentially challenging forms of political action.

The concern about inadequate housing was emblematic of the wider importance of welfare state issues where entitlements are derived from legal residence rather than nationality (Guiraudon, 2000b). Social and economic rights and the fight against discrimination were at the forefront of the agenda of immigrant groups in France (Miller, 1981; Wihtol de Wenden, 1988). In the 1980s, the focus broadened to also include political claims-making based on religion with a growing numbers of organisations established by Muslims (Kepel, 1987).

The relaxation in 1981 by the Socialist government of the laws on association created a window of opportunity for political activity by foreigners. This replaced a decree issued in 1939 by the Daladier government, which insisted on the political neutrality of immigrants borne from the fear that the Nazi and Fascist regimes might use associations of their nationals to undermine the French government. The 1981 law gave associations of foreigners the right to organise on the same basis as French associations, i.e., via a simple declaration to the interior ministry. This also gave immigrant associations access to the FAS, with immigrants participating in the FAS administrative council from 1983 onwards.

Immigrant organisation and la droit à la différence

Between 1981 and 1983 the social and political tensions surrounding immigration and nationality had increased. In the 'hot summer' of 1981 there was disorder in Lyon and strikes in car factories. The Socialist government stepped in to create educational priority zones in areas with large immigrant populations and provided more money from the FAS. It was also during this period in the early 1980s that activism by second generation North Africans (*beurs*) became evident and was characterised as a form of 'identity politics' (Wihtol de Wenden, 1988). At this time, the Socialists were caught between a flirtation with ethnic pluralism and the assimilationist model. Vulnerability to a right-wing backlash coupled with adherence of leading socialists to republican ideas saw the Socialists move quite rapidly from the language of multiculturalism and *la droit à la différence* towards a more assimilationist model captured by their 1986 election slogan of *vivre ensemble* (living together).

Initial attempts to consolidate immigration organisations had a class basis reflected in the aim of the *Conseil des Associations Immigrées en France* (CAIF, Council of immigrant Associations in France) to create a 'single immigrant worker organisation'. In the mid-1980s other broad-based organisations emerged. *SOS-racisme* was established in 1984 under the leadership of Harlem Désir, who had close connections with the Socialist government. The organisation pursued a rather vague and eclectic multiculturalist agenda that sought to move from the ambiguity of the 'right to difference' and embrace a no less ambiguous 'right to resemblance' (the slogan became the 'right to indifference' – *droit à l'indifférence*) coupled with a commitment to anti-discrimination under the slogan *'ne touche pas à mon pôte'* (don't touch my mate). A rival organisation *France-plus* pursued a more electoralist agenda by seeking to encourage young people of Franco-Maghrebi origin to engage with the political process both as voters and as candidates for elected office.

From the mid-1980s the presence of a Muslim population estimated at between 5 and 6 million people (Tribalat, 1995) was perceived by some as threatening the assimilationist foundations of French nationhood. The

Socialist Prime Minister, Pierre Mauroy revealed that these concerns existed at the heart of government when he spoke of religious groups 'acting on agendas that have little to do with French social realities'. A *cause célèbre* was the Foulard Affair of 1989 when three Muslim schoolgirls attending the College Gabriel Havez in the town of Creil were expelled from school for wearing the *hajib* (a scarf covering the head and neck) because their teachers saw this as counter to *laïcité*. The Foulard Affair 'revived existing controversies, played on French fears of a fundamentalist Islam, and dramatised anew continuing concerns about the future of immigrant communities in France' (Feldblum, 1999: 136). Schools were supposed to play a key role as agents of socialisation with ethnic differences left at the school door. By October 1989, the right were using the Foulard Affair as the basis for initiating a discussion of immigration control and more restrictive nationality laws. The issue also blurred lines between left and right. For instance, the leading Socialist politician Jean Pierre Chevenement stated in an interview with *Le Monde* that the 'right to difference' and what he called the 'American model' were a route to 'a Lebanon very simply' (cited in Feldblum, 1999: 140). The then education minister, Lionel Jospin, asked the Council of State for its advice and then, when a case-by-case approach was recommended, followed it. This is important to the extent that it shows that Jospin tried to diffuse and restrict the debate to a legal question. In such terms, Guiraudon (2000a) argues that this is an example of an attempt to reduce the scope and terms of debate through a change in institutional venue (the executive to the courts in this case).

The issue was particularly difficult for the Socialists because their official policy pronouncements rejected the notion of ethnic politics, or as Prime Minister Rocard put it to the executive committee of the Socialist Party, 'the juxtaposition of communities', the creation of geographic and cultural 'ghettos' and 'soft forms of apartheid' (cited in Feldblum, 1999: 142–3). As affirmation of this policy direction the *Haut Conseil à l'Intégration* (HCI) was established as a think tank in 1990 under the direction of a Secretary-General for integration based in the Prime Minister's office to deal with a range of integration concerns, although immigration was obviously near the top of the agenda. The HCI's first report in 1991 was entitled 'For a French model of integration' informed by 'a logic of equality and not a logic of minorities' (HCI, 1991: 19).

A central question was the relation between the French state and France's Muslim population whose loyalty and assimilability had been questioned by politicians of left and right. Hargreaves (1995) discusses the pursuit of a policy of co-option pursued by both left and right as a way of weakening the potential for the perceived threat of Islamic fundamentalism. Through the 1980s there were attempts to establish consultative structures and co-opt the representatives of France's Muslim population, although it was difficult to know with whom to speak because Islam in France was diffuse, diverse and non-hierarchical. The search for intermediary institutions has been seen as a usual strategy seeking 'conformity between a centralised state and the representative elements of specific communities' (Amiraux, 2000: 236). There were attempts by the state to sponsor a French Islam. In March 1990, the interior minister Pierre Joxe established the *Conseil de Réflexion sur l'Islam en France* (CORIF) in an attempt to incorporate representatives of France's Muslim communities in the wake of the Foulard Affair. It was also an attempt to dissociate these groups from their countries of origin. This desire to create a 'French Islam' was continued by the right when they returned to power. In 1994, the hard-line interior minister Charles Pasqua said 'It is no longer enough to talk of Islam in France. There has to be a French Islam. The French Republic is ready for this'. A recurring cause of concern for the French authorities – exacerbated by the terrorist attacks on New York on September 11 2001 – was that many mosques, Muslim schools and Islamic cultural centres were financed by the governments of Muslim states such as Saudi Arabia and Algeria and supported an orthodox Islam. Many imams were trained outside Europe. After the 2001 municipal elections, President Chirac met with some of the new mayors from towns and cities across France. A topic for discussion was the creation of a 'French Islam'.

Hargreaves (1995: 208) calls this kind of activity a 'conjuring trick' by which the French state has tried to minimise and control the impact of diverse ethnic origins. This conjuring trick has been a central element of the politics of immigrant integration in France with some divergence between the powerful rhetoric of 'national integration' and practices that have often involved recognition of ethnic difference. But to what extent have these ideas and practices also been influenced by external factors? Have developments in other European countries and from beyond the nation state, such as the EU, had an influence?

New policy directions?

Concerns about racism and discrimination were evident in the activities of the Socialist government elected in 1997. A report from the *Commisison Nationale Consultative des Droits de l'Homme* (2001) provided evidence of perceptions of racism in France and the groups that are the main targets for it (see Tables 3.3 and 3.4). The tables showed the persistence of the perception of racist attitudes and some constancy in terms of the groups targeted. It can also be seen that the category 'native French' was added, which reflected the experience of field researchers that a substantial number of people had internalised the *Front National's* message that it was the 'native French' who were losing out when policies favoured immigrants.

An October 1998 circular from the Minister of Employment and Solidarity, Martine Aubry, to the Préfets, the Director of ANPE (the national agency for employment), and the Director of AFPA (national agency for

TABLE 3.3 Perceptions of the level of racism in France (%)

Q: Would you say that at this moment racism in France is very common, rather common, rather rare or very rare?

	02/90	10/90	11/91	11/92	11/93	11/94	11/95	11/96	11/97	11/98	11/99	10/00	Evolution 99/00
Very common	36	38	38	36	35	34	39	41	35	32	30	29	–1
Rather common	54	56	52	53	55	55	54	53	56	60	62	62	=
Rather rare	7	5	7	9	7	8	6	4	6	6	6	7	+1
Very rare	1	–	2	1	1	1	–	1	1	1	1	1	=
No opinion	2	1	1	1	2	2	1	1	2	1	1	1	+
Total	100	100	100	100	100	100	100	100	100	100	100	100	

Source: Commisison Nationale Consultative des Droits de l'Homme (2001)

TABLE 3.4 Perceptions of the principal victims of racism and xenophobia in France (%)

Q: In your opinion who are the principal victims of racism, xenophobia and discrimination in France?

	02/90	10/90	11/91	11/92	11/93	11/94	11/95	11/96	11/97	11/98	11/99	10/00	Evolution 99/00
Maghrebis	83	85	83	83	79	77	77	83	75	76	77	75	−2
Beurs	58	59	57	65	61	67	67	71	63	65	57	55	−2
Black Africans	38	35	37	38	37	35	33	43	42	41	41	44	+3
Travelling people	37	31	24	29	33	30	28	36	37	38	28	41	+13
Jews	18	24	20	23	19	16	16	16	19	20	14	19	+5
'Native' French	–	–	–	–	–	–	–	–	14	13	7	10	+3
Antilleans	11	7	7	6	8	6	7	8	7	8	7	10	+3
Mediterranean people*	8	6	4	5	5	4	4	4	5	5	5	8	+3
East Europeans	–	–	–	–	–	–	–	7	12	12	6	7	+1
Asians	9	7	7	7	6	8	5	6	5	7	6	6	=
Others	3	5	4	6	7	5	8	4	2	1	1	1	=
No opinion	5	3	3	3	4	6	5	3	3	3	3	3	=

*Greek, Spanish, Italian and Portugese

Source: Commisison Nationale Consultative des Droits de l'Homme (2001)

professional training) stated that the fight against racial discrimination was to be regarded as an important government priority. This policy emphasis was reflected in the report produced by the *Haut Conseil à l'Integration* entitled *Lutte contre les discriminations*, which proposed an anti-discrimination body with some similarities to the UK Commission for Racial equality (CRE). A report by a member of the *Conseil d'État*, Jean Michel Belorgey, also proposed an anti-discrimination body that would be similar to the CRE, although this idea seemed to lapse. Minister Aubry also established a *Groupe d'Etude sur les Discriminations* (GED), which began its work in late 1998 (which became the *Groupe d'Etudes et de Lutte Contre les Discriminations*, GELD, in autumn 2000) with the task of diffusing knowledge and good practice.

There was also continued emphasis on both access to citizenship and the utilisation of citizenship rights. The *Assises de la Citoyenneté* in March 2000 were attended by over 1000 young people from the *banlieues* and by Prime Minister Jospin with citizenship, housing and employment to the fore in discussion. There were, though, few concrete outcomes, although a freephone number (114) was established to report discrimination with cases referred to the Commission for Access to Citizenship (CODAC, established in February 1999).

By 2003, France will also be bound by the EU directives covering race equality and discrimination in the workplace. These suggest some EU influence on French ideas about immigrant integration, to be considered more fully in the next section, which explores the EU's impact on the politics of migration in France.

European integration

European co-operation and integration do not necessarily weaken states. They can strengthen the capacity of member states' to achieve immigration policy objectives through externalising controls. EU institutions can shape understandings of good and bad mobility. European integration can also, of course, lead to the creation of supranational policies and laws that bind participating states and raise the possibility of unintended effects. While in the short-term at least, a shift to Europe can reduce domestic legal and political constraints, in the longer term, European integration's effects can feed into national laws and practices and re-order domestic political opportunities. The adoption of restrictive immigration policy by French governments in the early 1990s used the developing European frame as a device for reducing the ability of asylum-seekers and other unwanted immigrants to enter French territory, and the creation of post-Amsterdam immigration and immigrant policies have implications for French ways of 'doing' migration politics.

France was a founding EU member state, as well as a founding signatory of the Schengen agreement that sought swifter movement towards a frontier-free Europe with compensating internal security measures, including immigration and asylum. France also participated since the mid-1970s in the Trevi Group of member states who co-operated on internal security issues. This helped put in place a security frame and routinised interaction between internal security ministers and officials that was to have important effects on the Europeanisation of migration as a security concern in post-Maastricht Europe. Guiraudon (2000a) argues that French support for common European responses to immigration and asylum developed in the early 1980s, when immigration and asylum were not highly salient political issues, but at a time when the French state had begun to encounter domestic legal and political constraints on its control capacity. This accords with Hollifield's (2000b) argument that such a preference is an attempt to externalise immigration controls and escape the unwelcome intervention of national courts. From this perspective, the changes made by Pasqua in 1993 to French asylum laws can be seen as an attempt to avoid domestic legal and political constraints. Moreover, when the perceived interests of the French state have been threatened then steps have been taken to minimise some implications of European integration. In April 1996 the French government announced to the Schengen Executive Committee that it would maintain controls on the borders with Belgium and Luxembourg because of fears about easy movement of soft drugs from the Netherlands. The Dutch noted that Schengen made no mention of a harmonised drugs policy. France had initially introduced border controls as a measure against terrorist attacks. When these ended the French government maintained controls because they said they were needed because of the problems caused by Dutch drugs policy.

Can a pattern in French policy preferences be detected as the basis for engagement with EU institutions? In the early 1990s the French Socialist government favoured deeper European integration of immigration and asylum during the inter-state negotiations leading up to the Maastricht Treaty and expressed dissatisfaction with the informal intergovernmental arrangements that had developed in the aftermath of the SEA. The French government was not alone in holding this preference. The majority of member states favoured deeper European integration, but in a decision-making environment reliant on unanimity then the preferences of more reluctant states such as the Danish and British governments had a decisive and limiting effect on the range of possible outcomes. The resulting 'pillared' structure of the Maastricht Treaty was criticised by the French government for being too minimalist, but accepted as a basis for future development.

Maastricht's pillars were then seen as legal sandstone and thus capable of erosion, rather than legal granite. During the negotiations preceding the Amsterdam Treaty the French government maintained a long-standing preference for deeper integration, albeit with resistance to the extension of European Court of Justice (ECJ) jurisdiction over internal security matters. Along with the German government, the French were key players in the pre-Amsterdam Treaty negotiations. Opposition to integration from a small number of states led to the consideration of an EU 'fast lane'. A joint Franco-German declaration of December 1995 identified internal security, including immigration and asylum, as priorities for reform. The French and German governments agreed on the supranationalisation of immigration and asylum policy, the strengthening of anti-racism and xeno-phobia provisions and accession by the EU to the European Convention on Human Rights (ECHR). A Declaration by Chancellor Kohl and President Chirac in December 1995 stated that: 'Where one of the partners faces temporary difficulties in keeping up with the pace of progress in the Union, it would be desirable and feasible to introduce a general clause in the Treaties enabling those Member States which have the will and the capacity to do so to develop closer co-operation among themselves within the institutional framework of the Union.' (quoted in Hix and Niessen, 1996: 49). A joint declaration by the French and German foreign ministers in October 1996 spoke of 'intensified co-operation in the light of the further deepening of European integration'. The Amsterdam Treaty contained a clause allowing for 'closer co-operation' between more integration-minded member states (Ehlermann, 1998: 6).

Debates about EU citizenship and European identity were also at the margins of discussion of French nationality in the late 1980s and early 1990s. The Commission of Experts convened to consider French nationality law in the wake of the failed 1986 legislation were asked in a rather vague way by the Prime Minister to bear in mind '1992', the year of intended completion of the European single market. The head of the Commission, Marceau Long, called for a form of European citizenship that would disentangle nationality and citizenship although this was long before EU citizenship was created by the Maastricht Treaty, which did no such thing. Another member of the Commission, the sociologist Alain Touraine, argued that European integration meant that French national identity was less clear than in the past. The Commission of Experts was understandably unsure about the meaning and extent of a form of European citizenship that had still to be agreed by EU member states.

It is difficult to argue that something that did not at the time exist drove debates in France. Feldblum (1999: 157–8) argues that there was a framing effect in that European citizenship stimulated republicans of both the left and right to 're-envision' French citizenship as part of a broader defence of national identity. Moreover, the transposition of a derived right of EU citizenship – i.e. derived from prior possession of national citizenship onto diverse criteria for allocation of nationality in member states, was bound to create some anomalies. Weil (1994: 184) notes that EU citizenship: 'runs the risk of accentuating the marginalisation of non-EU residents that began with the crisis in France's 'republican' institutions and the intensely political nature of the debate over immigration'. Along with the German and British governments, the French government opposed the extension of EU citizenship to legally resident TCNs. In a statement issued after the Tampere summit meeting of EU heads of government in October 1999 the French, German and UK governments noted that TCNs 'residing legally and long term were entitled to be fully integrated' and 'as soon as good integration has been achieved and confirmed, it is natural and desirable that the foreigners defined ... should acquire the nationality of their state of residence' (Statewatch, September–October 1999).

The French government has adopted the June 2000 EU Directives based on Article 13 of the Amsterdam treaty dealing with direct and indirect discrimination on grounds including race, ethnicity and religion. This will mean that EU law prohibits direct or indirect discrimination on grounds of race, ethnicity and religion in the workplace and in provision of public services such as housing and education. When transposing the legislation into national law the French government added three other motives for discrimination to the list: physical appearance, last name and sexual orientation. The significant point is that France accepted EU legislation that brought practices and ideas that seem to be more associated with Anglo-Dutch 'ethnic minorities' policies into its national legislation. During the 1990s, French immigrant associations had shown little to no interest in the EU dimension. A key factor in 2000 that influenced the French government's stance was the entry into the Austrian coalition government of Haider's extreme right-wing Freedom party. In these terms, the acceptance by the French government of the European Commission's anti-discrimination proposals could be seen as a reaction against racism and thus as a rather more 'traditional' form of anti-racist response to extreme right-wing politicians. The French government was a leader of the hostility to the Austrian coalition containing the Freedom Party. In these circumstances, it was difficult for the French to then reject EU anti-discrimination legislation (Geddes and Guiraudon, 2002).

The EU laws agreed in June 2000 provide a more prescriptive model for the evolution of debates about anti-discrimination in France and supplement the vague framing effects of the 1980s and 1990s. European integration could then affect domestic structures in France where the 'fit', in terms of ideas and practices, is not so strong compared to countries like the UK and Netherlands where anti-discrimination laws are well entrenched.

Conclusion

The questions of convergence, divergence and the development of a European politics of migration have had robust tests in the opening two chapters. Both Britain and France have developed distinct approaches to post-war migration. These distinct approaches are also accompanied by mutual incomprehension and suspicion that widens the conceptual gulf between the two countries. Yet, in both France and the UK there are some similarities at the horizontal level: post-war labour migration to fill labour market gaps with post-colonial effects that influenced responses to immigration and its sequels. Even so, strong elements of diversity in the French approach are linked to French history and to specific political-institutional channelling effects. At the same time, both cases also show how organisational contexts in both countries and changes in these contexts have important effects on the understanding of international migration and migrants. Despite the particularities, in both the UK and France the understandings of immigration as a problem were linked to other more deep seated social, political and economic changes. These changes and feelings of insecurity among some sections of the French electorate provided fertile soil for Le Pen's extreme right *Front National*. Le Pen's second place in the first round of the 2002 French presidential elections propelled security to the top of the French political agenda and re-emphasised the familiar extreme right-wing linkage between security/insecurity and immigration.

The social, economic and political changes that have affected France and that contextualised the domestic politics of migration and immigration have a supranational dimension too. This is not to make the extravagant claim that supra- or post-national developments have driven the French approach. At the risk of tautology, debates about immigration in France remain very French. These national and sub-national particularities need to be accounted for because they drive much of the explanation. But when some of the rhetoric is stripped away there are similarities in the response to the objectively similar phenomena associated with international migration that suggest some horizontal convergence associated with political processes in liberal states and some vertical impact from the EU on immigration and immigrant policies that together give us some idea of the parameters of a European politics of migration and immigration rather than a series of distinct national cases.

4

Germany: Normalised Immigration Politics?

Between 1988 and 1992 more than 4 million people moved to the Federal Republic of Germany (FRG) at a time when the Federal Republic was undergoing momentous changes linked with the end of the Cold War and reunification with the ex-East Germany. During the 1990s, Germany's foreign population rose from 4 million to 7.3 million. By 1999 14 per cent of Germany's population had not been born in Germany. Yet, in formal terms, Germany remained *kein Einwanderungsland* (not an immigration country). Even with an international migration profile more akin to the USA, this self-understanding was central to the politics of migration in Germany. This chapter examines the implications of what Thomas Faist (1994) called the 'counterfactual ideology' of *kein Einwanderungsland*.

In the 1990s Germany reached the end of what Dietrich Thränhardt (1999) called a provisional period lasting from the creation of West Germany in 1949 until reunification in 1990. During this time unique impediments were placed on the capacity of the Federal Republic to regulate international migration. The legacy of migration by guestworkers, relatively liberal asylum provisions and a right to return for ethnic Germans (*Aussiedler*), meant that Germany was the European country that was most open to international migration in the 1990s. Yet, all this occurred when Germany did not actually possess an immigration policy because it was officially *kein Einwanderungsland*. The chapter's discussion of immigrant policy focuses on the implications of the relationship between Germany as a welfare state and Germany as an ethno-cultural national community and the resultant articulations between inclusion and exclusion that this has generated.

As with Britain and France, there are national particularities, but there are some points of convergence affecting both immigration and immigrant policies. The impact of European integration is also assessed in order to demonstrate both the use by German governments of the EU as an institutional venue for attaining domestic policy objectives while also showing the EU's capacity to feed back into German debates. The EU's impact can be seen in relation to the externalisation of controls on extra-EU migration and in debates about free movement by EU 'posted workers'.

Immigration policy

The term *kein Einwanderungsland* was officially adopted in the 1977 naturalisation regulations, by which time there were already 4 million foreign immigrants in Germany. For Rogers Brubaker (1992: 174) the 'not a country of immigration' statement should be seen as neither a social nor a demographic fact because patently the reverse was true. Rather it should be seen as 'a political-cultural norm' and as an element of national self-understanding. As such the statement amounts to a normative assertion that 'was conditional on the context of *de facto* immigration because otherwise there would be no point raising it' (Joppke, 1999: 65). The underlying reasons for this are linked to West German history as a provisional state and incomplete nation geared to the recovery of national unity. While the Federal Republic was not an immigration country, it did offer a 'right of return' to ethnic Germans in other countries.

Immigration to a non-immigration country

There were four main sources of post-war migration to Germany. First, *Aussiedler* migration, which between 1945 and 1955 amounted to around 12 million people fleeing persecution in Soviet bloc countries. Article 116 of the 1949 Basic Law gave automatic German citizenship to people possessing 'German nationality or who as a refugee or as an expellee of German descent or as their spouse or descendant has found residence in the territory of the German Reich in its borders of 31 December 1937'. The *Aussiedler* 'were seen as part of the German 'community of fate' (*Schicksalsgemeinschaft*) even if they were geographically distant. By 1950, refugees and expellees accounted for 16 per cent of the FRG's population.

The second source was the recruitment of 'guestworkers'. Between 1945 and 1955 *Aussiedler* had initially filled labour market gaps, but their numbers were insufficient. Guestworker recruitment was requested first by agriculture and then by industry. The first formal agreement was signed with Italy in 1955, although the Farmer's League of Baden-Württemberg had begun to recruit Italian workers as early as 1953. The ten-year gap between the end of the Second World War and the beginning of guestworker recruitment allowed the recruitment scheme to be 'reconstructed at a temporal distance from the experience of national socialism' (Esser and Korte, 1985: 169). Decisions about recruitment were made in the corporatist context of the Federal Labour Ministry (the BfA) with representatives of employer's organisations, trade unions and government.

By July 1960, Germany had recruited some 280,000 guestworkers, of whom around 45 per cent were Italian. In 1960, further recruitment agreements were signed with Spain and Greece and in 1961 with Turkey. The construction of the Berlin Wall in August 1961 ended movement from East Germany and placed greater reliance on foreign labour to fuel economic growth. Between 1961 and 1967 the FRG entered what Esser and Korte (1985: 169) referred to as a period of 'uncontrolled expansion'. This continued until the economic recession of 1966–67. Additional recruitment agreements were signed with Portugal (1964), Tunisia (1965) and Morocco (1963 and 1966). In April 1965 a new Foreigner's Law was introduced to replace the 1938 Aliens Regulations. The new law explicitly attempted to ensure that the state governed access to the FRG's territory while also attempting to ensure exit from it (Esser and Korte, 1985).

The recruitment of guestworkers was subjugated to the economic interests of the Federal Republic. Article 2(1) of the 1965 Law stated that a residence permit 'may be issued if the presence of the foreigner does not harm the interests of the FRG'. Conditions for these residence permits were all dependent on executive discretion. Residence permits were linked to work permits and both these types of permit were subordinated to West Germany's economic interests.

Two aspects of the 1965 legislation were particularly significant. First, the issuing of residence permits was a matter for the *länder* and dependent to a considerable extent on the political complexion of these 11 regional governments. Conservative Bavaria and Baden Württemberg were, for instance, more restrictive than liberal Hesse. Second, the 1965 legislation made no provision for family reunification. Such legislation was not put in place until 1981.

The number of guestworkers in Germany peaked at 1.3 million in 1966, but the recession of 1966–7 appeared to validate the expectation of return migration by the 'guests' because between 1966 and 1967 the number of guestworkers fell from 1.3 million to 0.9 million. Numbers picked up as the economy recovered between 1967 and 1973, but the ethnic composition of the guestworker population changed. There were fewer Italians and Yugoslavs and more Turks. At the beginning of the 1970s, 13 per cent of the foreign population were Turks, by 1980 33 per cent were (Esser and Korte, 1985: 172).

TABLE 4.1   *The foreign population of the Federal Republic of Germany, 1973–80*

	Guestworkers	Total foreign population
1973	2,595,000	3,966,000
1980	2,070,000	4,450,000

Source: Esser and Korte, 1985

The third major source of post-war movement to Germany was by the family members of guestworkers. As we saw in France and Britain, the end of labour migration did not mean the end of immigration. After the so-called immigration-stop the foreign population actually increased, as Table 4.1 shows.

The fourth main source was asylum seekers, whose rights were protected by the comparatively liberal provisions of Article 16 of the German constitution that recognised the right of the asylum applicant to make a claim rather than the obligation of the state to consider a claim made. The German government backtracked from this commitment during the 1990s: the symbolic right to asylum remained, but the actual ability to exercise the right by entering German state territory was reduced.

Immigration after the immigration-stop

Why did the FRG continue to accept immigrants after it had declared the intention to end the recruitment of migrant workers? Between 1955 and 1973 economic interests and labour market pressures underpinned the policy of expansiveness. After 1973 economic conditions did not favour the large-scale recruitment of migrant workers. There was some fluctuation in business attitudes to immigration. As Thränhardt (1999: 35) put it: employers and industrialists 'oscillate between their conservative leanings, ideas that immigration is an economic necessity in a time of demographic change, and an interest in a cheap and motivated labour force'. Economic interests were central to the period of large-scale recruitment, but are less helpful in explaining why immigration continued during the economic slowdown after the recruitment-stop.

Perhaps a sense of moral obligation to the guestworkers could explain continued openness to immigration? In 1982, Interior Minister Gerhard Baum stated that: 'We have brought them to this country since 1955 ... Even if they are without jobs we have obligations towards them'. But how could this vague commitment be given legal or political effect? In answer to this question, Joppke (1999: 69–70) identifies the role of law and the courts utilising two of the FRG's basic constitutional principles:

- the subordination of state power to the rights of the individual and
- the granting of the rights enshrined in the Basic Law to all irrespective of their nationality.

The effect, Joppke (1999) argues, was that the FRG's sovereignty was 'self-limited'. This is an argument with more general implications because it counters post-national claims about the power of international legal standards – externally constrained sovereignty – by contending that it was in fact domestic laws that limited states. In practical terms, this meant that resident foreigners were able to access formal legal and social rights and enjoy equal protection of the law. These rights increased with the duration of their residence because of the 'legal fate of dependency': long-term resident foreigners had nowhere else to go and thus should be formally treated in the same way as other Germans.

Three landmark rulings in the 1970s and 1980s confirmed these principles in cases where individual rights conflicted with state interest. The 1973 'Arab case' limited the state's powers of deportation. The 1978 'Indian case' allowed automatic renewal of residence permits. Previously, long-term residence had actually been a reason not to extend a resident permit because the FRG was *kein Einwanderungsland*. The 'Turkish' and 'Yugoslav' cases of 1987 were more complex. They dealt with the issue of family reunification and thus with new residence permits rather than the renewal of existing permits. Following a December 1981 ruling by the Federal government, measures had been introduced to allow family reunification, albeit with an 8-year residence qualification for the spouse and a 1-year wait outside the FRG for the partner (ultra-restrictive Bavaria imposed a 3-year wait for partners). This appeared to conflict with Article 6 of the Basic Law, which guaranteed the rights of the family, and a challenge was made to these family reunification measures on this basis. The Constitutional Court upheld the 8-year/1-year rule, but disallowed the additional Bavarian stringency. The Constitutional Court confirmed the state's sovereign power to control access to the state territory, but at the same time reduced the capacity of the state to control family migration in the sense that an automatic right (albeit restrictive) to family migration was established (Joppke, 1999).

During the period of socialist rule, East Germany had also recruited foreign workers, but also never defined itself as an immigration country. Foreign policy interests determined the DDR's recruitment of mainly male contract workers aged between 18 and 35 from other socialist states such as Poland, Hungary, Angola, Mozambique, North Korea and Vietnam. By 1989 there were 190,000 foreign workers in the GDR (1.2 per cent of the total population). There were no special integration measures because, according to Marxist-Leninist ideology, nationalism divided the working class while racism and xenophobia did not officially exist

(Ireland, 1997). This was convenient because it allowed contract workers to be housed in military style barracks on the edges of towns and cities. The collapse of the DDR in 1989 contributed to fears of large-scale east-west migration, which reinforced restrictive policies. The possibility of large-scale migration affected the reunification debate with the attitude of east Germans summed up by the phrase *Kommt die Deutschmark, bleiben wir; kommt sie nicht, geh'n zu ihr* (if the DM comes we stay, if not, then we leave for it).

Post Cold-War transformation and the reassertion of controls

The end of the Cold War transformed the migration context in the FRG. The 'right to return' was exercised by hundreds of thousands of *Aussiedler* in what Thränhardt (1999: 36) called 'the largest single state organised migration flow in the world'. Brubaker (1992: 171) notes that 'what was intended as a transitional legal provision [when the FRG was created in 1949] ... became something quite different: an open door to immigration and automatic citizenship for ethnic German immigrants from Eastern Europe and the Soviet Union'. Until the late 1980s this movement was uncontroversial because it vindicated the FRG's superiority. The presence of ethnic Germans did, however, become controversial as their numbers increased and the costs of special measures became more apparent following the 1988 Special Programme for *Aussiedler*, which provided DM2.2 billion for the construction of special housing. *Aussiedler* had never been particularly popular on the left. They were seen as natural supporters of the CDU/CSU.

By the early 1990s in a reunified Germany the 'incomplete nation' arguments that underpinned *Aussiedler* migration no longer held such force. The lack of sympathy on the left for the *Aussiedler* led to a preference for ethnic Germans being characterised as an undesirable *Deutschtumelei* (Germanishness) when asylum seekers were seen as possessing a greater moral claim (Thränhardt, 2000). There was also growing pressure from the *Länder* because of the costs of looking after the *Aussiedler*. The growing resentment on the left and pressure for some limitation from local government led to measures to limit the 'special treatment' received by the *Aussiedler*.

How could this migration be reduced given that ethnic Germans had a right to move to Germany? The first step was to externalise the controls. The 1990 Ethnic German Reception Law stipulated that an application to move to Germany had to be made from the country of origin. This placed greater emphasis on lengthy and complicated admission processes managed in sending countries such as Kazakhstan and Belarus. Further limits were placed in 1992 when quotas were placed on ethnic German immigration by a law that limited the right to claim *Aussiedler* status to people born before September 1 1993, with a 225,000 annual quota (plus or minus

10 per cent at the discretion of the Federal Reception Office in Cologne). *Aussiedler* arriving after 1992 were redefined as *Spätaussiedler* (late resettlers). From 1996, local authorities were given the right to disperse *Spätaussiedler* similar to the ways in which asylum-seekers were dispersed. These measures gave the state authorities increased powers to monitor, observe and regulate the lives of the *Aussiedler*, which placed them in a similar position to other immigrants (Bommes, 2000). The German government used external (application processes in countries of origin) and internal (dispersal and welfare state exclusion) measures to reassert its ability to regulate this form of migration (Bommes, 2000).

The growth in *Aussiedler* migration after the end of the Cold War was matched by a rapid growth in asylum-seeking migration. The FRG was the destination of choice for most asylum seekers in Europe. Thomas Faist (1994) argued that asylum actually served as a symbolic concern in German politics that shielded discussion of more fundamental issues such as immigration policy, social rights and nationality law. Article 16 of the Basic Law enshrined the right of the politically persecuted to enjoy the right to asylum. This recognised the right of the asylum-seeker to make an application rather than – as in other European countries – the responsibility of the state to consider a claim. The result was that asylum seekers in Germany were empowered by these provisions while the authority of the state to regulate access to the territory was undermined. In addition, Article 19 of the Basic Law offered the scope for lengthy and exhaustive legal redress. Even if an application was rejected there was scope for a follow-up application that could spin the process out for 8 years or more, after which time deportation would probably be ruled out for humanitarian reasons. In the peak year of 1992, 438,191 asylum applications were made in Germany (80 per cent of asylum applications in western Europe). This was in addition to the 1 million ethnic Germans who moved to Germany between 1989 and 1992. Between 1987 and 1995, 1.83 million applications for asylum were lodged. Of these 125,000 were granted refugee status, 130,000 were deported, 130,000 left voluntarily, 83,000 had cases that were still pending, 277,000 had not been decided by the courts, while 1.1 million either stayed in Germany, moved on or returned to their country of origin (Marshall, 2000: 40).

The problem as seen by the German government and as widely discussed in public debate was that Article 16 constrained the state's capacity to regulate access to its territory. The reasons for this lay in the FRG's special obligations after the Second World War. But by the 1980s and 1990s the FRG was trying to retreat from the asylum implications of these obligations in debates about immigration, which although tending not to be overtly nationalistic, were certainly more state-centred. The development of EU co-operation policy on asylum also provided an opportunity for Germany to avoid these obligations. European co-operation on asylum strengthened rather than weakened German capacity to regulate access to the state territory through measures such as the recognition of 'safe third countries', 'safe countries of origin' and fast-track procedures for 'manifestly unfounded applications'. The construction of a central and east European buffer zone around the EU and the forging by the German government of bi-lateral ties with its neighbours to the east was a key element of the reassertion of control by the German government.

That said, the questioning of the right to asylum could be traced to the 1970s when the changed political and ethnic composition of asylum-seekers began to be seen as problematic. Prior to the 1970s, most asylum seekers were fleeing totalitarian regimes in Soviet bloc countries. Following the arrival of left-wing refugees in the aftermath of the Chilean coup there were fears among some CDU/CSU politicians that these refugees brought with them the possibility of Communist subversion (Thränhardt, 2000). Asylum began to develop as a left-right issue. The right identified with the *Aussiedler*, the left with asylum seekers. In 1973, Interior Minister Genscher (FDP) used the term *Asylßbrauch* (abuse of the asylum procedure). In 1974, visa requirements were imposed on Palestinians and in 1980 for Afghans, Sri Lankans and Turks. In 1974 the *Länder* interior ministers agreed a formula for the dispersal of asylum-seekers. Between 1978 and 1981, eight federal laws shortened the asylum adjudication process. The main effect was, however, to increase the financial costs for the *Länder* who were responsible for housing asylum seekers. The regional governments pressed for change.

. From 1981 a transition was made from cash paid benefits to payment-in-kind with asylum-seekers turned into passive recipients of state handouts. The system of in-kind payments was, however, far more expensive at a cost of around DM5 billion per annum. The basis for an asylum claim was also amended. In 1982 a federal law dropped the category of 'Convention Refugee' as defined by the 1951 Geneva Convention because it was argued that the political persecution clause of Article 16 of the Basic Law already covered this. The key difference, however, was that the Convention spoke of *subjective* fear while Article 16 was based on the *objective* fact of persecution. A result of the law change was that by the mid-1980s 95 per cent of applications were being rejected. However, non-refoulement provisions meant that most stayed because of what became known as 'little asylum'. Only 1–2 per cent of rejected applicants were deported. So long as asylum-seeking migration continued then Article 16 would remain the key issue. The attacks on Article 16 intensified during the 1980s, particularly from the right. In 1986 Chancellor Kohl spoke of *Wirtschaftsasylanten* (economic asylum-seekers).

Restricting asylum

The increase in asylum after the end of the Cold War exacerbated some existing tensions rather than being the sole cause of them. A September

1991 opinion poll showed that 76 per cent of respondents favoured revision of Article 16. In the same poll, 96 per cent said that they wanted to end economic migration while 73 per cent favoured amending the Basic Law to restrict ethnic German migration (Marshall, 2000: 71). This discontent created some space for the extreme right to exploit the issue. The National Democrats (NDP), the German People's Party (DVU) and the Republican Party made some electoral gains. In 1991, the DVU got 6.2 per cent of the vote in traditionally liberal Bremen while in April 1992 the Republican Party picked up 10.9 per cent of the vote in Baden Württemberg. As with the rise of the French *Front National*, the rise of the German extreme right was more a symptom of the politicisation of immigration than a cause. But pressure from the extreme right did induce an eagerness to be tough on immigration and immigrants from mainstream right-wing parties (the CDU/CSU). The mainstream right began to argue that the position *ex ante* was no longer sustainable. The prominent CDU politician Alfred Dregger argued that 'Every state has to serve its own citizens first and only secondarily the rest of the world. Germany cannot become everyone's country' (cited in Joppke, 1999: 92). This was countered with an argument from the left that human rights interests obliged a continued commitment to the principles of Article 16.

Debates about Article 16 of the constitution were the key. The debate centred on seven issues. First, the 'not an immigration country' maxim still possessed resonance among the German population. Second, many asylum seekers were portrayed as 'bogus'. Third, the measures adopted in the 1970s and 1980s had already eroded in both material and symbolic terms the status of many asylum-seekers. Fourth, the perceived migration crisis following the end of the Cold War and German reunification led to migration issues leaving relatively shielded corporatist or judicial arenas and entering the wider political arena. Fifth, there was pressure from the *Länder* for changes because they picked up the costs of accommodating asylum seekers. Sixth, the centre-right governing CDU/CSU coalition felt pressured by the growth in support for extreme right-wing parties such as the NDP and the Republikaner. Seventh, racist outrages contributed to pressure for a more restricted right to asylum. In November 1992 after the murderous attack on a hostel housing foreigners in the east German town of Rostock an opinion poll found that 68 per cent of respondents thought that asylum seekers were abusing the system, 78 per cent favoured immediate deportation to 'safe countries', while 90 per cent were concerned about extreme right-wing violence.

All these factors contributed to pressure for a move away from the FRG's 'special obligations'. The EU provided a route. The amendment made to Article 16 by the Asylum Compromise of 1993 brought German law and practices into line with other EU member states and with the Dublin Convention agreed by those states in 1990 (Joppke, 1997). The 1993 legislation provided for:

- fast track applications deemed to be 'manifestly unfounded' because of, for instance, forged documents;
- 'safe third countries' including Poland and the Czech Republic to which asylum seekers could be returned;
- 'safe countries of origin' to which applicants could be returned;
- fast track adjudication procedures in extra-territorial space inside airports.

The numbers of asylum applicants fell while the asylum issue faded as a matter of public concern, although stabilisation in the Balkans in the mid-1990s also eased the flow of asylum-seekers. In 1992, 78 per cent of Germans saw asylum as the most important issue confronting the FRG. By 1993 this had fallen to 32 per cent and by 1995 to a mere 7 per cent. The potency of the 'anti-asylum card' in the hands of extreme right political parties faded. The asylum compromise was challenged in the courts, but in May 1996 the Constitutional Court ruled that: 'the concerns of the state – particularly in dealing with the problems arising from the large numbers of asylum seekers – had priority' (cited in Marshall, 2000: 95). A dissenting judgement noted that 'with this [legislation] the executive is given a free hand' (Marshall, 2000: 104). That may be true, but the Constitutional Court maintained that the right to determine access to the state territory was a key aspect of the sovereign authority of the German state. The fact that this had been in doubt does indicate the particularities of German immigration politics until the early 1990s and a 'normalisation' in the sense that there was a retreat from 'special obligations' with asylum practices becoming similar to those in other European countries, with the developing EU context playing an important role.

Towards an immigration policy?

Germany has not had a system for the regulation of immigration or the integration of migrant newcomers. This changed with the election of the Social Democrat/Green coalition in 1998. The question of immigration policy, or more precisely the lack of one, had lurked in the background. The issue was addressed by a group of leading academics that produced the *Manifest der 60: Deutschland und die Einwanderung* (Manifesto of the 60: Germany and Immigration). The Manifesto searched for concepts that could underpin an immigration policy informed by both humanitarian obligations and economic interests (Bade, 1994). There had been some attempt to promote some short-term and rotation migration as a labour market 'safety valve' (Rudolph, 1996). There were, however, growing concerns by the late 1990s about labour shortages in key economic sectors, such as IT. The SPD/Green coalition proposed that, in response to skills shortages in the IT sector, the German government begin to issue 'green cards' to IT specialists. The government's plan was to issue 20,000 of these five-year work visas. The proposals were portrayed as an attempt to attract Indian IT workers to Germany, and were attacked by the right who argued that German children should be trained rather than foreign workers recruited, particularly when unemployment in Germany was high. Take-up was low, which could be explained by the fact that Germany is not alone in entering the global competition for skilled migrant workers, while continued hostility in some quarters to this labour migration was not likely to help the recruitment drive.

In summer 2001 a Commission established by the SPD/Green coalition reviewed German immigration policy. The report of the Commission published in summer 2001 began by stating that Germany needs immigrants and that it needed to successfully integrate them. The Commission looked across the border to Dutch policy to argue that foreigners should learn German and raised the possibility of 'integration contracts' offering a quicker path to an unlimited residence or work permit for foreigners who passed a German language test, and penalties such as delayed family unification for immigrants that did not learn German. The Commission also proposed that more German language courses be offered to resident foreigners, with funding doubled to DM615 million annually to teach 220,000 foreigners a year.

On August 3, 2001, Interior Minister Otto Schilly proposed a bill that would give Germany its firstever regulated immigration system. The legislation was delayed following the terrorist attack of September 11, 2001, which led to increased emphasis on security issues. In August, though, Schilly did make the symbolically important declaration that 'Germany is an immigration country'. He also linked German labour market needs to a developing global competition for high-skilled immigrants: 'There's competition among the industrialised countries for the best minds. That's why we have to direct our immigration law more strongly toward our own economic interests' (*Migration News*, September 2001). The introduction of legislation was complicated by the fact that 2002 was the year of legislative elections with the Christian Democrat leader, Edmund Stoiber, indicating that he intended to make immigration an election issue (*Financial Times*, May 25, 2002).

Interior Minister Schilly's proposal would convert the present Federal Office for the Recognition of Refugees into a Federal Office for Migration and Refugees. Schilly was unprepared to follow all the advice of the immigration commission. He ruled out specific immigration quotas. This does, however, mark a substantial re-orientation of German policy on top of the restrictions on asylum and *Aussiedler* migration. Germany has recognised that it is an immigration country, that it needs some migrant workers to fill labour market gaps, and that the integration of these immigrants is an issue that the state needs to address. In the 1990s, the German government also reasserted its capacity to regulate access to the state territory through restrictions on ethnic migration and asylum seeking. Finally, these measures were attained within an EU context that has also allowed Germany to use EU venues as a way to attain domestic policy objectives, particularly in relation to asylum.

Immigrant policy

Because Germany had neither immigration nor immigrant policies did not mean that there was no concern about the inclusion of migrants and their descendants. This section of the chapter explores the articulation between Germany as a welfare state and the understanding of the German national community as a community of descent based on ethnic ties.

Germany's guestworker migrants were 'denizens'. They possessed legal, social, but not political rights. Exclusive nationality laws meant that this incomplete membership status was likely to persist into later generations with the result that children born in Germany of foreign parents would also be 'foreign'. In contrast to France – the country with which comparison is most usually made – Germany was conceived as a community of descent (*jus sanguinis*) rather than a territorial community (*jus soli*). Naturalisation was extremely difficult and, until 1990, entirely at the discretion of the state authorities. Things changed during the 1990s. Nationality laws were revised to allow for as-of-right naturalisation while there was also increased emphasis on a tighter demarcation of the territorial and conceptual borders of the national welfare state. This has been identified as a downplaying of national semantics with less emphasis on belonging to the imagined community of descent and more emphasis on belonging to the imagined community of GNP contributors (Bommes, 2000).

The role of the welfare state

The FRG's identity as a welfare state had important implications for non-national migrants. Foreign workers and their families were given access to social rights on a par with Germans. Article 20(1) of the Basic Law commits the FRG to the social inclusion of all citizens. The Social Security Code 'essentially makes no distinction between Germans and foreigners, but is geared to the residence of the beneficiaries in Germany' (Guiraudon, 2000b: 79). Upon arrival, guestworker migrants had similar working conditions to Germans, although they were housed in poor conditions in hostels and then in public housing, which was often of the lowest quality, in high-rise blocks on the edges of major towns and cities. In 1964 the federal government introduced measures covering accommodation and social provision for guestworkers, but these were geared entirely towards their temporary presence rather than permanent settlement (Esser and Korte, 1985).

The 1973 Federal Government Programme for the Employment of Immigrant Labour was the first attempt to deal with some of the social implications of long-term settlement for foreign workers. In the same year a committee was established in the Federal Chancellery to formulate some policy guidelines. The resultant *integration auf zeit* (temporary integration) paradigm prompted simultaneous emphasis on measures aimed at integration with others geared towards repatriation. These could be contradictory. For instance, a 1975 regulation on child allowances led to wide differentials between allowances payable to children in sending countries and children in the FRG, which actually stimulated family migration to West Germany (Esser and Korte, 1985: 177).

In 1978 an Ombudsman for the Advancement of the Integration of Foreign Workers and their Families was appointed. The first report by Ombudsman Heinz Kühn (SPD) was highly ambitious because not only did it identify Germany as an immigration country, but also argued for *jus soli* and local voting rights for foreigners. Once the palpitations had subsided, the government's response was far more cautious. The November 1979 guidelines called for the integration of the second generation into social and economic life, but not political life, and made no reference to nationality. Moreover, the guidelines continued to point in the direction of repatriation with a reference to the maintenance of ties with sending countries (Marshall, 2000: 13). Ombudsman Kühn resigned in frustration and was replaced by Liselotte Funke from the liberal Free Democrats. She pursued a three-fold strategy redolent of the approach being pursued in the UK and France: external frontier controls, repatriation if possible, integration of the already settled.

Private welfare organisations 'represented' the immigrants. The Catholic organisation Caritas looked after Catholics from Italy, Portugal and Spain. The protestant *Diakonie* acted for non-Catholic Christians from Greece while the non-denominational *Arbeitwohlfahrt* with trade union links assumed responsibility for Turks and Maghrebis. The result was the creation of cultures based on religious identities that many of the immigrants had not chosen for themselves. Migrants were turned whether they liked it or not into representatives of their national culture (Radtke, 1994).

Foreign workers were able to build social networks linked to the labour market, particularly the manufacturing industry. One effect was low levels of social mobility and a vulnerability to downturns in manufacturing. Foreigners in Germany could not participate in the formal political process, but they did have voting rights and eligibility to stand for the *betriebsrat* (works councils). Works councils in Germany have real influence over work time, dismissals and a wide range of other measures. As Thränhardt (2000: 179) puts it: 'participation makes sense for both foreign and indigenous workers, and co-operation strengthens the worker's position'. The apprenticeship system was also open to the children of foreign workers. There were some variations within the German foreign population with the emergence of what Esser and Korte (1985: 196) call 'ethnic strat-ification' with Yugoslavs at the top of the pile and Turks at the bottom. This was not necessarily because Turks were the least qualified group or poorly equipped for life in the FRG. Turks arrived last and had to accept jobs that left them at a higher risk of unemployment when labour market conditions changed.

The increased number of Turks also made them more visible with some attempts to 'demarcate an ethnic boundary' (Esser and Korte, 1985: 201). An aspect of this was religious identity. In 1982 the Turkish Islamic Union (DITIB) was founded as the German branch of the Turkish government's Directorate of Religious Affairs (*Diyanet*). By 1987, more than 50 per cent of the 1.7 million Muslims in Germany were practising this form of Islam that conformed with the ideology of the Kemalist state (Amiraux, 2000). In Germany, as in France, adherence to Islam has been construed as reac-tionary or as evidence of an unwillingness to integrate. Bastenier (1994) argues that the utilisation of aspects of ethnic identity – such as religion – as the basis for political action can signify a reworking of older disputes to explain current status and discrimination. The result is that 'the importance of ethnicity as a category of social practices arises out of and is measured by the social advantage one gains by invoking it. It is indicative of the wish to be included in the society, despite the obstacles faced, rather than being indicative of the existence of a hard core of cultural identities averse to any compromise' (Bastenier, 1994: 54).

On these grounds, it is wrong to see a permanent antithetical relation-ship between 'hosts' and 'immigrants' as though either of these constructs is static and unchanging. This static perception homogenises the host society and imputes to it a coherence that usually makes little sense while also assuming that ethnic identifications are regressive and potentially dangerous. Moreover, the 'ethnic' component of such mobilisation may also reflect the way in which the German state was actively complicit in the creation of 'ethnic minorities' through the ways in which migrant workers were dealt with as though they were defined by their national cultural origins whether they liked it or not (Radtke, 1994).

Another example of the disjunction between Germany as a welfare state and as an ethnic nation state is provided by the case of the *Aussiedler* whose status as 'ethnic belongers' and welfare state membership was redefined in a way akin to immigrant groups. Until the early 1990s the *Aussiedler* were treated as though they had lived in Germany for their whole lives. They were entitled to the same unemployment and pension benefits as other Germans and were given direct access to the health insurance system and to special educational and housing programmes. The 'deviating' welfare state biographies of the *Aussiedler* were thus 'repaired' (Bommes, 2000: 100–2). In the 1990s, however, the welfare state position of the *Aussiedler* was redefined to the extent that their treatment came to resemble that of foreign immigrants rather than Germans. This redefinition occurred via incremental decision-making processes in the neo-corporatist system within which the *Aussiedler* had no special interest groups to represent their interests. Bommes (2000) argues that by the 1990s an idea of Germany as a 'community of belonging' had been replaced by a 'community of contributors to the GNP'. This community of GNP contributors included – albeit at a lower level – the foreign population of guestworkers and their descendants, while excluding those deemed 'undeserving' such as asylum-seekers, refugees, contract labourers and *Spätaussiedler*.

From 1993, the entitlement of *Spätaussiedler* to unemployment benefits on their arrival was replaced by *übergangsgeld* (transition payments) linked to attendance at a language course. In 1995 these language courses were reduced to 6-months duration, which was insufficient in many cases for the acquisition of linguistic competencies necessary for success in the labour market. The 1994 Asylum Seekers Benefit Law reduced welfare benefits for asylum seekers. Within a 6-year period, welfare benefits available to *Aussiedler* became a question of social rather than national integration, which meant the adoption of a policy frame previously used for labour migrants.

Ethno-cultural nationality laws

The discussion of the role of social and labour market policy in the socio-economic integration of immigrants tends to be submerged by discussion of German nationality law. Analysts have highlighted the key role played by nationality law (for example, Brubaker, 1992; Wilpert, 1993; Levy, 1999). Indeed, Wilpert (1993) argues that German nationality laws were a form of 'institutional racism' because of their ethno-cultural foundations and exclusion of non-Germans.

There was no German nation state and no German citizenship until 1871. German national sentiment predated the creation of the nation state, which contrasts with post-1789 France where the opposite was true (Brubaker, 1992). The current provisions on nationality can be traced to the 1913 Nationality Law. Following the creation of the FRG in 1949 there was no separate West German citizenship. The citizenship laws of the FRG after the Second World War were seen as provisional in the incomplete nation and remained so even after East Germany established its own citizenship laws in 1967. The FRG's citizenship laws were geared to the recovery of national unity.

The 1913 Nationality Law conceptualised the German nation as a community of descent based on *jus sanguinis*. This placed formidable obstacles in the path of non-Germans because to become German was not simply a question of naturalisation or acquisition of nationality *à la français* but rather 'involved a social transubstantiation that immigrants have difficulty imagining, let alone desiring' (Brubaker, 1992: 78). In contrast to

France, national feeling developed in Germany before the creation of the nation state. The German nation was conceived as an organic cultural community, a *volksgemeinschaft* within which 'nationhood is an ethno-cultural, not a political fact' (Brubaker, 1992: 1). Even so, there has been tension in German politics between 'ethno-national' ideologies that see the state as an expression of the people, and 'state-national' ideologies that view the *staatsvolk* as the creation of the state. In the latter case, there is potential for the *staatsvolk* to be redefined, for instance, through nationality laws that make it easier for foreigners to become German.

Until 1990 the conditions for naturalisation were covered by Section 8 of the 1913 Nationality Law, which left the matter entirely to the discretion of the authorities. The 1977 Naturalisation Guidelines required spoken and written German, knowledge of the FRG's political system and at least 10 years residence. Even then nationality would only be granted if it served the public interest because, according to paragraph 2.3 of the regulations: 'The Federal Republic is not a country of immigration, it does not seek to deliberately increase the number of German citizens through naturalisation.' The regulations went on to state that 'The personal wishes and economic interests of the applicant cannot be decisive'. In addition to socio-economic integration there was also discretion at *Länder* level to require evidence of cultural assimilation. In Bavaria, for instance, knowledge of the first verse of the Bavarian national anthem was required.

The consequence of these kinds of restrictive measures was an annual naturalisation rate during the 1980s of less than 0.5 per cent of the foreign population. Dual nationality was not simply ruled out, it was described as 'evil' by a 1976 Constitutional Court ruling. In practice, dual nationality became increasingly common. Of the 630,000 naturalisations between 1975 and 1990, 430,000 entailed dual nationality for *Aussiedler* unable to relinquish their previous nationality.

These nationality provisions were heavily criticised from the left. This coincided with a more general left-wing distaste for the nation state and a belief that post-national forms of organisation would be more progressive. There were calls for a civic model that did not rest on 'blood' ties and that could facilitate 'post-national federative institutions'. This would rid Germany (and the rest of Europe) of 'obsolete nation state traditions that are centred on ethno-nationalism' (Fijalkowski, 1995: 862–3). From the right too there was an unwillingness to force the issue of naturalisation. For instance, Michael Glos of the right-wing Bavarian CSU, perhaps rather disingenuously given the exclusionary stance adopted by Bavaria, argued that naturalisation was undesirable because it would lead to 'forced Germanism' (*Zwagsgermanisierung*).

The issue of nationality also caused tensions during the 1980s within the governing coalition between the conservative-inclined CDU/CSU and the more liberal FDP. In 1982 the return to power of the CDU/CSU-led coalition prompted plans for a new Foreigners Law to replace the 1965 legislation. The new law would have banned marriage immigration for the second generation, but was shelved because the CDU/CSU coalition partners in the FDP opposed it. A further attempt to introduce hardline legislation which sought 'the maintenance of national character' with the guestworker period defined as 'an historically unique, finite event' and future stays by foreigners limited to 8 years was also abandoned in the face of widespread opposition including from more liberal elements within the CDU (Joppke, 1999: 83).

Towards a civic model?

The successful third attempt was made by interior minister Wolfgang Schauble and was more moderate in tone. The legislation recognised that by 1990 more than 70 per cent of the foreign population had lived in Germany for more than ten years and that since 1970 around 1.5 million so-called foreigners had actually been born in Germany. The legislation was agreed in April 1990 and entered into effect in 1991. The new law provided for:

- Naturalisation for foreigners with at least 15 years residence and for those of the 2nd and 3rd generation aged between 16 and 25 with at least 8 years residence.

- Family reunification for children under 16 no longer at *Länder* discretion.

- Foreigners given statutory residence and family rights.

- The one-year waiting period for spouses to be abolished.

- Spouses and children to be given residence rights independently of the head of the family.

- Second and third generation foreigners who had temporarily returned to their home country to be allowed to return to Germany.

This revised foreigners legislation tried to turn the page on the guestworker period as a unique and not to be repeated event. The basis for this limited openness towards the resident foreign population would be accompanied by restrictive measures to keep out further immigrants. Foreigners were given greater legal security, but access to German nationality still remained very difficult. Dietrich Thränhardt (1999) argues that the 1990 Foreigners Law ended the divergence between the French and German models with a move on the German side away from *jus sanguinis* to an element of *jus soli*. Christian Joppke (1999: 200) contends that the changes 'swept away cultural assimilation' with Germany recasting itself as a civic nation. In fact, if we compare debates in France with those in Germany we can see that overt displays of nationalism were far more evident during the 1980s and 1990s in 'civic' France (see Feldblum, 1999 for a comparison).

Despite the new legislation, naturalisation figures have remained low. In 1995 the naturalisation rate, excluding *Aussiedler*, stood at a mere 1 per cent. In 1995 there was some relaxation of nationality laws on the Turkish side when rules on property inheritance were relaxed and former nationals were allowed to reacquire Turkish nationality if they so desired. The national election victory in 1998 of the SPD/Green coalition brought to power two parties far more amenable to the civic model of the nation. The coalition agreement between the SPD and Greens acknowledged an irreversible process of immigration and argued that the aim of policy should be the integration of the resident foreign population. The government proposed that children born in Germany would obtain German nationality if one parent had been born in Germany or come to Germany while under the age of 14. This further reinforced *jus soli*, albeit without automatic acquisition of German nationality because parents had to apply on behalf of their children before they reached the age of 6. The new coalition also proposed that foreign spouses would be able to obtain citizenship independently of their partners, whereas before they lost their residence permit if the marriage broke up.

The opposition CDU/CSU criticised the proposals. Between January and February 1999 the opposition claimed to have got over 1 million signatures on a petition 'For integration – but against dual nationality'. A debate about the meaning of German national identity led to some attempts to define a 'guiding culture'. In February 1999 the right took control of traditionally liberal Hesse in the *Länder* elections. Of those who switched to the CDU, 61 per cent gave the foreigners issue as their main reason (Marshall, 2000). This electoral setback led to revised proposals from the government, which allowed dual nationality up to the age of 23 for the children of foreigners at which point a choice had to be made. The changes to the naturalisation law came into effect on January 1 2001. Around 200,000 foreigners applied to become Germans. There were also 300,000 foreign children under 18 who could have applied for automatic German citizenship, and then been dual nationals until age 23, but only 30,000 did so (*Migration News*, March 2001). The DM500 cost per application was identified as one explanation for this. The 1990s saw moves to a combination of *jus sanguinis* and *jus soli* that makes sense in a reunified Germany where the special circumstances of the provisional state and incomplete nation no longer hold such sway. To what extent were these changes driven by domestic political factors or by external factors such as European integration and ideas about European citizenship?

European integration

Integration into a federal Europe has been seen as part of the natural evolution of the German state. Yet, hard-headed concerns have also been involved in this preference for deeper integration. The 1993 asylum compromise showed that the German government could – without ditching its constitutional commitment to the rights of the politically persecuted – use European co-operation to slip domestic legal and political constraints through the creation of European institutions that helped reduce the numbers of asylum seekers entering the state territory and thus defuse the asylum crisis. The Federal Republic was also a founder member of Schengen and an active participant in the development of 'compensating' immigration and asylum measures. A particular concern has been with the migration effects of EU enlargement. The German government has expressed concerns about immediate extension of free movement rights to citizens of new member states. German governments have also sought to co-opt their central and eastern neighbours into a tight framework of immigration controls.

Throughout the 1990s, Germany was keen to seek a common European response to help resolve the asylum issues that it faced. The attempt to establish some redistributive solidarity, or 'burden sharing' as it was more commonly known, met a frosty response from neighbouring states who felt no obligation to assume responsibility for this political headache. The Schengen agreement – based as it was on international law and thus with problems of enforcement – provided little scope for the redistribution of asylum seekers. During the Maastricht negotiations, the German government expressed a preference for more elaborate Treaty provisions to overcome the decisional and democratic deficiencies of the post-SEA informal arrangements. Even though the majority of states favoured some form of supranationalisation of immigration and asylum the preference of a minority of member states for a 'pillared' intergovernmental structure held sway.

As with the French government, the German government also saw the Justice and Home Affairs pillar as a short-term measure on the route to more common policies covering key aspects of immigration and asylum. This preference was again evident within the Intergovernmental Conference that negotiated the Amsterdam Treaty. The German government expressed a preference for some further integration of immigration and asylum with a transfer from the intergovernmental JHA first pillar. As already noted in the chapter on France, the development of provisions for 'flexible co-operation' was an innovation of the Amsterdam Treaty and raises the possibility of a smaller group of states creating some kind of inner circle of deeply integrated countries and a Europe of 'variable geometry' (Geddes, 2000a: 115–17).

German governments have resisted any amendment to the provisions on EU citizenship that go beyond the derivative character established by the Maastricht Treaty. Naturalisation was confirmed as the route to the repair of the incomplete membership status of denizenship at the Tampere summit meeting of EU heads of government held in October 1999. A declaration by the French, British and German governments affirmed their commitment to the approximation of the rights of third country nationals, but with a firm statement that the nationality of a member state would remain the route to access EU rights. At least, German nationality law now seemed to allow this possibility.

The picture painted so far is of an 'escape to Europe' where the EU offers a chance for ministers and officials to dodge domestic legal and political constraints in the pursuit of restrictive immigration and asylum policies formulated in executive-friendly Euro-forums. This combines with a resistance to European integration where provisions such as EU citizenship rights for legally resident third country nationals would challenge national approaches to immigrant policy. This rests uneasily with a deeper ideological commitment to European integration that has been the hallmark of German policy. In fact, what it might show is that the combination of idealism and realism is a key element of the shift to EU co-operation. There is a preference for Europe but also a belief that Europe can help resolve some of the practical policy issues that states face. Indeed, in some senses, the EU can actually facilitate the reassertion of state control over 'unwanted' forms of migration.

Yet, the EU is much more than just an external venue to which member states escape. More than 40 years of European integration means that European integration has become part of the political process in member states and influences policy preferences. There is also the prospect of deeper integration in the wake of Title IV of the Amsterdam Treaty, which specifies common policies in areas related to free movement, immigration and asylum. Moreover, the anti-discrimination laws agreed in June 2000 empower both EU citizens of immigrant and ethnic minority origin as well as third country nationals. As Germany looks for concepts to inform its immigrant policies then the EU is likely to provide a powerful frame backed by legal and symbolic resources.

There are other ways in which the effects of European integration have been visible in Germany. The EU has responsibilities in the areas of labour, social and migration policy. This is most clearly evident in provisions for the free movement of workers, goods, services and capital within the single market. Free movement for service providers provoked a debate in Germany about EU migration when fears that cheaper labour from other EU member states could expose German 'consensus capitalism' to a challenge from a more liberalised, deregulated 'Anglo-American model'. The debate about these posted workers centred on the utilisation of rights established by the Treaty of Rome that guaranteed free movement for service providers (i.e. for workers to be posted by these service providers). The wages and non-wage social costs of these workers were paid in their country of origin. Germany has both relatively high wages and non-wage social costs. The effects were particularly noticeable in the construction sector where cheaper labour from Ireland, Portugal and the UK undercut German workers. There was an important difference between this 'posted worker' migration and 'guestworker' migration. Posted workers were labour market substitutes, guestworkers were complements. By 1999 there were an estimated 200,000 workers from other EU member states employed on German construction sites. This led to fears of European 'wage dumping' because German workers cost around DM40 per hour including their social security payments, but foreign workers cost much less. The 1996 Foreign Employees Posting Act and the EU's 1996 Posted Workers directive sought to eliminate wage dumping. The 1996 Act requires that collective wage agreements should apply to posted workers, but agreement on wage levels was difficult to reach and there were numerous violations (Hunger, 2000). Germany's attempts at re-regulation have also been challenged in the European Court of Justice and future rulings may undermine this attempt to re-regulate the labour market because such powers have been ceded to the EU. This while the FRG was able to reassert its authority to determine access by ethnic Germans and asylum-seekers: its ability to regulate and limit movement by EU citizens exercising rights under the Treaty is more limited.

The EU's social, labour and migration policy competencies can affect domestic contexts. The restoration of the principle of welfare state territoriality is difficult to reconcile with Germany's binding EU commitments. Yet, at the same time, a post/supra national alternative – some kind of European welfare state, for instance, is not in view (Halfmann, 2000). Welfare state and fiscal differences seem likely to persist.

In the late 1990s the German government was also concerned about EU enlargement to central and eastern Europe. Throughout the 1990s Germany had been concerned about the potential large-scale migration from central and eastern Europe and participated in a range of bilateral and multilateral forums to enhance the restrictive potential of its neighbours to the east. In 2001, Germany called for a seven-year moratorium on free movement for citizens of new member states. This is motivated by the hope that economic growth will occur on such a scale in central European member states as a result of accession that migratory potential diminishes. These issues will be discussed more fully in Chapter 8.

Conclusion

This chapter began by seeking to explore the particularities of the German case while also exploring the extent to which German immigration policy and politics have become convergent with policies pursued in other European countries. There are clear points of divergence in both the history of migration and the absence in Germany of either immigration or immigrant policies given the official denial (until recently) that Germany was an immigration country. That said, there are some points of convergence that became clearer during the 1990s as the provisional period of immigration policy in the 'incomplete state' ended. Like France and the

UK, Germany sought to retreat from prior commitments that inhibited the capacity of the German state to control access to its territory. This involved measures to restrict labour migration, asylum-seeking and *Aussiedler* migration. In respect to all these types of migration there were legal and political impediments on immigration controls. German governments also sought to externalise controls, through both bilateral agreements with surrounding states and EU co-operation, while retreating from the commitment to asylum made in Article 16. The German state was thus able to redefine its relationship with the international asylum system in ways that enhanced the ability of the German authorities to control access to the state territory.

Some of the most significant changes have occurred in nationality law. In the 1990s, Germany moved towards a civic model with a combination of *jus soli* and *jus sanguinis*. This indicates some ability to re-imagine and re-conceptualise the *staatsvolk* although, again, the reasons for this re-envisioning of national citizenship appear linked to domestic legal and political processes. The role of EU citizenship was very much at the margins while the German government has made it clear that their preferred route to the 'repair' of the incomplete membership status of denizenship is the acquisition of German nationality. The formal access to citizenship does not guarantee effective utilisation of citizenship rights. In this respect, the articulation between Germany as a welfare state and as an ethnic nation state was identified as key to the discussion of the inclusion and exclusion of Germany's immigrant population. The role of more general labour market and welfare state policies and institutions was identified as playing a central role in the inclusion of immigrant newcomers, albeit at a relatively low socio-economic level and with lower levels of social mobility. There has been a downplaying of national semantics linked to the imagined community of descent – although such ideas continue to resonate, particularly on the right – and an accentuation of membership of the imagined community of GNP contributors.

The dramatic debates about international migration that occurred in Germany in the 1990s were largely couched in national terms even though European integration is seen as part of the natural evolution of the Federal Republic, and German governments have been key players in developments both outside (Schengen) and within the EU Treaties. EU competencies have had some uncomfortable effects. Intra-EU migration coupled with EU labour and social regulations have affected the German labour market and welfare state and raised the spectre of dreaded 'Anglo-American' liberalisation and deregulation. EU anti-discrimination laws agreed in June 2000 could also provide legal and symbolic resources for immigrants in Germany. So, while national particularities remain strong, there are elements of convergence in both horizontal terms that link German responses to migration (both wanted and unwanted) with other European countries. Social and political processes in a liberal, welfare state were identified as the key in this respect. In addition to this, a vertical dimension exists that connects Germany to an integrating EU both as a problem solving venue, but also with the capacity to feed into German debates and affect laws, institutions, policies and collective identities.

The next chapter develops this focus on responses to international migration in highly organised societies with developed welfare states. Responses in the Netherlands and Sweden are particularly interesting because they indicate a move away from 'multicultural' responses to immigration towards a stronger emphasis on integration and civic nationalism. They also indicate once again the importance of exploring the ways in which national and supranational organisation – and changes in them – shape understandings of migration and migrants.

5

Multicultural Dilemmas in Sweden and the Netherlands

This chapter examines the impact of international migration on highly organised welfare states. It also asks why the Netherlands and Sweden developed 'multicultural' responses to immigration and why both moved towards approaches that emphasise socio-economic integration and adaptation by immigrant newcomers. While both are multi-ethnic societies they no longer pursue multicultural policies. It is also shown that 'multiculturalism' and 'integration' Dutch- and Swedish-style are related to the background conditions of corporatist decision-making and the welfare state (Sweden) and 'pillarisation' (Netherlands).

The chapter initially notes some similarities in Dutch and Swedish attempts to regulate international migration. Both are open, trading economies with a strong international outlook, but both have developed and consolidated their capacity to control forms of migration defined by state policies as unwanted. They have also expanded the array of mechanisms to allow them to achieve these objectives to include external (visas, in particular) and internal (welfare state-related) dimensions. The Netherlands has been more closely linked to the EU as a founder member and Schengen state compared to Sweden, which did not join the EU until 1995 and has free movement links to Nordic Council states dating back to 1954.

The chapter then analyses ideas and practices in the Netherlands and Sweden about multiculturalism and immigrant policies. Multiculturalism refers to interactions in culturally diverse societies with its particular form depending on the types of diversity (Guttmann, 1994; Kymlicka, 1995). Charles Taylor (1992) links the idea to 'the politics of recognition' and argues that withholding recognition of cultural differences can be a form of oppression. Parekh (2000: 3), however, cautions that 'multiculturalism is not about identity *per se* but about those embedded in and sustained by a culture; that is a body of beliefs and practices in terms of which a group of people understand themselves and the world and organise their individual and collective lives'. As such these culturally derived differences have a 'measure of authority' (Parekh, 2000: 3). Multicultural policies thus go beyond a plea for tolerance and involve the public affirmation of difference as socially desirable. This seems to suggest that cultural rights can be added to the Marshallian idea of legal, political and social rights as the hallmarks of modern citizenship in an integrated national community.

Yet, in Sweden and the Netherlands – which are both clearly multiethnic societies – the move away from identity-affirming policies was justified by arguments that such approaches maintained social distance between immigrants and newcomers and contributed to social marginalisation. Maritta Soininen (1999: 691) observes strong similarities between the Dutch and Swedish cases and the move away from multicultural approaches: 'Even the arguments for this orientation raise the same points. Namely that the accentuation of values deemed deviant by majority cultural standards risks making integration more difficult and that certain values are in conflict with the fundamental principles of the Dutch and Swedish societies'. A focus on culture and identity can however, mask broader effects of economic change, welfare state reform, neo-conservative welfare state ideologies, diminished trust in politicians, and the rise of communitarian politics with ideas about the responsibilities of individuals that can quite easily translate into adaptive pressures for immigrant newcomers. 'Integration' is an expectation for everyone, but is brought particularly into focus by the presence of immigrant newcomers. Welfare state pressures, as well as changes in their organisation and ideologies, have important effects on understandings of migration and migrants.

Immigration policy

Dutch and Swedish governments have used external measures and internal mechanisms to regulate international migration. Both states have an international outlook, but both have become more specifically European in their pursuit of the regulation of international migration.

TABLE 5.1   *Dutch population by ethnic origin, 1997 (thousands)**

Population group	Number
Native Dutch	12,890
Ethnic minorities, Of which:	
*Main policy target groups***	1,063
Turks	280
Moroccans	233
Surinamese	287
Antilleans/Arubans	95
Greeks	11
Italians	32
(former) Yugoslavians	60
Cape Verdians	17
Portuguese	13
Spaniards	29
Tunisians	6
Others	1,613
Total population	15,567

*Ethnic origin: definition combining a person's birthplace and his or her parents' birthplaces; if one of the three birthplaces is outside the Netherlands, the person is considered to belong to an ethnic minority.
**In addition, Moluccans, refugees (with legal status), caravan-dwellers and gypsies also belong to the target group of the 'integration policy' for ethnic minorities.
Source: Centraal Buro Voor de Statistiek (1998, p. 59)

Dutch immigration policies

One person in six in the Netherlands belongs to an ethnic minority group, defined as either being born or having a parent who was born outside of the Netherlands (see Table 5.1). This is more or less the same proportion as in the USA, but it wasn't until the late 1990s that a Dutch minister officially recognised that the Netherlands was indeed a country of immigration. For most of the post-war period, the word immigrant with its connotations of permanent settlement was not used. The Dutch government actively sought to promote emigration to Australia, Canada and New Zealand. Partly this was because of a perception of the Netherlands as a small, overcrowded country without the resources to accommodate large numbers of immigrants. As in other European countries, the expectation of temporariness was unrealised.

There were three main sources of post-war migrants to the Netherlands. First, colonial repatriates who were relatively easily integrated because of their familiarity with Dutch language and culture. Second, people from former Dutch colonies that arrived as Dutch passport holders and came mainly from Surinam and the Netherlands Antilles. From 1954 Dutch nationality law recognised only one form of Dutch citizenship, although like the 1948 British Nationality Act this was not intended to be a stimulus for migration from former colonies. The extent of migration was a main reason why Surinam was encouraged to become independent in 1975. The majority of post-war migrants came from Surinam. Of these around 50 per cent were of African origin, the rest were descended from Indian and Indonesian origin contract workers. Third, 'guestworkers' arrived from mainly Mediterranean countries. The Netherlands signed recruitment agreements with Italy (1960), Spain (1961), Portugal (1963), Turkey (1964), Greece (1966), Morocco (1969), Yugoslavia and Tunisia (1970). As was generally the case, these agreements tended to recognise rather than create migration flows. Prior to these agreements, migrant workers were able to enter the Netherlands and then, after finding a job, register with a local magistrate and acquire the necessary documents.

There was early hostility to immigrants and some evidence of a nativist backlash. In 1962 there was violence in the eastern textile manufacturing towns of Enschede, Hengelo and Almelo. There was also trade union concern stemming from fears that immigrants could undercut Dutch workers. Recruitment agreements with sending countries were a way to regulate migration flows that had been largely organised by employers, as well as an attempt to specify workplace standards. Recruitment agreements specified that the mode of entry would be a work permit, which was to be obtained in the country of origin. As was the case in Sweden after 1965, the work permit became the main mechanism to regulate labour migration. Not all employers and migrants played by the rules and some migrants fell into the category of illegality. The questions of the legal status of immigrants became a matter for the courts, which van Amersfoort (1999: 147) argued tended to decide in favour of immigrants with the effect that length of residence was considered the basis for the acquisition of denizenship status even if that status had been irregular. The government attempted to resolve the situation in 1975 with a general regularisation for illegals.

Political-historical ties and labour recruitment agreements structured much movement to the Netherlands. These became the basis for the establishment of migration networks. The Netherlands also experienced new migration flows in the 1990s linked in particular to asylum seeking. This led to greater diversity among the immigrant-origin population. Between 1965 and 1970, six countries accounted for 75 per cent of all immigrants. Between 1990 and 1994 the corresponding number had risen to 20 (Entzinger, 2002). This presented particular challenges to multiculturalism Dutch-style because many of these new immigrants had no previous ties with the Netherlands. These issues also have a strong local dimension because the Dutch immigrant-origin population is particularly concentrated in towns and cities on the western seaboard such as Amsterdam, Rotterdam, The Hague and Utrecht.

The Dutch government responded to the oil crisis of 1973 by ending labour migration. The issuance of new work permits ceased and sanctions against employers hiring illegals were introduced, although these were weak. The ending of labour migration did not lead to an end to migration *per se* because family migration continued. Family migration also contributed to a change in the profile of the immigrant-origin population with a changed gender and age distribution and an increased level of engagement with key Dutch social institutions, particularly the labour market, welfare state and political system. Attempts to regulate family migration, such as reducing the age limit from 21 to 18, or specifying minimum income for the entry of marriage partners, were difficult to implement. The Dutch government also tried to stimulate return migration through the short-lived REMPLOD programme co-ordinated by the Ministry for Overseas Development, although with a similar lack of effect as other European countries such as France that pursued similar policies.

Between 1965 and 2001, the 1965 Aliens Act regulated Dutch asylum policy. Dutch policy distinguishes between 'invited refugees', of which there are around 500 each year and whose refugee status has already been confirmed by the UNHCR, and asylum-seekers making a claim under the terms of the Geneva Convention. The suspicion about the status of some asylum applicants has been linked to increased use of visas to regulate this new migration flow. The Netherlands identified 'risk countries' such as Turkey and Morocco from which travellers would require visas. The role of visas as an external regulatory mechanism for the regulation of migration has shifted the location at which migration control occurs from the Dutch border to Dutch consulates in sending countries.

The arrival of Tamil asylum-seekers in 1985 led for the first time to a broader political debate about asylum seeking. There was a growing perception of a system in crisis: numbers were rising (peaking at 52,000 in 1994), adjudication procedures were lengthy (taking up to 3 years), removal rates were low (11,000 between 1980 and 1999, according to UNHCR figures) (Vink, 2001a: 13–4). Since the 1980s reception policies have moved from providing accommodation, welfare state benefits and labour market access to policies that are 'humane, but austere' (van Amersfoort, 1999: 151). Asylum-seekers are housed and become reliant on a low-level welfare state safety net. They are viewed with suspicion by the authorities until their refugee status can be confirmed. These measures mark a determination to ensure that this form of migration, unlike others, can be reversible through the removal of rejected applicants – although enforcement presents its own difficulties because of the number of cases to be dealt with and the length of the adjudication process. In July 1994, the *Wet Identificatieplicht* increased the number of occasions where documentation needed to be produced and required employers to keep copies of residence and work permits of foreign employees. The 1995 *Koppelingswet* (Linkage Act) connected social benefits to legal residency in an attempt to curtail illegal residency. There was a counter-mobilisation against this harsh and restrictive legislation that could deny basic social rights to irregular migrants. The 2001 Aliens Act sought faster adjudication, but also hoped to link Dutch policies to EU structures that could secure a more even distribution of asylum-seekers across the EU.

To sum up, post-colonial ties and labour recruitment agreements structured much post-war migration to the Netherlands. Attempts were made to close the door to labour migration, but immigration continued in the form of family migration. Increased asylum-seeking migration led to the use of visas as an external control device supplemented by internal labour market and welfare state-related measures. Dutch governments have also sought to use the EU as a vehicle for attainment of immigration and asylum policy objectives, more of which later.

Swedish immigration policies

There was swift recognition by the Swedish authorities of permanent immigration with the aim of ushering immigrants as swiftly as possible from denizenship to citizenship. Tomas Hammar (1999: 195) characterised Swedish immigration policy as 'pragmatic and reactive', which is 'apt for an area in which decisions must be based on shaky forecasts and without full knowledge of all the facts'. Since the 1990s, he argues that there have been attempts to develop a more preventative, long-term and European approach. Sweden's control capacity has been aided by its geographical position. Its only land border is to the north with Finland, with whom it has long had a free movement arrangement as part of the Nordic Council framework and now within the EU. This goes to the more general point that Sweden is closely linked to its Scandinavian neighbours through the Nordic Council (Denmark, the Faroe Islands, Finland, Iceland and Norway). Until the 1970s, the main migration flows into Sweden came from other Nordic countries, particularly Finland. Since 1954 there has been free movement within the Nordic labour market for citizens of member states and the right to reside and work in other member states. These provisions are similar to those of the EU. Another similarity is that third country nationals cannot move freely unless covered by other agreements (Fischer and Straubhaar, 1996). Sweden and Finland joined the EU while other Nordic states stayed out, although Norway and Iceland are Schengen 'observers'.

Sweden was not a large-scale recruiter of migrant workers until the 1960s. The main sources of recruitment were Greece, Turkey and Yugoslavia. In 1965, the unexpected arrival of workers from Yugoslavia prompted an Aliens Decree, which was issued without reference to the *Risksdag*, the Swedish Parliament. This specified that in order to enter Sweden, migrants needed to apply for a work permit in their country of origin. In 1968, guidelines to regulate migration were issued and the

TABLE 5.2 *Swedish population by citizenship, 1980–97*

Country of citizenship	1980	1990	1997
Swedish Citizens	7,896,270	8,106,926	8,325,576
Aliens (Overall)	421,667	483,704	522,049
Nordic countries	240,857	191,772	162,221
Other Europe	113,161	117,375	180,001
Africa	6,882	17,375	27,873
North America	6,989	11,982	14,605
South America	13,364	25,762	18,385
Asia	36,315	101,971	103,264
USSR	937	2,119	982
Oceania	620	1,473	1,989
Stateless persons	2,052	8,259	6,139
Unknown country	490	5,616	6,590
Total	8,317,937	8,590,630	8,847,625

Source: Swedish Migration Board (2001)

Swedish Immigration Board was established with responsibility both for regulating migration and the integration of immigrants. Sweden has since elaborated a system of controls that combines external controls (visas) with internal controls (residence and work permits).

Labour migration reached its peak in 1969–70. The Swedish trade unions accepted immigration so long as migrant workers were entitled to the same conditions as other workers. Immigrants also received the same social benefits as Swedes, including unemployment benefit. This welfare state reception was in line with the rapid acceptance of permanent immigration and was accompanied by liberal nationality laws. In contrast with the Netherlands, Sweden explicitly pursued an immigration policy rather than a guestworker paradigm predicated on the flawed assumption of temporariness. After one or two years in Sweden, migrants could establish permanent resident status with the rights of denizenship and after five could become Swedish citizens.

Expansive recruitment policies ended during a short economic recession in 1972. Again, a major decision on immigration was made without reference to Parliament. As Hammar (1999: 174) puts it: 'the political system was not involved, and the general public was not informed'. Hammar calls this an 'apolitical tradition', although the corporatist origins of this particular form of 'apolitical politics' are revealed when it is noted that the Swedish trade unions' *Landsorganisation* vetoed continued labour migration. The trade unions were worried about labour migration's impact on the salaries and working conditions of their members. In 1973, the closing of the immigration door was made abundantly clear when a new law forced all employers of any foreign worker to pay 400 hours of full salary for Swedish language classes.

After 1972, four migration routes remained. First, there was free movement for people from Nordic Council states, extended after 1995 to

TABLE 5.3   Asylum seekers in Sweden
1984–2000 (thousands)

1984	2,000
1985	4,500
1986	14,600
1987	18,114
1988	19,595
1989	30,335
1990	29,420
1991	27,351
1992	84,018
1993	37,581
1994	18,640
1995	9,047
1996	5,753
1997	9,662
1998	12,844
1999	11,231
2000	16,303

Source: Swedish Migration Board (2001)

include EU citizens. Second, limited labour migration regulated by perceptions of Sweden's capacity to provide employment, housing and social support for migrants on the same terms as Swedes. To do otherwise, it was supposed, would erode the key welfare state principle of egalitarianism. Housing was a key concern. In order to alleviate shortages, the Swedish government embarked in the mid-1970s on what was known as the 'one million programme'. In terms of numbers built the programme was relatively successful, but they were often the lowest quality housing stock with a bad physical environment and poor access to services and employment. The high concentration of immigrants in this new housing stock also led to residential segregation. The third route was family migration, which was protected by law and continued after the ending of large-scale labour migration in 1972. As in the Netherlands, family migration changed the profile of the immigrant population in terms of its age and gender distribution and increased the points of engagement with the Swedish welfare state. The fourth route was asylum-seeking migration, which has been at the centre of the politicisation of immigration in Sweden since the late 1980s (see Table 5.3).

Migration became politicised since the late 1980s, mainly around the issue of asylum seeking. Hammar (1999) identifies three reasons for this. First, the end of the Cold War led to movement from and across former Soviet bloc countries. Second, increased asylum-seeking migration linked to economic internationalisation and the development of travel possibilities. Taken together, these two factors meant that Sweden was not as remote as it had once been. Third, labour market deregulation and the weakening of forms of social control that had tightly regulated the Swedish labour market and welfare state access created some spaces for irregular migration. To this could be added that these welfare state and labour market changes affected the perception of migrations with some development of welfare state chauvinism. This is not to say that previous forms of Swedish social organisation have been uprooted and transformed by these changes. Research suggests that the Swedish welfare state has been resilient (Lindbom, 2001). Rather, it is to argue that economic, labour market and welfare state practices affect the practices and ideas that underpin immigration and immigrant policies.

The two main asylum routes into Sweden are 'quota refugees', agreed with the UNHCR and managed by the Swedish Migration Board, coupled with those seeking recognition under the terms of the Geneva Convention. Since 1997, Sweden also recognises three other grounds: a well-founded fear of capital or corporal punishment; protection from non-state persecution (civil war, external conflict or environmental disaster) and; a well-founded fear of persecution because of gender or sexual orientation.

In the early 1980s, the numbers of asylum seekers had been low, at around 5000 each year. This increased to around 12,000 to 15,000 between 1985 and 1988 and to around 30,000 a year between 1988 and 1991. The peak was reached in 1992 when 84,000 asylum seekers entered Sweden, mainly from former Yugoslavia. During the 1990s, asylum-seeking migration increased the range and diversity of migrant-origin groups in Sweden. The numbers of migrants from other Nordic countries fell to around 30 per cent of the total from nearer 70 per cent while the number of people from outside Europe grew to around 50 per cent of the total with increased numbers of Kurds, Iranians, Iraqis and Lebanese.

Sweden developed a dispersal policy for the reception of asylum-seekers. Prior to 1985, the Swedish Labour Market Board which was the institutional legacy of past flows of labour migrants, managed dispersal. This form of management has been seen as beneficial in that it maintained strong links to the labour market (Ålund, Edin and Fredriksen, 2001). In 1985 responsibilities were transferred to the Swedish Immigration Board. Initially, asylum-seekers were accommodated in 60 of Sweden's 284 municipalities deemed to have suitable characteristics for reception. By 1989 and in the face of increased numbers, 277 of the 284 were involved. Previously, housing, education and future employment had all been considered as relevant factors. By the late 1980s the concern was mainly with the availability of accommodation. The broadening of the reception scheme exposed corporatist and relatively insulated decision-making to a populist backlash. In 1987 in the town of Sjöbo in southern Sweden the local council refused to participate in the refugee resettlement programme and was strongly supported by a local referendum in which 65 per cent of those who voted backed the town council's stance. The anti-immigration New Democracy Party played to this anti-immigration sentiment and was able to get 8 per cent of the vote in the 1991 national elections. There were also racist attacks that provoked national self-reflection. In 1993 in Tröllhatten two Somalis were badly beaten while the local Mosque was burnt to the ground. The media were able to find local people only too willing to express openly racist sentiments. This was not the tolerant Sweden of the popular imagination.

The government's response was to reduce the ability of asylum seekers to enter Sweden while also introducing measures to tackle racism and xenophobia, particularly among young people. If the success of these measures were to be assessed then the falling numbers of asylum-seekers and the fact that no anti-immigration or xenophobic parties secured parliamentary representation in the 1998 elections could be brought forward as evidence. At the same time, the problem was identified as the numbers of asylum-seekers. This repeats a familiar mantra: large numbers of immigrants – or at least the perception of large numbers given that relative to the size of the population numbers are quite small – threaten social peace. The Swedish government sought to reassert its sovereign right to determine who could enter the state territory. They did this by maintaining a commitment to the right to asylum, dealing with some of the managerial and administrative headaches such as the backlog of cases, and introducing measures designed to make it more difficult for asylum-seekers to enter Sweden. Immigration legislation in 1989 established adjudication centres in 9 cities managed by the Swedish Migration Board. Some dispensations were granted with permanent resident status given to certain types of asylum-seekers, such as those with young children. The 1989 legislation was accompanied by a political declaration that Sweden did not have the resources to integrate new immigrants.

Visas played a key role in the regulation of asylum. A decision in 1993 exemplified the logic of internal inclusion for those already in Sweden and external closure for potential newcomers. Permanent residence status was granted to Bosnian refugees already in Sweden while visas were required for all new arrivals from that country. This almost completely stopped the flows because the journey became near impossible. In 1997, legislation abolished the categories of *de facto* refugees, war refusers and the granting of residence permits on humanitarian grounds. At the same time, the 1997 legislation also introduced the three new categories referred to above (capital/corporal punishment, non-state persecution, gender and sexual orientation). Enforcement was problematic because many asylum-seekers arrived without documentation that would allow their country of origin to be easily ascertained. The Swedish authorities employed linguistic experts in a bid to return rejected applicants to their countries of origin. This approach was dismissed by academic linguists as flawed and unreliable, but indicates the determination of the Swedish authorities to tackle this form of migration (Hammar, 1999). The number of rejected asylum-seekers hovered at between 8,000–10,000 a year through the 1990s. A sanctuary movement developed to protect asylum seekers in response to what was seen as draconian encroachment by the state on migrants' rights and a breach with Swedish traditions of international solidarity.

Although figures are, of course, difficult to ascertain, the numbers of illegal immigrants in Sweden has remained relatively low. Getting to Sweden would obviously be part of the problem. Another is that Swedish society has been tightly regulated and the 'spaces' for irregular status are small as a result. For instance, the Swedish ID system means that people are issued with personal ID numbers with their date of birth and a personal code that connects them to the population register and tax system. A bank account cannot be opened or health care accessed without this code. At the same time, corporatist structures with institutionalised dialogue between the trade unions and employers' organisations have led to tightly regulated working conditions. Hammar (1999) argues that trends towards deregulation have created more spaces for irregular status with the informal economy estimated to account for between 4 and 5 per cent of Swedish GNP in 1997.

Swedish governments have also pressed for more international co-operation on the regulation of migration, or 'burden sharing' in a European context. Attempts to pursue such policies have floundered because European states seem thus far to have opted for a beggar thy neighbour approach rather than solidarity. Sweden's insertion in the EU policy frame is considered more fully later.

Immigrant policy

There are similarities between Sweden and the Netherlands in that both initially recognised group rights for immigrants and adopted identity-affirming multicultural policies. These policies were channelled through Dutch 'pillarisation' and the Swedish social democratic welfare state and corporatism. Changes in immigrant integration policies also need to be located in relation to these socio-economic changes that have prompted a move away from group rights and multiculturalism Dutch- and Swedish-style towards an approach emphasising individual rights and adaptation to the host society. The Swedish approach began to change in the late 1970s while change occurred a decade later in the Netherlands.

From minorities policy to integration policy in the Netherlands

The Netherlands has moved from minorities policy to integration policy. As one of the most influential academic commentators (and indeed influences on both policy frames) has put it, there has been 'a renewed emphasis on citizenship and shared values in response to earlier tendencies towards postnationalism and multiculturalism' (Entzinger, 2002). Multicultural policies came under fire in the 1980s and 1990s for maintaining social distance between immigrants and the Dutch, for contributing to social exclusion, and for not pushing Dutch institutions to become more accommodating of newcomers. The new approach involves more emphasis on socio-economic integration and *inburgering* (a form of civic education) for new immigrants with 500 hours of training on 'being Dutch', including language training.

According to the 2001 EUMC survey of attitudes in the EU towards minority groups, the Dutch were strong supporters of policies promoting equal opportunities and had positive attitudes regarding the benefits of cultural diversity, which suggests some multicultural optimism. In policy terms, however, the Dutch favoured cultural assimilation more strongly that most other Europeans. According to the survey, a fairly sizeable minority of 35 per cent of Dutch respondents thought that in order to become fully accepted then people belonging to minority groups should give up their own culture (only Belgium on 36 per cent ranked higher). Seventy-five per cent thought that people belonging to minority groups must give up those parts of their religion and culture that conflict with Dutch law. Only Denmark, 85 per cent, and Sweden, 79 per cent, ranked higher, with an EU average of 56 per cent (EUMC, 2001: pp. 48–9).

This raises the issue of the link between public opinion and policy change. Instead of seeking to unravel this particular Gordian knot the discussion that follows takes a different route. It links background conditions – namely 'pillarisation' and socio-economic change – to public attitudes about migration. Large-scale public opinion surveys are not well placed to help us identify the ways in which public attitudes are affected by social settings that give meaning to ideas about immigrant integration in the first place. To say that the Dutch are more 'culturally assimilationist' may reflect an understanding by Dutch respondents of a question about the form of social integration necessary if core elements of Dutch social life that they value are to be maintained.

This allows us to explore the impact of a particular form of Dutch social organisation labelled *verzuiling* (pillarisation) the approach to the resolution of social problems that it has implied, and the implications of the declining social relevance of the ideological *zuilen* (pillars). The *zuilen* offered 'cradle to grave' membership, social belonging and protection akin to welfare organisations for their members. These services were provided on the basis of identity and offered a route to social participation. The pillars were also identity-affirming. Institutionalised separateness within the pillars was resolved at elite level by consultation, dialogue and compromise as the basis for decision-making with a pre-disposition to technocratic solutions to take the heat out of potentially divisive social and political problems. Experts could thus assume a prominent role in the development of policy ideas while, in turn, their input would be informed by an idea of community service (Rath, 1999).

Pillarisation had implications for the way of 'doing' politics. Politics was both sectarian in the sense that the faith-based and secular pillars helped inculcate a strong sense of identity in their members while also potentially open in that the pillars could provide a model for the inclusion in Dutch institutions of immigrant newcomers.

Even though the pillars declined in social relevance from the 1960s because of social modernisation, key assumptions lingered to inform the development of minorities policy in terms of both the key concepts (identity-affirming) and the organisation of the response (technocratic). In 1978, the Ministry of Culture, Recreation and Work established an Advisory Committee on Ethnic Minorities whose work influenced a 1979 report published by the Scientific Council for Government Policy (the WRR to use the Dutch acronym) entitled *Ethnic Minorities*. The underlying approach that would inform this 'minorities policy' frame was influenced by academic research on the formation of ethnic minorities in Dutch society (van Amersfoort, 1982). As in the UK, the term 'ethnic minorities' has acquired an everyday currency in Dutch policy. This is a contingent rather than necessary effect of responses to immigration as the chapters on France and Germany have indicated only too clearly.

Minorities policy saw the Netherlands as a multi-ethnic society with the expression of ethnic differences by immigrants an important part of their social identity, which should be protected. A 1981 government report and subsequent legislation in 1983 defined the policy objective as 'Achieving a society in which all members of minority groups in the Netherlands, individually and also as groups, are in a situation of equality and have full opportunities for their development'. Or put another way 'integration with retention of cultural identity' (Entzinger, 2002). Indeed, the retention of cultural identity was seen as a route to integration and is in turn linked to a type of pluralistic integration associated with pillarisation and the politics of accommodation (Lijphart, 1975).

In practical terms this approach meant three things: emancipation in a multicultural society, equality before the law and equal opportunity (Entzinger, 2002). Emancipation meant that money was provided for cultural and social organisations. Provision was also made for mother tongue teaching for the children of immigrants as part of the core school curriculum.

Equality before the law meant the extension of rights to immigrants without non-nationals necessarily being required to acquire Dutch nationality. Emphasis was placed on closing the socio-economic gap, tackling discrimination and encouraging participation in Dutch society. One of the key elements of this was the extension in 1975 of local voting rights to legally resident immigrants after three years in the Netherlands (although turnout among immigrant groups has been very low). Naturalisation provisions were open and liberal. They had their origins in the French Napoleonic code and were more open than, for instance, the ethnic-based provisions of their German neighbours.

Efforts to promote equal opportunity meant action in areas such as housing, education, employment and health care while legislation tackled both direct and indirect discrimination in a manner similar to UK race relation's legislation. The measuring scale was to be 'proportionality': immigrants should participate in key Dutch institutions in numbers proportional to their presence in the population. In these terms, the policy failed. Levels of unemployment were very high, particularly for 'targeted' ethnic minority groups (Turks, Moroccans, Surinamese, Antilleans and Arubans), while those that were employed were often in low skilled positions and vulnerable to economic change and industrial restructuring.

Within ten years of establishing minorities policy many of the same people who had been influential in its formation were present at the funeral. Research suggested marginalisation and social distance between immigrants and the Dutch while social and political institutions remained closed to immigrant newcomers. In turn, prominent voices began to challenge the consensus. The leader of the liberal party (the VVD), Frits Bolkestein argued for a greater emphasis on 'the Dutch way of life'. This view attacked key multicultural ideas, as well as the foundations of the legitimisation of difference provided by Dutch pillarisation. Bolkestein struck a chord and the VVD profited at the polls.

Many of the same experts who had influenced the development of minorities policy now turned their attention to its failings. As an observer from across the border in Germany noted: 'a well-intentioned and carefully constructed policy may have some counter-productive results in the economic and social field' (Thränhardt, 2000: 178). It was argued that the downside of policy was that immigrants were targeted as 'needy' and 'under-achieving' (Thränhardt, p. 178). This criticism draws from analysis within the Netherlands of the 'minorising' effects of policy. If the dividing lines between ethnic minorities and the host society are stressed and identified as a 'problem' then minorities can be placed outside of the Dutch imagined national community. The policy will reproduce their 'otherness' with minorities tolerated without becoming full members of Dutch society (Rath, 1992).

Other factors were at play too. The size of the ethnic minority population had doubled in size since minorities policy was developed. Moreover, there was more diversity in terms of country of origin among immigrant groups. Many new immigrants had no previous point of contact with the Netherlands and little knowledge of Dutch language or society. At the same time, increased unemployment, welfare state restructuring and the rise of neo-conservative welfare state ideologies favoured an emphasis on individuals and their responsibilities rather than groups and their entitlements.

In 1989 a WRR report entitled *Immigrant Policy* argued that too much emphasis had been placed on multiculturalism and not enough on the integration of immigrants into the wider society. This implied that the integration of immigrants needed to be considered as a more general social policy issue. The 1994 election defeat of the Christian Democrats was important because they were the main advocates of pillarisation. Indeed, the shift to a policy emphasis on socio-economic integration has been a particularly noticeable feature in the Netherlands since the mid-1990s. The secular parties (the Labour party, the VVD and Democrats 66) were less keen to stress the cultural dimension. Legislation introduced by the new coalition in 1994 replaced minorities policy with integration policy. Integration was redefined as 'a process leading to the full and equal participation of individuals and groups in society, for which mutual respect for identity is seen as a necessary condition' (cited in Entzinger, 2002). The definition was bland and 'mutual respect for identity' sounds fairly similar to the minorities policy approach. This bland definition did, however, disguise some of the more significant shifts that were occurring beneath the surface linked, for instance, to welfare state pressures.

The integration policy emphasised equal opportunities, but for individuals not groups. Immigrant participation in Dutch society was stressed, which meant some identification with and commitment to Dutch society from newcomers. A politics of belonging was to be inculcated based on shared values, but whose values? How would they be inculcated? Would immigrants who didn't accept these values be required to leave?

The new approach implied socio-economic and civic integration with individuals the focus, not groups. Culture, identity and post-national trends would be replaced by an emphasis on Dutch society and its values. Immigrants would be encouraged to 'seize opportunities', as a report of the Minister for Urban Integration Policy put it. The minister, Roger van Boxtel, argued that: 'Members of ethnic minorities can be expected to do their utmost in order to acquire an independent position in our country as soon as possible. This requires them to choose for this society and to take responsibility for making use of the many facilities that our country offers its new compatriots. Mastering the Dutch language is a crucial aspect of this' (cited in Entzinger, 2002).

This leads to the second policy strand: civic integration and *inburgering* (civic integration) policy. A policy report by two academics contended that high levels of ethnic minority unemployment were not so much a result of demand-side factors such as racism and discrimination but of supply-side effects such as lower levels of educational attainment and the absence of social networks linking immigrants to the labour market. The suggestion of compulsory civic integration courses was the most controversial proposal. This would involve 500 hours of language training and

100 hours of civic education. The Law on the Civic Integration of Newcomers came into effect in September 1998. Denmark, the UK and Germany seem to have been very much taken by this Dutch approach with its emphasis on individual self-reliance and its re-assertion of a form of civic nationalism that stresses the ties that bind the 'national community'. Changes to Dutch nationality law are interesting with regards to this debate about civic integration. The 1985 nationality law emphasised the rule of one nationality. This changed when a 1992 circular permitted dual nationality, but this decision was reversed in 1997 after opposition from the CDA and VVD (Vink, 2001b).

The Dutch were in the vanguard of ethnic minority politics, but have since embraced a form of civic nationalism and moved away from minorities policy. Han Entzinger (2002: 1) identifies what he sees as 'a respectable non racist assimilationist view that can be opposed to the long-standing multicultural option'. Yet, 'culture' and 'identity' alone are not driving policy change. The decline of pillarisation, welfare state restructuring, neo-Conservative welfare state ideologies, privatisation, the internationalisation of the Dutch economy and Europeanisation have given the Dutch approach a decidedly more individualistic flavour.

Lurking beneath the surface are also fears about immigrant loyalty, or disloyalty. In 1998 the Dutch historian and Labour Party member Paul Scheffer wrote a much-debated article in the *NRC Handelsblad* in which he discussed the 'multicultural tragedy': the development of an 'ethnic underclass' that was unwilling and unable to integrate. He called for a 'civilisation offensive' with efforts to tackle deprivation (the class-based reference does hint that 'culture' and 'identity' are not doing all the work here) combined with more emphasis on assimilation to 'our' culture and history. Scheffer overstates the case by adopting a stereotypical approach to immigrants in Dutch society and neglects to say that there has been fairly substantial integration. In a sense, a 'crisis of integration' is actually part of the integration process itself. There are countless historical parallels from across Europe that demonstrate how the 'deviance' of new immigrant groups and their lack of orientation to the host society has been seen as subversive. Yet, these fears have faded only to be replaced by concerns about the next wave of immigrants and their perceived inassimilability.

The debates about immigration, integration and multiculturalism have created some space for populist exploitation of anti-immigration sentiment. In the March 2002 local elections a party founded only in 1998 called *Leefbaar Nederland* (Liveable Netherlands) became the largest party in Rotterdam with 34.7 per cent of the votes. With national elections due in 2002, the populist anti-immigration message of *Leefbaar Nederland* threatened the main Dutch political parties and highlighted disillusion with both the governing centre-left coalition and multi-party coalition governments. The party was strident in its opposition to immigration, although its former leader, Pim Fortuyn, was sacked following anti-Muslim remarks. Fortuyn then established his own list that picked up

17 seats in Rotterdam. Fortuyn's own party, the List Pim Fortuyn (LPF) became a Dutch political phenomenon in the run-up to the 2002 general election. Fortuyn was an unusual figure who defied an easy categorisation. He used his own homosexuality and social liberalism to condemn Islam as a 'backward' faith and to argue that the Netherlands was 'full' and could receive no more immigrants. He vigorously rejected comparison with more traditional extreme right figures such as France's Jean Marie Le Pen, but advanced a strong critique of immigration and immigration-related diversity that has been at the core of the extreme right's message. Fortuyn's assassination by an animal rights fanatic on May 6 2002 robbed the movement of its leader but gave an enormous boost to the electoral fortunes of the LPF, who rode a wave of popular revulsion at the murder of Fortuyn and sympathy for his core message. In a dramatic political shake-up the LPF secured 26 seats (three more than the Dutch Labour Party whose support collapsed) in the 150-seat Dutch parliament to become the second largest party.

The reaction to the death of Fortuyn may have turned him into a secular saint, but his disciples within the LPF appeared on the verge of disintegration in the absence of their leader as they faced up to the issue of negotiating a coalition agreement with the Christian Democrats, which won 43 parliamentary seats. The broader issues that Fortuyn raised struck at the heart of traditionally liberal responses to immigration and immigration-related diversity in the Netherlands. They reveal a growing sense of uncertainty, insecurity and dissatisfaction among some sections of the Dutch population with the remedies proposed by existing parties. The dissatisfaction that Fortuyn expressed does, however, also reflect a growing uncertainty about immigration and immigrant integration policies that can be dated back to the early 1990s. Fortuyn's populism focused international attention on the Netherlands, but the subjects he raised had been major topics of discussion for more than 10 years.

From multicultural policy to integration policy in Sweden

In 2002, the murder by her father of Fadime Sahindal, focused attention on the relationship between young women immigrants in Sweden torn between liberal Swedish society and the traditional upbringing that some parents want to maintain. Fadime Sahindal had become well known when she brought a court case against her father and brother when they threatened to kill her after she had established a relationship with a Swedish man. The murder provoked a broader debate about how to integrate immigrants into Swedish society.

Four elements characterise initial Swedish responses to immigration in the 1970s. First, the swift recognition of permanent immigration compared to the flawed expectation of temporariness in other European countries of immigration. Second, the social democratic welfare state that provided 'cradle to grave' protection founded on strongly egalitarian principles meant that immigrants were swiftly included as welfare state members. Third, a corporatist policy style resulted in an emphasis on consultation and dialogue between key social interests. Fourth, there were ideas about international solidarity and the responsibilities of richer countries to less economically developed countries. All have implications for ideas about the sovereign authority of the Swedish state: its ability to regulate the state territory, to provide for social inclusion, and to express international identity in a political universe of other nation states.

All four elements have come under pressure and reflect changed perceptions of the sovereign authority of the Swedish state. First, new migration, particularly asylum-seeking, has been the target of restrictive policies designed to reduce asylum seekers' ability to enter the Swedish state territory and secure access to the welfare state. Swedish immigration policies have, as Hammar (1999) puts it, tried to close the door to the Swedish welfare state. Second, economic change and trends towards individualisation have weakened corporatist structures. These structures were already problematic in that they were based on class interests and had difficulty dealing with either gender or ethnic identities (Soininen, 1999). Third, the international orientation has been joined by a more specifically European orientation because of Sweden's links to EU policies centred on tight immigration restrictions.

In sum, new migration has coincided with relative economic decline, welfare state pressures, the weakening of corporatist structures, individualisation and Europeanisation. All dent the perceived ability of the Swedish state to act as the sovereign arbiter of inclusion and exclusion. This is not to say that the Swedish model has been cast asunder and that Swedish society has been plunged into a crisis of uncertainty. Rather, previous assumptions have been questioned with implications for ideas about immigrant integration. Indeed, immigrant newcomers can be identified as the most visible manifestation of these changes with the possibility of scapegoating. So, while a lack of orientation to Swedish society by immigrants was seen as a problem, a deeper problem was that Swedish identity and values were themselves under examination. A renewed emphasis on newcomers acquiring these values occurred at a time when these values were in flux.

Evidence from the EU Monitoring Centre on Racism and Xenophobia (EUMC, 2001) survey of attitudes towards minorities does show that the Swedes display positive attitudes towards minorities and are supportive of participation by minorities in social and political life. On most of the Eurobarometer survey measures, Swedish respondents were usually among the most multiculturally optimistic Europeans. In fact, 75 per cent of Swedes agreed that people from minority groups were enriching Swedish cultural life (EUMC, 2001: 43). The attitudes harden when questions about abuse of the welfare system, preferential treatment for immigrants, and immigrants causing unemployment are asked. The opinions of Swedish respondents then fall into line with more general EU attitudes towards social conflict, loss of welfare and feelings of disturbance.

As with the Netherlands, this survey data needs to be linked to the institutional context that gives meaning to ideas about immigrant integration. Sweden swiftly affirmed the rights of migrants to participate in Swedish society and politics, but did so for reasons linked to welfare state organisation, egalitarian principles and corporatist decision-making. The long-standing commitment to equal rights, participation and anti-discrimination is reflected in Swedish attitudes towards immigrant minorities. Particular tensions have arisen in welfare related areas, which underpins attempts to restrict new immigration while shifting the policy focus towards socio-economic integration. Yasemin Soysal (1994: 80) argues that Sweden's multicultural approach defined 'migrant groups as ethnic minority communities, and ... aims at equality between ethnic groups while emphasising separate existences ... and collective identities'. Maritta Soininen (1999: 686) stresses the importance of corporatist structures as 'the government's way of understanding and identifying the problems of the rights and needs of immigrants and the context within which actual immigrant interests are mobilised'.

Five periods of Swedish immigrant policy have been identified (Hammar, 1999: 172). Before 1945 there was little non-Nordic migration and no integration policy. This was, though, a rather sinister aspect of this period. Ideas about the superiority of the Swedish people were prevalent in both social democratic and right-wing thought. In 1921, the *Riksdag* created an Institute for Racial Hygiene. The sterilisation of people seen as unsuitable parents persisted into the 1970s with some estimates of around 60,000 people being subjected to this scheme (*Time Magazine*, September 22 1997). Ideas about race and racial superiority were evident in Sweden. Indeed, a parallel can be drawn with broader debates about Social Darwinism. In his analysis of the USA, Richard Hofstadter (1955: 146) notes that 'the eugenics craze had about it the air of a "reform". Like the reform movements, it accepted the principle of state action toward a common end, and spoke in terms of the collective destiny of the group rather than individual success'.

Between 1945 and 1964, Swedish responses to immigration rested on an expectation of assimilation. Between 1964 and 1975 there was a shift towards 'mutual adaptation' with the provision of language training, home language instruction and the creation of local immigrants' councils. Foreign workers were assigned denizenship status to ensure their welfare state integration. Hammar (1999: 178) describes the measures between 1968 and 1975 as 'social engineering', with attempts to extend the principle of equality to all legal residents with the social and political participation of newcomers as an objective coupled with 'vague ideas' about ethnic minority rights in a multicultural Sweden. These measures were remarkably inclusive, particularly when it's remembered that other European countries were still struggling to recognise that the 'guests' had stayed. Another element of this approach was that immigration and immigrant policies were dealt with in corporatist arenas. Decisions tended to be made in shielded bureaucratic and legislative arenas without wider political debate. Sweden also made it easy for immigrants to become Swedish. Naturalisation was relatively quick and easy with high naturalisation rates. Brubaker (1989: 10) links this to a faith in the ability of welfare state institutions to level out inequalities in the same way that French institutions were supposed to level out cultural inequalities.

In 1974, a parliamentary commission on immigration mapped out a multicultural Sweden with 'equality', 'freedom of choice' and 'partnership'. Equality meant living conditions comparable with Swedes. Freedom of choice meant a genuine choice about retaining cultural identity. Partnership meant co-operation and solidarity between Swedes and newcomers. Ålund and Schierup (1993: 99) described the policy as an 'ambitious attempt to create social equality among ethnic groups [with] its respect for immigrant culture and its emphasis on providing immigrants with resources with which to exercise political influence'. The policy also demonstrated a confidence in the ability of the Swedish state to act as the sovereign guarantor of inclusion – a confidence that has since diminished.

The fourth period between 1975 and 1985 saw these ideas about a multicultural Sweden put into effect. As well as full welfare state membership, from 1975, local voting rights were extended after 36 months legal residence. Immigrant associations were subsidised. From 1976, Swedish nationality could be obtained after five years of residence. From 1977 the children of immigrants had the right to be taught their native language. Yet, by the early 1980s, there was concern that the policy was not contributing to the social inclusion of immigrants. A 1984 parliamentary report linked future migration to Sweden's ability to integrate newcomers. The report also argued that the previous approach was too broad in terms of its recognition of group rights. Instead, it was proposed to distinguish between national and immigrant minorities. It was argued that immigrant minorities could not have the status of 'ethnic minorities' such as the Saami, Tornedal Finns, Swedish Finns, Roma and Jews did. Since June 1999 these groups have been regarded as national minorities in accordance with the Council of Europe's Framework Convention for the Protection of National Minorities. Postwar immigrants could not be considered as national minorities even if they had developed their own forms of ethnic and cultural-based organisation in Sweden. The parliamentary report went on to argue that there needed to be some adaptation by immigrants. Their language and culture could be protected, but in a more limited sense that did not conflict with core Swedish values. On the issue of assimilation the Swedish state declared itself to be neutral: it would neither promote nor oppose it.

After 1985, there was a move away from multicultural policy towards an approach that placed more emphasis on Swedish language and culture and adaptation by immigrants. This coincided with evidence that the employment and income levels of immigrant-origin people were lagging behind those of other Swedes. Moreover, the Swedish economy entered recession, unemployment increased and welfare state pressures emerged. Concern about 'ethnic segregation' coincided with a more general lack of confidence in central planning. There was the transfer of some state enterprises to the private sector and a more neo-liberal policy approach (Rothstein, 1998). Soininen (1999: 691) argues that: 'The source of the government's recent stance on immigrants can be traced to this change in the Swedish model'.

In 1996 a designated minister with responsibility for integration policy was established. Greater emphasis was placed on individual rights while terms such as self-sufficiency and self-support were adopted in order to encourage immigrant participation in Swedish society. While Sweden was recognised as 'an unavoidably multicultural society', this was seen as an argument for the maintenance of 'Swedish cultural heritage' and the basic principles of Swedish law and democracy (cited in Soininen, 1999: 692).

The shift towards integration policy was confirmed by legislation on immigrant integration that came into force on January 1 1998. This created a National Integration Office with specific responsibilities to develop programmes for and monitor the (particularly socio-economic) integration of immigrants. New anti-discrimination measures came into force on May 1 1999, which prohibited direct or indirect discrimination. This built on the 1986 Act on Discrimination at Work and the creation of the Office of the Ombudsman against Ethnic Discrimination.

The impact of denizenship provisions that included local voting rights and relatively straightforward access to Swedish nationality was one focus of the 1997 Swedish Democratic Audit, which referred to the unusually poor realisation of the democratic ideals of equality for Swedish immigrants with passivity and powerlessness and a marked lack of interest in exercising local voting rights (cited in Soininen, 1999: 694). In 1994, only 40 per cent of eligible denizens voted in the local elections, compared to 80 per cent of Swedes. This is linked to a structurally weak labour market position, which in turn is further undermined by a decline in the availability of public sector employment. In 1998, 5.3 per cent of Swedes were unemployed compared to 27 per cent of immigrants. The approach to be pursued by the National Integration Office (set up in 1998) was outlined in a government report entitled 'Sweden, the Future and the Plural Society – From Immigration Policy to Integration Policy'. The report calls for the mainstreaming of immigrant integration measures across social and labour market policies based on the principles of non-discrimination, equality, diversity and mutual respect. The policy places far more emphasis on individual self-reliance.

European integration

How have relatively small EU member states sought to exert influence in EU structures? The Netherlands and Sweden have both sought to become more European in their approaches to the regulation of international migration.

The Netherlands is a longer-standing EU member state than Sweden, which was tied to the Nordic Council's free movement frame and only joined the EU in 1995. The Netherlands has left an indelible mark on the recent history of European integration as the location at which the Maastricht and Amsterdam Treaties were finally negotiated. The Netherlands was also a frontrunner in key EU initiatives such as CIREA, the centre for sharing information on asylum, the Eurodac scheme for keeping personal data on asylum-seekers, and the High Level Working Group on Immigration, which links the internal security frame of the old JHA pillar with the foreign and security policy pillar (van Selm, 2002).

A key reason why both member states have sought European co-operation and integration is that along with Germany both are in the top-three asylum-receiving states in per capita terms (UNHCR, 2000). Countries that receive most asylum-seekers and push for distributive solidarity can also 'face pressure from their domestic electorates to stop the "streams of asylum seekers" by counteracting the free-riders behaviour ... while on the other hand, humanitarian norms (embodied in international conventions or domestic constitutional traditions) may prevent them from engaging in such a race to the bottom' (Vink, 2001a: 5). In the 1996 Intergovernmental Conference during which the Amsterdam treaty was negotiated, both the Dutch and Swedish governments pushed for the transfer of competencies from the JHA pillar to the 'Community' pillar, which would imply roles for the ECJ, Parliament and Commission. The Swedish government did, though, indicate a preference for continued use of unanimity as the basis of decision-making in this area (Hix and Niessen, 1996: 56–7). The Netherlands was an integrative maximalist in pursuit of policies that could allow EU cooperation at a level commensurate with the Dutch approach.

An interesting issue is the way in which EU outcomes can depart from national laws and practices. For instance, structures for democratic control and accountability are notoriously weak at EU level. Why should member states that often speak of their desire to see the EU become more democratic and open accept practices that fall far short of these standards? Or as Maarten Vink (2001a: 16) bluntly puts it: 'how does the government get away with it?'. In his analysis of the Netherlands, Maarten Vink argues that ratification of the Dublin Convention occurred despite Dutch parliamentary concerns about the absence of an ECJ role. Ratification of the Eurodac Convention took place even though there were concerns that the outcome would be a shift to EU co-operation that strengthened the executive and weakened the scope for legislative and judicial oversight. In both the Dublin and Eurodac cases, the Dutch government argued and Parliament eventually accepted that not to ratify would be a breach of European obligations and that change could be lobbied for from within existing structures after ratification had take place. 'Defection', Vink (2001a: 21) argues 'is generally not an option for a small, but pro-active country ... there may be no other choice than to follow the lowest common denominator-compromise of other European countries'.

Not all EU measures suggest a race to the bottom with minimum standards. It is possible to put in place structures at EU level that exceed the standards evident in many member states. Examples of this are the anti-discrimination directives agreed in June 2000, which cover direct and indirect discrimination on the grounds of race, ethnicity and religion. Two Directives were introduced in June 2000 covering direct and indirect discrimination on grounds of race, ethnicity and religion. This developing EU anti-discrimination frame suggests that countries such as the Netherlands, Sweden and the UK, which have a relatively long-standing commitment to tackling direct and indirect discrimination have, in a sense, hit a 'national home run' (Héritier, 1997) in that they have managed to put in place EU level structures that replicate to a considerable extent existing national practices. This new EU legislation goes considerably further than provisions in other member states that were either non-existent or lodged in the criminal code where the burden of proof is very heavier. These developments are considered more fully in the next chapter.

Conclusion

The Netherlands and Sweden were in the vanguard of ethnic minority politics, but now seem to be at the forefront of moves towards civic nationalism, socio-economic integration, even assimilation. This chapter has also shown how the regulation of international migration and immigrant integration are related to background institutional factors: economic restructuring, welfare state pressures, privatisation, internationalisation and Europeanisation that have led to pressure to close the doors to the Dutch and Swedish welfare state and drawing a tighter line around the community of legitimate receivers of welfare state beneficiaries. Factoring in these broader institutional factors means 'popping' the immigration bubble and examining what lurks behind debates about the 'culture' and 'identity' of immigrants and the host society. The regulation of international migration and changed ideas about immigrant integration do not reside in a carefully demarcated area called 'immigration politics', they need to be related to the background institutional context that, for instance, can weaken group-based ties and legitimate moves by individually-oriented policy approaches that stress the moral relevance of community and thus strike at liberal universal values of openness towards immigrants.

While these background factors are strongly rooted in the Dutch and Swedish national contexts, there are also broad similarities with other 'older' European immigration countries. There has been a strengthened commitment to tackling forms of migration defined by state policies as unwanted, particularly asylum seeking. What is more, the array of devices to attain this has expanded to include external measures such as increased use of visa, recognition of safe third countries and co-operation at EU level. In this sense, the EU provides a frame for policy development through both market integration and the developing immigration and asylum *acquis*.

Internally, the rules governing welfare state and labour market access have been used to place unwanted immigrants such as asylum seekers in a more tenuous position in relation to the community of legitimate receivers of welfare state benefits, at least while their claims are being processed. This tends to derive from an internal political dynamic centred on an apparent reassertion of civic nationalism even though these societies have changed and become more diverse, with the effect that 'integration' becomes more difficult to specify. In this sense, too, and even though there is a domestic political dynamic at work, both the Netherlands and Sweden display tendencies that are evident in other older immigration countries to try to restrict welfare state access to those deemed to be 'undeserving' of welfare state benefits.

In broader terms, this chapter has demonstrated that responses remain decidedly 'national' in relation to the background institutional setting, but also that what we mean by 'national' in an integrating Europe has changed. Both the Netherlands and Sweden have tightened their immigration controls and moved towards immigrant policies that place more adaptational pressure on newcomers. In this kind of context the EU is not necessarily either an abrogation of sovereign authority or an indication that states are losing control. Instead, it can serve as a new venue for the attainment of domestic policy objectives. The next chapter analyses the shift to EU level co-operation and integration on migration policy. It seeks to explain the time, content and form of policy co-operation while also seeking to explain the effects that policy co-operation can have on member states. These points are then developed more fully in chapters that follow on immigration politics in southern, central and eastern Europe.

6

The Politics of Migration in an Integrating Europe

CONTENTS

If there are diverse responses at national level to international migration then why have EU member states ceded migration policy responsibilities to EU institutions and what effects do these competencies have on laws, institutions, policies and collective identities in the member states? These questions are at the heart of this chapter's analysis. The ceding of policy responsibilities to the EU could hinder the ability of EU member states to pursue their preferred response. Yet, since the 1980s EU co-operation and integration have intensified. This has important implications for the politics of migration and immigration in Europe and what can be called its four Europeanised faces – free movement, aspects of immigration and asylum policy, the creation of EU citizenship, and anti-discrimination laws.

This chapter brings together the themes discussed in previous chapters and sets the scene for the discussion of the politics of migration in newer immigration countries in southern, central and eastern Europe, which have been particularly influenced by the migration policy obligations of EU membership. The chapter also tries to cut through some of the EU jargon and highlight key points about the thinking behind policy development, the new institutional responsibilities that have been created, and what this means for European countries.

The chapter's next section outlines competing explanations for the development of EU co-operation. The two explanations that are put forward highlight different underlying processes with important implications for the driving forces behind integration and the actors empowered. Sections that mimic earlier chapters by focusing on the EU's impact on immigration and immigrant policies follow this.

Why Europe?

Why would European countries voluntarily cede aspects of their migration responsibilities to supranational institutions? EU migration policy development could be linked to economic interdependence and globalisation that have driven European integration while eroding the territorial and functional foundations of the nation state. This could be called the 'losing control' hypothesis in the sense that the internationalisation of the economy has diminished state sovereignty (Sassen, 1998, 1999). The EU represents the erosion of core nation state functions with regards to border control and the mediation of membership and belonging. Sassen (1999) argues that 'much as states have resisted and found it incompatible with their sovereign power, they have had to relinquish some forms of border control and have had to accept court rulings which support the human rights of immigrants and the civil rights of their citizens to sue their own government'. The EU is becoming 'a testing ground for the relationship between the national state and supranational or transnational actors' (Sassen 1999). In turn, this view can be linked with broader analyses of supranational governance that identify self-reinforcing processes associated with the development of transnational society, the pro-integration activities of supranational institutions and the density of supranational rules which 'gradually, but inevitably, reduce the capacity of the member states to control outcomes' (Stone Sweet and Sandholtz, 1997: 299).

Alternatively, the 'escape to Europe' hypothesis contends that EU co-operation and integration have allowed member states to avoid domestic legal and political constraints to attain their domestic policy objectives (Joppke, 1997; Freeman, 1998; Guiraudon, 1998; Hollifield, 2000b; Vink, 2001a). From this perspective, the development of EU immigration and asylum co-operation and integration is a reassertion of control capacity and as such strengthens rather than weakens state sovereignty (Freeman, 1998). EU migration policy can thus be understood as an attempt by the member states to resolve problems of international regulatory failure in new *external* venues at European level (Stetter, 2000). Externalisation allows member states to pursue their domestic migration policy objectives by other means. As Hollifield (2000b: 110) argues: 'The Schengen agreement is a classic example of extra territorial control. It has helped to create buffer states, and to shift some of the burdens and dilemmas of control outside the jurisdiction of liberal states in western Europe'. He goes on to contend that liberal states will prefer this escape route because the alternative is to roll back the rights of their resident foreign populations, which is likely to be legally and politically untenable. 'Ideas, institutions and culture, as well as certain segments of civil society, which may resist encroachments by the state on negative and/or positive freedoms, impose limits of control'.

These two hypotheses – 'losing control' and the 'escape to Europe' – distinguish between domestic and international factors in an attempt to explain EU policy development. They specify different motive forces, highlight the role of different actors, and identify different EU-level 'political opportunities' that arise as a result of economic and political integration. In short, both approaches would offer a distinct explanation for the timing of the shift to Europe, the content of policy, and the actors who have tended to predominate.

There is still a gap in the discussion. We have focused on the shift to EU level co-operation and integration. But what effects does this shift have on member states and surrounding states and regions? The EU cannot be neatly separated from national contexts. Nor can we pretend that the effects on all European countries of immigration will be more or less the same. For instance, newer immigration countries in southern Europe and those states seeking membership of the EU have been particularly influenced by EU migration policy developments. In turn, this raises issues of institutional compatibility or 'goodness of fit', which have become particularly important because of the geo-political and conceptual widening of the migration issue to include more states and new types of international migration.

Immigration policy

In this chapter's introduction, two explanations for the 'shift' to Europe were sketched. One emphasised the dynamics of the international system. The other focused on state interests. There is some risk of a false dichotomy because the global and national are linked, as international migration demonstrates *par excellence*. The two explanations do, however, offer competing accounts of the reasons for European co-operation and integration, the form that policy has taken, and the actors that have tended to predominate.

To get a full picture of the shift to Europe and the implications of this shift, we have to consider the policy preferences of member states as a basis for their actions and the attempts to accommodate these preferences at European level in treaties and laws, as well as more informal co-operation. The treaties signed by the member states' have the potential to be turned by Community political and legal processes into laws that bind those states. Thus, the EU's supranational processes – which are its unique and distinguishing feature as an international organisation – can lead to 'constitutionalisation' with laws established above the member states that over-ride nationals laws. These can then 'domestify' European politics with the effect that the European order becomes more hierarchical and rule bound and thus acquires some of the characteristics of a political system in its own right (Caporaso, 1996; Hix, 1998). This 'constitutionalisation' means that political actors face new structures of political opportunity as a result of European integration and may redirect their activities in response to the new constellation of political authority. European integration and co-operation can thus affect the expectations of political actors about the location of power, authority and capacity. At the very least, this indicates to us that we might need to reconsider a vocabulary of political analysis 'indelibly impregnated with assumptions about the state' (Schmitter, 1996: 132). This is a useful observation to bear in mind because as we have seen both immigration and immigrant policies are closely linked to nation state and national society points of reference. European integration suggests that these may no longer be sufficient.

Free movement

The right of free movement for EU citizens is a supranational right guaranteed by European laws that over-ride member state laws. This has created an intra-EU migration policy that is linked to (i) market integration and (ii) the possession of the citizenship of a member state (with some exceptions).

The origins of EU free movement can be traced back to the Treaty of Rome (1957). This provided free movement for workers, services, goods and capital. These 'four freedoms' were central to the development of the 'Common Market' after its inception in 1968. The right to free movement was initially linked to economic function. It was a right for workers, not a generalised right open to all. It has since been expanded to include other categories such as students and retired people with the proviso that people are able to support themselves. Free movement has been supranationalised and Community law has been established that is supreme and has direct effect – it over-rides national law and must be implemented by the member states. The effect has been that the EU's free movement framework constrains the member states, reduces their capacity to control international migration, and also demonstrates how market-making and economic integration have long been key drivers of European integration (Handoll, 1995; O'Leary, 1996; Guild, 1998).

The creation of the single market has resulted in a form of member labelled 'economic citizenship', which places greater emphasis on civil rights than on the development of social and political rights (Everson, 1995). Limited social rights are extended to EU citizens who move within the Union and can take their social entitlements with them (Ireland, 1995; Eichenhofer, 1997; Geddes, 2000a). This is not akin to the creation of a European welfare state. Welfare states are national and are likely to remain so because of the diverse levels of provision within EU welfare states and the different ways in which they are organised (Bommes and Geddes, 2000). The EU's social policy provisions were co-ordination measure enacted to ensure the portability of social entitlements because if such provisions were not made then there would obviously be a powerful disincentive to movement.

Where did people who were not nationals of EU member states stand in relation to this intra-EU migration framework? As we have seen, the legacy of guestworker recruitment was a permanently resident population of non-nationals that could find it difficult to acquire the nationality of the state to which they had moved (Turks in Germany are a good example) and thus would be excluded from the rights extended to nationals of member states. An exception is that some third country nationals such as citizens of European Economic Area countries such as Norway and Iceland have acquired rights of free movement as a result of agreements between the EU and third countries.

This supranationalised intra-EU migration did not automatically 'spillover' to cover related issues such as immigration, asylum and nationality laws. Until the 1990s these issues remained strictly national concerns although there were developments outside of the formal Treaty structure. Since the mid-1970s the member states had co-operated on internal security measures. The Trevi group initially discussed member state responses to terrorism, but provided a setting for a wider range of issues as European integration progressed through the 1980s. Trevi provided a 'security' frame into which migration issues were inserted when they rose up the political agenda from the late 1980s. In addition to this was the Schengen Agreement (1985) – initially between France, Germany and the Benelux countries – that sought to realise the speedier attainment of a frontier-free Europe. This required that attention also be paid to 'compensating' immigration and asylum measures.

Trevi and Schengen developed before the Single European Act (1986) created the commitment to single market integration. So, while single market integration provided a crucial impetus to co-operation on immigration and asylum it is rather difficult to argue that single market integration alone caused this co-operation, which had begun to develop prior to the SEA and was linked to attempts to consolidate control over international migration in the face of some domestic constraints. In her study of three Schengen founder members, France, Germany and the Netherlands, Guiraudon (1998) argues that a growing realisation of domestic legal and political constraints on immigration control capacity prompted these countries to seek new European level venues where co-operation could be insulated from these constraints. In these terms, co-operation on immigration and asylum were tied to state interests.

To illustrate the ways in which the member states have tried to keep a tight control on co-operation and integration – and also how this control might be slipping – we can distinguish between four periods in the development of EU co-operation and integration on immigration and asylum.

Minimal immigration policy involvement (1957–86)

During this period immigration policy was firmly a national prerogative. Attempts to include measures relating to the social integration of TCNs in the EC's first Social Action Programme of 1974 were rebuffed by the Council, as too was a proposed Commission directive on clandestine immigration. In 1985 the Commission proposed Guidelines for a Community Policy on Migration (CEC, 1985), which spoke of consultation, experimentation and information rather than legislation (Handoll, 1995: 355). The Commission then proposed a non-binding Decision to establish prior consultation and communication procedures on migration policy that would require member states to give advance notice of measures they intended to take that affected TCNs and their families (similar to the measures outlined in the Commission's 2001 communication on the co-ordination of national immigration policies, CEC 2001a). Denmark, France, Germany, the Netherlands and the UK challenged the Commission proposal and argued that it exceeded Commission competence. In July 1987 the Court annulled certain aspects of the decision, but did allow for a consultation procedure. Even the consultation mechanisms were not used (European Parliament, 1991).

While formal moves within the Community method of decision-making were being rebuffed, there were significant developments within Trevi and, after 1984, Schengen. Belgium, Luxembourg and the Netherlands had created a 'mini-Schengen' in 1970. Further impetus came from protests in 1984 by lorry drivers angered by delays at the Franco-German border that led to a Franco-German agreement signed at Saarbrucken on July 13 1984. The Schengen Agreement of June 14 1985 brought France, Germany and the Benelux countries together in a far-reaching attempt to abolish border controls with compensating internal security measures including immigration and asylum. An implementing convention was then agreed in June 1990, which came into effect 6 years later. The effect was that internal frontiers between participating states were removed. Passports are still shown when entering the Schengen area, but, after that, journeys between Schengen states are classed as internal. By 1997, 13 EU member states (excluding the UK and Ireland) were Schengen members with Iceland and Norway as observers because their Nordic Council partners Denmark, Finland and Sweden are in Schengenland. Schengen, therefore, was a parallel development that saw intensive patterns of co-operation on free movement and internal security. Moreover, the Schengen Agreement formally became part of the EU's *acquis* following the ratification of the Amsterdam Treaty in 1999.

Schengen could be seen as a forum for the pursuit of state interests because it allowed member states to pursue market integration accompanied by restrictive immigration and asylum policies. Schengen was, however, more than a vehicle solely designed for the pursuit of state interests. It put in place structures that indicated deeper integrative intent among a core group of member states. In this sense, Schengen was a testing ground – a laboratory as Monar (2001), puts it – for the future developments within the formal Treaty structure. Schengen also demonstrated the willingness of member states to pursue more 'flexible' forms of co-operation and integration with smaller groups of pioneer states pushing for closer integration.

Informal intergovernmentalism (1986–93)

Within the EC there was strong opposition from some member states to extended supranational competencies. British governments, for example, have consistently supported intergovernmental co-operation but opposed any EU measures that would jeopardise their use of external frontier controls. Even so, the commitment in the Single European Act to create an area without internal frontiers raised immigration and asylum issues. A political declaration by the member states that was attached to the SEA noted that the member states were to co-operate on the entry, movement and residence of TCNs while, at the same time, stating that nothing contained within the SEA affected their immigration control policies. States were keen to pursue their domestic immigration control objectives at EU level without empowering EU institutions and to extend the restrictive policy frame to newer member states in southern Europe (Greece joined in 1981, Portugal and Spain joined in 1986).

Various mechanisms were established to try and do this. In 1986 the Ad Hoc Working Group on Immigration (AHWGI) was established, which was composed of high-level immigration policy officials from the member states and dealt with asylum, external frontiers, forged papers, admissions, deportations, and the exchange of information. The ECJ and EP had no powers to scrutinise the AHWGI's work and the Commission was only loosely associated with developments. Indeed, this form of co-operation was a problem for the Commission, which wanted to see supranational integration but was, at the same time, eager to participate in developments in migration policy areas that connected with core EC objectives (Monar, 1994).

In December 1988 the member states established a Group of Co-ordinators with the task of co-ordinating between the free movement measures and the internal security implications. The resultant 'Palma Programme' led directly to measures covering asylum and external frontier control. The main problem with these measures was that the member states had to rely on conventions in international law. Unlike supranational laws made by the Council and that bind the member states, international conventions relied on ratification in each member state.

The key asylum measure was the June 1990 Dublin Convention on the state responsible for examining applications for asylum lodged in one member state (Handoll, 1995: 419–25). The Convention sought to end the possibility for 'asylum shopping' where asylum-seekers make applications in more than one member state. Member states were also to maintain information on rejected asylum claims in the Eurodac database. The Dublin Convention did not harmonise the rules so that procedures in member states became the same; rather it sought approximation with the effect that only one member state would be responsible for judging an asylum application.

The core elements of the Dublin framework were put in place at a meeting of immigration ministers held in London between 30 November and 1 December 1992. What is interesting is the ways in which these measures have had particular effects on central and eastern European countries that were not EU member states but were required to adapt to these measures as a requirement for membership and thus become a 'buffer zone' to absorb migration pressures on EU member states (see Chapter 8). A non-binding resolution on 'manifestly unfounded applications for asylum' was adopted, which meant that an application could be judged manifestly unfounded if it was not covered by either the Geneva Convention or New York Protocol, because there was no fear of persecution in the applicant's own country, or because the claim was based on deception or an abuse of procedures. A resolution on 'a harmonised approach to host third countries' was also agreed at the London meeting, which intended to return rejected asylum-seekers to 'safe third countries'. Central and eastern European countries were defined as safe, with the effect that asylum seekers entering the EU from central and eastern European countries could be returned to them. Germany had received more asylum seekers than any other European country, but was able to use these EU devices in order to maintain its symbolic commitment to asylum while also drastically reducing the ability of asylum-seekers to enter the state territory. The London meeting also established Centres for Information, Discussion and Exchange on Asylum (CIREA) and Information, Discussion and Exchange on the Crossing of Borders and Immigration (CIREFI).

The Dublin Convention was not ratified until September 1997. These ratification problems were also evident in the travails experienced by the External Frontiers Convention, initially agreed in September 1991, but remained unsigned by the British and Spanish governments because of a dispute about the status of Gibraltar. The draft External Frontiers Convention (EFC) of June 1991 outlined the general principles concerning the crossing, surveillance, control and nature of the controls at external frontiers, as well as surveillance at airports.

The two main weaknesses of this informal approach were that it was inefficient because it was difficult to ratify agreed measures and that it was undemocratic because decisions were made in secretive forums without democratic or judicial accountability at national or European level. What the informal co-operation did achieve, however, was routinised interaction between interior ministers and officials and the development of a security frame that was to be expanded to include immigration and asylum in the 1990s. It is important to identify the actors associated with the process. In this case, co-operation was largely colonised by those with a security-centred understanding of migration and migrants and a determination to restrict those forms of migration defined as unwanted. Pressure grew during the negotiations preceding the Maastricht Treaty for more formalised co-operation within the Treaty and a more developed role for supranational institutions. This was likely to be controversial given the reluctance of Denmark and the UK to integrate in these areas.

Formal Intergovernmental Cooperation (1993–99)

Immigration and asylum's heightened post-Cold War salience helped prompt agreement that informal intergovernmentalism was problematic, but there was still disagreement about what should replace it. The German government was particularly keen to advocate distributive solidarity or 'burden sharing' with a redistribution of asylum seekers between member states. The basic problem was that if the Treaties were to be reformed and if expanded immigration competencies were to be established then the consent of all member states was needed. This was a problem because the British and Danish governments made it very clear that they would not countenance common policies.

Some compromise was needed. The member states were presented with four options – ranging from the status quo to fully integrated common policies – by the Luxembourg government that held the presidency of the EC in the first six months of 1991. The preference for intergovernmentalism and the status quo of Denmark, the UK, Greece and Ireland meant that the basis for an accommodation between the member states would be likely to centre on a form of intergovernmentalism that pushed immigration and asylum closer to the legal framework of the Treaty but fell short of full incorporation. The proposed solution was the establishment of an intergovernmental pillar dealing with Justice and Home Affairs (JHA) with a similar pillar dealing with equally sensitive Common Foreign and Security Policy (CFSP).

The three 'pillars' covering Justice and Home Affairs, Common Foreign and Security Policy and the Community pillar would be the foundations of the newly created European Union. This division was artificial in the sense that internal (JHA) and external (CFSP) security have become closely linked during the 1990s, but the deal satisfied the requirements of member states at the Maastricht summit. The divisions between the pillars have been eroded since the late 1990s as links between foreign and interior policy have become more apparent (Pastore, 2001a).

The Maastricht Treaty recognised the following immigration and asylum issues as being of 'common interest' (*nota bene*, not common policies):

- Asylum policy.

- External frontiers – particularly the crossing of these frontiers and the exercise of controls.

- Immigration policy and policy regarding TCNs.

- Conditions of entry and movement by nationals of third countries on the territory of member states.

- Conditions of residence by nationals of third countries on the territory of Member States, including family reunion and access to employment.

- Combating unauthorised immigration, residence and work by TCNs.

There was some complication because a new Article 100c was added to the Community pillar that covered visa policies (also mentioned in the JHA pillar) and allowed the Council, acting unanimously, to draw up a list of third countries whose nationals needed visas to enter EU member states. Article 100c meant that visa policy was to be dealt with in the Community pillar and by Articles K.1 (2) and (3) in the third pillar. This delightful situation was further complicated when regulations establishing a uniform visa format and listing the countries whose nationals needed visas were introduced were struck down by the European Court of Justice because of the failure to consult the European Parliament.

If we try and cut through some of the EU jargon, we can delineate the key features of the vision of a 'pillared' Europe devised at Maastricht. The analogy was to a Greek temple that would rest on three pillars: the main Community pillar and the two new flanking pillars for JHA and CFSP. The allusion to classical symmetry was flawed because these arrangements were decidedly asymmetrical. The much larger Community pillar remained the point of reference while there were functional and institutional linkages between them. In this context, Müller-Graf (1994) talks about the 'legal sandstone' of the third pillar and argues that pressure was likely to grow for measures to be located within the main 'Community' pillar because of these linkages.

The main advantage of the pillared arrangement for those states that preferred intergovernmentalism was that it minimised the involvement of supranational institutions. The British government preferred their system of external controls with dominance by the executive branch of government. Thus, co-operation at EU-level between ministers and officials could be supported, but extended powers for the European Commission or European Court of Justice were to be avoided because these could alter a system that had delivered stringent restrictions on immigration based on a system of executive dominance and external frontier controls that did not fit with the Schengenland model. The *modus operandi* was decision-making in the Council of Ministers based on unanimity. Although the possibility did exist for the ECJ to be given powers to adjudicate, these were never actually extended. The Commission's role was also limited, . although the Commission was eager to secure a seat for itself at the inter-governmental negotiating table because of the broader implications of immigration and asylum co-operation for Community competencies.

The period between 1993 and 1999 was distinguished by a proliferation of non-binding measures concerning immigration and asylum, of which there were over 70 produced between 1993 and 1998. Even though these were of obscure legal standing, the effects of co-operation were highly sig-nificant for countries in central and eastern Europe that had to adapt this framework as a requirement for membership. Adaptation was made more difficult by the fact that it was an evolving and moving target.

Concerns about both efficiency and democracy remained. Yet, at the same time, the Maastricht period had demonstrated that states kept a tight grip on the process and that the role of supranational institutions had been minimised. Measures such as the Dublin Convention and the recognition of 'safe third countries' allowed the member states to pursue their restrictive policy objectives and to off-load responsibility for control to a central and eastern European 'buffer zone'.

By the mid-1990s, there was renewed discussion about the status of immigration and asylum policies. Would the 'legal sandstone' of the JHA pillar be eroded because of perceptions by more integration-minded member states of the deficiencies of intergovernmental co-operation? If states were only interested in using the EU to pursue their domestic objec-tives then it could be argued that they'd be happy with the status quo. In fact, as the discussion of the Amsterdam Treaty shows, the state-centred explanation appears particularly well-suited to the era of 'pillarised' co-operation between 1993 and 1999 and is perhaps questioned by the 'communitarisation' of immigration and asylum in the late 1990s. This could be because the state-centred explanation fires on one cylinder. It neglects functional, political and institutional linkages connecting immi-gration and asylum to free movement that blurred the distinction between the JHA and Community pillars. Yet, the clear merit of the state-centred explanation is its demonstration that states have been able to use the EU as a new venue to pursue domestic policy objectives.

Communitarisation

Amsterdam has been acknowledged as a landmark in that, as Peers (1998: 1235) puts it: 'The argument over competence is over; long live the argument over substance'. Hailbronner (1998: 1048) contends that 'the establishment of an immigration control system has to be considered as a primary objective which is closely connected with the abolition of internal border controls and the establishment of the single market'. The Amsterdam Treaty brought immigration and asylum into the Community pillar in a new Treaty title covering free movement, immigration and asylum; but at the same time confirmed intergovernmentalism as the basis for decision-making until at least 2004 (five years after the Treaty came into force). Immigration and asylum were thus 'communitarised' in the sense that they moved to the Community pillar, but were not 'supranationalised' in the sense of being made subject to day-to-day processes of integration.

The Amsterdam Treaty's centrepiece was a new Treaty objective that defined the Union as 'an area of freedom, security and justice' and a new Title IV added to the Treaty dealing with free movement, immigration and asylum together. Title IV gave the Council of Ministers the responsibility to ensure within five years of Treaty ratification (2004) the free movement of persons and related external border control, asylum and immigration measures. Amsterdam also incorporated the Schengen Agreement of 1985 and Implementing Accord of 1990, plus all the associated decisions that had emerged since. The list of Schengen documents itself was 18 pages long and contained 172 documents covering all aspects of the 142 articles of the Schengen Agreement. The Schengen *acquis* was to be incorporated into either the new Title IV (dealing with free movement, immigration and asylum) or into the pillar dealing with judicial and police co-operation (the old JHA pillar). The British and Irish governments opted-out of Title IV – with the possibility of opting back in on a case-by-case basis – and affirmed their right to exercise their own external frontier controls. Denmark is a Schengen member state, but reserved the right to opt-out of Title IV measures that would 'communitarise' measures previously determined intergovernmentally. An element of 'flexibility' was thus introduced.

In its December 1998 'Action Plan' the Commission emphasised the need to move away from the 'soft law' of the post-Maastricht period to supranational laws and enact asylum and immigration measures (CEC, 1999). The Tampere summit meeting of heads of government in October 1999 called for a common EU migration and provided political impetus from the highest governmental level. The common policy was to be based on:

- Partnership with countries of origin. The post-Amsterdam role of the High Level Working Group on Immigration and Asylum has been crucial here. Not only because it illustrates the links between internal security concerns and foreign policy, but also because it has been seen as displaying the EU's intention to try to keep migrants closer to their countries of origin (Van Selm, 2002). As has already been noted, there was an air of artificiality about the division between JHA and CFSP. Ferruccio Pastore (2001a: 1) draws from a Machiavellian analogy to argue that internal and external threats to the power of the Prince used to be distinct but that 'recent trends towards an ever stronger internationalisation of economic and social processes have blurred the traditional distinction between internal and external security (and related policy fields) world-wide'. EU responses highlight the blurring of this distinction and the tendencies towards what is known as 'crosspillarisation' with functional linkages made between the concerns dealt with by the CFSP and JHA pillars (and thus between the concerns of foreign and interior ministries).

- Asylum measures were specified to include a workable determination of the State responsible for the examination of an asylum application, common standards on processing applications, common minimum conditions of reception of asylum seekers, and the approximation of rules on the recognition and content of the refugee status. This would be accompanied by measures on temporary protection for displaced people (based on solidarity between member states). In the longer term, the member states proposed that Community rules should lead to a common asylum procedure and a uniform status for those who are granted asylum valid throughout the Union. The Commission was asked to prepare within one year a communication on this matter (which it did, see CEC, 2000b). The Council of Minister was also urged to finalise its work on the system for the identification of asylum seekers (Eurodac).

- Fair treatment for third country nationals who reside legally on the territory of its Member States. The member states talked about 'more vigorous' policies aimed at granting TCNs rights and obligations comparable to those of EU citizens with measures to enforce the principle of equal treatment in economic, social and cultural life. There was also a call for measures to combat racism and xenophobia (see the next section of the chapter for more information on these measures, including antidiscrimination laws).

- The management of migration flows based on co-operation with countries of origin and transit, of information campaigns on the actual possibilities for legal immigration, and the prevention of trafficking in human beings. The heads of government also called for common policies on visas and false documents, including closer co-operation between EU consulates in third countries and, where necessary, the establishment of common EU visa issuing offices. The member states also reaffirmed their determination to tackle illegal immigration and those who traffick in human beings and economically exploit migrants. There was also renewed commitment to closer co-operation and mutual technical assistance between member states on border controls and technology transfer, especially on maritime borders, and for the rapid inclusion of the applicant states in this co-operation. It was also stated that applicant countries must accept the Schengen *acquis* in full. Finally, the Amsterdam Treaty conferred powers on the Community for readmission. The Council was mandated to conclude readmission agreements or to include standard readmission clauses in other agreements between the European Community and relevant third countries or groups of countries.

Towards common European policies?

How successful has the EU been in achieving these objectives and moving towards common EU policies, and what have developments meant for the role of supranational institutions? There is quite a convenient source of information when answering the first question because the Commission helpfully publishes a biennial 'scoreboard' specifying progress towards the attainment of the Tampere objectives. In its summary of developments in the second half of 2001, the Commission notes that 'It would be satisfying to be able to report to the European Council that the "pillar switch" has led to a greater sense of urgency and flexibility than was the case before the Amsterdam Treaty came into force, particularly in the light of the clear deadlines set at the highest level [at Tampere]. Unfortunately, that is not yet the case' (CEC, 2001b: 6). It reports some positive developments, such as the creation of a European Refugee Fund, a directive on Temporary Protection and the setting up of the Eurodac system. In other areas the Commission reports that the 'familiar phenomenon' of reluctance by one or more member states to proposed measures can hinder the whole process. The requirement for unanimity acts as a brake on common decision-making.

To take the second question, what do the Amsterdam measures and the developments since mean for supranational institutions? Both the Commission and ECJ have had limited involvement in immigration and asylum measures and extensive involvement in free movement. Emek Uçarer (2000) argues that the impact of Amsterdam is such that the Commission is a 'sidekick' no more and that it has become a key player in the evolving immigration and asylum policy. The Communication issued by the Commission on asylum policy, immigration policy and on the co-ordination of national migration policies could be brought forward as evidence of this activism (CEC 2000a, 2000b, 2001a). As too could the reorganisation of the Commission which has involved the establishment of a JHA Directorate with around 250 staff members. This suggests some scope for supranational leadership or entrepreneurialism, but what would this imply? Moravcsik (1999: 272) defines supranational entrepreneurialism as 'exploitation by international officials of asymmetrical control over scarce information or ideas to influence the outcome of multilateral negotiations through initiation, mediation and mobilisation'.

If supranational leadership is a significant factor then these informational and ideational asymmetries need to be identified and its needs to be explained how and why supranational institutions fill them. Uçarer argues that the delegation of authority by the Amsterdam Treaty coupled with operational resources and capabilities have led to incipient task expansiveness. The Commission has been emboldened by the creation of a new Directorate General dealing with Justice and Home Affairs and is eager to flex its muscles in the area of migration policy. In addition to this, the Commission is an active alliance-builder. The Commission and European Parliament have forged a closer relationship to counterbalance restrictive national policies.

This argument about leadership tends to be based on the formal delegation of responsibility and organisational changes within the Commission that have both empowered and boosted the credibility of the Justice and Home affairs directorate. We can distinguish between *formal* and *informal* agenda setting capabilities when assessing claims about supranational leadership. Formally, the Amsterdam Treaty 'communitarised' immigration and asylum by bringing them into a new Title IV from Maastricht's JHA pillar. The issues were 'communitarised' not 'supranationalised' because the Commission, ECJ and European Parliament are constrained for at least five years after Treaty ratification. Commission activity in these areas has been quite impressive. But activity does not necessarily mean that the Commission is in the driving seat. Pollack (1999: 7) suggests that 'for the first five years of the new Treaty, the Commission will effectively be 'on trial' in its proposals to the Council which will weight its decision to move to QMV accordingly'.

Limitations on formal agenda setting can be countered if there is space for informal agenda-setting activity. Informal agenda setting activity includes the highlighting of problems, advancing proposals, and identifying the possible material benefits of integration. Pro-migrant lobby groups at supranational level have sought to exercise informal agenda-setting influence and have established mutually reinforcing pro-European integration alliances with Community institutions in the quest for 'more Europe' to counter what they see as lowest common denominator inter-governmental decision-making in the Council of Ministers (Geddes, 2000b). The EU executive is seen as potentially progressive, while national executives are not. The solution from this perspective to the problem of 'fortress Europe' – understood as meaning tightly restrictive policies – is not a return to state sovereignty, but rather consolidated powers for the Commission, European Court of Justice (ECJ) and European Parliament. This means *more* not *less* Europe in response to supposed 'fortress' like tendencies (Geddes, 2000b).

The Commission faces both formal and informal constraints on its agenda-setting role plus the limitations that arise from continued reliance on unanimity. More interesting perhaps is the way that the Commission has proposed in its July 2001 communication on the co-ordination of migration policies to act as the information store in an information-poor environment (CEC, 2001a). The Commission proposes to co-ordinate national action plans for migration drafted by the member states related to the management of migration flows, admission of economic migrants, partnership with third countries, and the integration of third country nationals (redolent of the Commission's plans in the mid-1980s that encountered fierce opposition from some member states). These reports will then be submitted to the Commission, which will prepare a synthesis report and identify 'European solutions to common problems' (CEC, 2001a: 12). This ostensibly rational approach to the management of labour migration based on the identification of needs and the recruitment of workers to fill them is predicated on the assumption that the policy environment is stable, information is available, and that actors are able to attain policy objectives. On the contrary, argues Sciortino (2000), the immigration policy environment is better understood as being unstable and state actors are often unable to meet their policy objectives. Nevertheless, the Commission appears to be positioning itself in a key co-ordinating role responsible for initiation, mobilisation and mediation. Informational asymmetries are thus utilised as an opportunity for supranational activity, but whether the member states will agree to expanded Community competencies remains unclear.

The ECJ's role is also important because it is well documented that national courts have helped open – at least in formal terms – 'social and political spaces' for migrants and their descendants (Hollifield, 1992; Joppke, 2001). Garrett and Tsebelis (2001) present 'a unified model of EU politics' in which they identify a 'third epoch' during which time the development of co-decision since the Maastricht Treaty has increased the potential for legislative deadlock between the Council and European Parliament with the result being enhanced discretionary space for the Commission to implement policy and the ECJ to adjudicate. This theoretical discretion can be limited if the ECJ encounters 'legitimacy constraints' when acting in areas that are at the core of member state sovereignty (Mattli and Slaughter, 1998). The Amsterdam Treaty also constrains the ECJ's migration policy competencies by stipulating that preliminary rulings can only be sought against decisions for which there is no judicial remedy under national law. This was seen by Pollack (1999) as reducing the access of lower courts to the ECJ and thus countering the impact that preliminary rulings based on referrals from these lower courts have had on the expansion of Community law. However, Hailbronner (1998: 1056) notes that lower courts may face an increasing number of decisions based on secondary European legislation without the possibility of seeking a preliminary ruling. This could lead to requests for judicial protection by migrants because national restrictions are argued to be incompatible with Community law and thus 'until a final ruling by the European Court can be obtained, national administrations and Courts would be obliged to implement Community legislation in favour of the applicant'. The ECJ is also excluded from measures relating to the maintenance of law and order and the safeguarding of national security, although given that it is the ECJ that rules on these issues it is thought unlikely that it will act to tie its own hands.

There has been a slow move towards communitarisation of migration issues, coupled with reluctance among member states to empower supranational integration in these areas and some 'flexibility' in the form of integration. Why have European countries moved into these areas? We have seen that single market integration played a key role, but so too did the growing awareness of domestic constraints and the search for new policy arenas that could facilitate the reassertion of immigration control. A classic analysis of the relationship between state interests and European integration argued that states would shy away from integration in areas of 'high politics' that impinged directly on state sovereignty because 'Russian roulette is fine only as long as the gun is filled with blanks' (Hoffmann, 1966: 882). Yet, in the 1990s there has been a blurring of the distinction between the intra-EU migration regime centred on market-making and the extra-EU migration regime that is bundled up with population control and security concerns. The parameters of a common policy have begun to emerge, with some Commission prompting, but questions remain about the political will of the member states. In addition to this, policy development has so far been deficient in terms of what Scharpf (2000) calls 'input oriented authenticity' (accountability and scrutiny), while doubts remains about 'output-oriented effectiveness' (the capacity to deliver policy objectives).

Immigrant policies

The preceding chapters of this book have located immigrant integration policies within the bounds of nation state and national society approaches. As Adrian Favell (2001) has pointed out this may not be entirely appropriate. He suggests that other intervening variables can also play a role, by which he means that local/city level and developments 'above' the nation state such as the EU and the development of transnational communities. This section examines the EU's immigrant policy role, the development of pro-migrant political mobilisation, and the emergence of EU anti-discrimination laws. These developments confound both a narrow state-centrism by showing the establishment of rights at EU level, but also question post-national universalism in the sense that these rights draw from Europeanised rather than universalised ideas about membership and belonging. Moreover, the forms of inclusion generated at EU level tend to be closely related to core EU-market-making functions and the development of a form of 'economic citizenship' that is designed to complement rather than replace national citizenship.

The EU migrant inclusion agenda

Until the late 1990s, EU migration policy development was unbalanced in the sense that there was a strong emphasis on restricting immigration and much less emphasis on immigrant policies covering both legally resident third country nationals and citizens of member states of immigrant and ethnic minority origin. This changed with the 1997 Amsterdam Treaty, which introduced a new Article 13 that extended the anti-discrimination provisions to include gender, race, ethnicity, religion, age, disability and sexual orientation. The Commission was given the power to make policy proposals in this area with the Council making decisions on the basis of unanimity. Two Directives were issued in June 2000 covering the principle of equal treatment irrespective of race or ethnic origin and the establishment of a general framework for equal treatment in employment and occupation. The 'race equality' directive applies to the public and private sectors, including public bodies and thus eliminates the 'state action' hurdle, which had hampered anti-discrimination law enforcement in other contexts. The Directive applies to access to employment, including self-employment and occupation, vocational training and working conditions; social security and healthcare; social advantages; education; and the provision of goods and services which are available to the public, including housing. These are, of course, precisely the areas in which racial discrimination is most evident. The Directive also presents scope for 'positive action' in order 'to prevent or compensate for disadvantages linked to racial or ethnic origin'. The deadline for implementation of the equal treatment directive is July 19 2003 and for the employment/occupation directive is December 2 2003 (Tyson, 2001; Chopin and Niessen, 2001).

These two Directives are important because the EU legislation aims to tackle both direct and indirect forms of discrimination and thus goes beyond provisions in many member states (European Parliament, 1998). Indeed, it could be argued that the measures draw from a UK and Dutch-style policy frame where legislation has focused on direct and indirect discrimination and where terms such as 'ethnic minorities' have acquired everyday policy currency. This contrasts with the situation in France, for instance, where in official terms at least, the policy discourse has disavowed notions of ethnic minorities on the basis that French Republicanism rests on a logic of equality and not minorities. The EU has also stepped up measures to tackle racism and xenophobia. 1997 was declared to be the European Year Against Racism while the European Union Monitoring Centre on Racism and Xenophobia was set-up in Vienna in 1998.

What lay behind this rapid development? As Tyson (2001) points out, the two directives based on Article 13 set 'world records' for this type of legislation not based on existing EU law in terms of their progress from proposals to legislation. The Council agreed the initial proposals made in

December 1999 with agreement reached in June 2000. Three factors help explain this. First, the role played by pro-migrant NGOs and their cultivation of alliances with supranational institutions. During the 1990s, ideas that drew heavily from UK and Dutch anti-discrimination laws became part of a developing EU migrant inclusion agenda. This was not a levelling down or a lowest common denominator policy. In fact, UK and Dutch standards with provisions on direct and indirect discrimination far exceed those in many member states. Second, in the wake of an increase in racist and xenophobic attacks there was a general view among member states that 'something needed to be done', although precisely what was a more difficult question. Third, the crystallising influence that brought supranational entrepreneurialism and state preferences together was the entry into the Austrian governmental coalition in October 1999 of the extreme right-wing Freedom Party.

Pro-migrant mobilisation at EU level

New forms of pro-migrant political action have developed since the 1990s that address EU sources of power and push for expanded EU competencies. Much of this mobilisation was closely linked to EU institutions to the extent that the Commission venue set and funded the European Union Migrants' Forum in a bid to consult and thus add legitimacy to policy development (Danese, 1998; Geddes, 2000b). Pro-migrant NGOs tend to be relatively weak because public opinion across the EU tends to be anti-immigration and anti-immigrant while non-national migrants have limited access to local and national political systems, never mind to the EU political system. Yet, this need not stultify the scope for pro-migrant advocacy. Political opportunities can arise where decision-makers are relatively shielded from anti-immigration/immigrant pressures, such as behind the 'closed doors' of the European Commission. In this sense, the EU's 'democratic deficit' understood as relative insulation from direct political pressures, could offer new political opportunities and more progressive outcomes.

The migrant inclusion agenda that developed at EU level in the 1990s had three main elements: EU citizenship rights for third country nationals; enhanced anti-discrimination provisions to cover race, ethnicity and religion; and treatment of asylum-seekers that accord with international standards.

The most problematic issue has been the rights of asylum-seekers. Policies across the EU have sought (i) to reduce the ability of asylum seekers to access the territory of EU member states and (ii) to use internal measures such as dispersal systems, accommodation centres, the denial of labour market access, and the use of vouchers rather than cash paid welfare state benefits. External measures have centred on visa requirements, recognition of safe third countries, carrier sanctions, as well as the cross pillar work of the HLWG. The rights of asylum-seekers in EU member states have also been questioned because of the widely expressed view that many claims are 'bogus'. Prominent NGOs such as ECRE have been strong critics of what they see as a race to the bottom by EU member states that bears only tenuous relation to the international commitments of EU member states. This may also reinforce the point made in the introduction to this chapter. EU co-operation and integration may actually have enabled the member states to develop new ways of regulating those forms of migration that their policies define as 'unwanted'. EU member states can thus retain a symbolic commitment to the right to asylum while eroding the ability of people who want to enter the territory of EU member states and exercise this right.

Why anti-discrimination legislation and not citizenship rights for third country nationals?

Why did anti-discrimination become part of the EU's legal framework while proposals for EU citizenship rights for legally resident third country nationals flounder? In the pre-Amsterdam intergovernmental conference during which Treaty changes were discussed, the EUMF proposed to amend Article 8a of the EU Treaty on EU citizenship with the effect that it would read: 'Citizenship of the Union is hereby established. Every person holding a nationality of a member state *or who has been lawfully residing in the territory of a member state for five years* shall be a citizen of the EU' (italics added). It was then proposed to amend Articles 48-66 covering free movement so that these rights would also be extended to third country nationals on the basis of legal residence rather than prior possession of the nationality of a member state (EUMF, 1996). The problem was that the EU was specifically precluded by declarations attached to the Maastricht and Amsterdam Treaties from involvement in the nationality laws of the member states. The idea that Europeanised denizenship with free movement rights extended to include legally resident TCNs was mentioned in the Commission's 1998 Action Plan on free movement, immigration and asylum. However, the Tampere summit supported 'approximation' of the legal rather than harmonisation of the status of third country nationals with 'uniform rights that are as near as possible to those enjoyed by EU citizens' with the long-term objective that they acquire the nationality of their state of residence. The French, German and UK governments issued a declaration that acquisition of nationality was the route to repairing incomplete membership rather than Europeanised denizenship that could undermine member state nationality laws.

In contrast, there were legal resources that could be used to support the claim for extended anti-discrimination provisions. What is more, these could be connected with the EU's market-making objectives. The EU has been committed to anti-discrimination since the Treaty of Rome (gender and nationality originally). It is also committed to the principle of equal treatment (Directive 76/207EEC of 1976). Consequently, legal, political and symbolic resources exist for successful mobilisation in the area of anti-discrimination while groups arguing for EU citizenship for third country nationals face an uphill task to put it mildly. When we move on to analyse the attitudes of member states it is important to note that inter-governmental impetus was given because of member state concern about racism and xenophobia. The French and German governments were instrumental in the creation of the Kahn Committee, which called for expanded anti-discrimination legislation (ECCRX, 1995). The entry into the Austrian coalition of six Freedom Party ministers also had a major impact. The anti-discrimination proposals were already on the table. Countries with policy approaches to immigrant integration that appeared less amenable to the kind of anti-discrimination policy that was being proposed were also the most vocal in their condemnation of the new Austrian government. The French and Belgian social affairs ministers refused to participate in the usual group photo with the new Austrian government ministers. The French were now keen to see the race directive passed as part of an anti-racist stance rather than as an approach to the integration of ethnic minorities that drew quite heavily from the kinds of 'ethnic minority' policies that had traditionally been anathema to the French approach to these questions. It has also been argued that the initial *policy linkage* between anti-discrimination and the Austrian far right ensured that the dossier would be given priority and that the Austrian delegation would be extremely co-operative during the negotiations. The same can be said of the German delegation that feared to be associated with Austria. No member state wanted to be the backstop in these parti-cular negotiations (Geddes and Guiraudon, 2002).

Conclusion

Changes in relations between states can also play an important part in shaping understandings of 'good' and 'bad' forms of migration. The EU has created a supranationalised free movement framework for the citi-zens of its member states and has labelled them as EU citizens. There has also been co-operation since the 1980s geared towards restrictions on those forms of migration defined as unwanted. In this sense, the EU has been a new venue for the pursuit of domestic policy objectives. It has also provided the context for the diffusion of policy ideas and practices to newer immigration countries in southern, central and eastern Europe.

The inclusion of migration as an EU concern also illustrates the contin-ued tensions between open economies and closed states and the kinds of boundary issues that arise as a result of attempts to reconcile forms of openness derived from EU market-making and the kinds of closure associated with nation states. International migration has become one of the most salient of these boundary issues since the mid-1980s because of its links to the kinds of economic migration within the single market that are prized by the EU coupled with changing ideas and practices concerning security and insecurity.

The EU project combines both boundary-removing and boundary-building aspects. It seeks an area without internal frontiers within which people (meaning mainly EU citizens) can move freely coupled with restrictions on those forms of migration defined by state policies as unwanted. In these terms, the EU defines a narrow state-centrism because states have ceded decision-making powers in important areas that erode in some respects and with regards to some forms of movement their ability to determine who enters the state territory. At the same time, European integration also challenges post-national universalism because the boundary-building aspects of European integration create Europeanised forms of membership and belonging centred on rights of 'economic citizenship'. Perhaps this just serves to remind us of the EU's hybridity – its combination of intergovernmental and supranational influences. As we have seen, intergovernmental influences have shaped immigration and asylum co-operation and even after the Amsterdam Treaty communitarised these issues there has been reluctance to cede powers to supranational institutions and thus risk unexpected outcomes in sensitive political areas.

There has also been a more recent move by the EU into the area of immigrant policies. The progress of this legislation is fascinating because it does not fit easily with policies in many member states and because it creates Europeanised forms of social and political power that have the potential to make a real difference to immigration and ethnic minority communities within the EU. The anti-discrimination directives of June 2000 have put in place a policy frame that appears to draw heavily from UK and Dutch understandings of anti-discrimination. Such ideas have been anathema in the French context (officially at least), but the EU has created legal and political resources which offer a challenge to this national way of doing things, as well as resources to groups in France that want to mobilise against discrimination in these terms. Second, this new supranational legislation creates the possibility for groups representing Europe's immigrant and ethnic minority population to access the material and symbolic resources made available for them at EU level to press for their inclusion at domestic level. Keck and Sikkink (1998) discuss what they call a 'boomerang effect' by which they mean that relatively weak domestic actors can be strengthened by the material and symbolic sources of power associated with international organisations.

This chapter has focused in particular on the shift to Europe and the explanations for and implications of the development of EU migration policy responsibilities. In the next two chapters the impact of European integration is discussed in more detail. We examine the politics of migration in southern, central and eastern Europe. This allows us to explore the implications of the geopolitical and conceptual widening of the migration issue. This has implications for our understanding of national responses in national contexts that differ from those in 'older' immigration countries, as well as the place of these national responses in an integrating Europe.

7

Southern Europe: Immigration Politics in Newer Immigration Countries

Europe's migration frontiers have moved south and east since the 1980s. This represents a geopolitical conceptual widening with new types of migration and new forms of state response. This chapter explores the politics of migration and state responses in Greece, Italy, Portugal and Spain. It distinguishes between specific features of these countries that contribute to a domestic politics of immigration in each of them. It analyses factors that link them, in particular the relatively high levels of economic informality (or underground economy) and irregular immigration. It also assesses the impact of European integration.

How can policy developments in southern European countries be explained? Is the politics of migration in southern Europe distinct because these are newer immigration countries? This temporal dimension could imply catch-up as they become more like older immigration countries. Perhaps the politics of migration differ in southern Europe differs because these are southern European countries and in some way exceptional (and likely to remain so)? Underlying this could be the dubious assumption that these countries are in some sense 'backward' and not capable of dealing with the issues in the same way that older immigration countries have (for one thing this assumes great success and attainment of objectives in these older immigration countries). Giuseppe Sciortino (1999) is critical of the southern European exceptionalism school of thought which, he argues, runs as follows: weak border controls, leading to a tolerance of illegal immigration, creating havens for clandestine immigration. He argues that there has in fact been a remarkable turnaround in southern European immigration policies with the adoption of a 'stop and contain' approach centred on external frontier controls that is similar to other EU member states. That said, the perception that southern Europe remains Europe's 'soft underbelly' will not have been helped by events such as those in Sicily in March 2002 when – accompanied by a Europe-wide media frenzy – more than 900 Kurds arrived in the port of Catania.

That said, there are measures that aim to secure the external frontiers of southern European countries, which in an integrated Europe will become the EU's external frontiers. The Spanish police, for instance, are developing with EU financial support a \$150 million 'electronic wall' that will cover 350 miles of Spanish coastline from Huelva in south west Spain to Almeria in the south east that will be able to detect boats (particularly from North Africa) containing would-be migrants that are 7 miles out to sea and then dispatch police to intercept them (*Migration News*, September 2000). This arises from concern about the small boats packed with clandestine immigrants who make the perilous journey from North Africa to Spain. Concerns about porous borders have been evident in Italy where substantial efforts have been made – more money and a reorganisation of the frontier police – to increase the capacity to control the country's external frontiers at vulnerable points such as the land border with Slovenia and the coastline of the southern region of Puglia (Pastore, 2001b).

The external control dimension is only part of the story. What happens within these states is equally as important. The underlying issues in southern Europe have been the persistence of relatively high levels of economic informality and irregular migration. Maria Baganha (2000: 170) has written that economic informality is 'a distinctive feature of Southern European migratory processes' and creates spaces for irregular migrants. This is not to say that informality and irregularity are unique to southern Europe. There is informality and irregular immigration in older immigration countries too, but not on the same scale. Tackling informality through tough labour market regulation raises issues that go wider than immigration and touch upon state-society relations and social control more generally. Put bluntly, external controls impact on foreigners who can't vote; internal controls affect citizens who can.

A key aspect of the internal response to immigration in southern Europe has been the regularisation of the status of irregular migrants. These regularisations have more to do with prevailing informality than with EU policy. Indeed, if regularisations encourage further immigration, as some argue they do, then a principal policy instrument employed in southern Europe runs counter to the EU policy frame and is determined largely by domestic factors.

This chapter also develops two other issues that have been discussed in earlier chapters. First, links between migration and security/insecurity as both a perceived threat to borders and to internal cohesion within these states. The politicisation of migration as a security problem has provoked 'emergency' responses with an emphasis on external frontier control and the co-option of neighbouring and sending countries into these control measures. Second, connections between international migration, foreign policy and 'international migration relations' as the conceptual and spatial widening of the migration issue affects politics within states and relations between states. This is not new, but as Sarah Collinson (2000: 316) puts it, international migration and its impact on southern Europe and the Mediterranean countries reflects 'a new, more dynamic, geopolitical configuration, but also itself is playing a part in shaping that new configuration'.

Informality and irregularity

Economic informality and irregular migration connect southern European countries, although other factors are at work too. Russell King (2000: 8–12) develops a model that captures the dynamic context under-pinning migration into southern European countries:

- Diversion effects initially contributed to immigration in southern European countries because of stricter controls in north western Europe since the mid-1970s.

- Southern European countries are accessible because of the centrality of cities such as Athens, Lisbon, Madrid and Rome to global communications networks. Many 'illegals' enter legally, as tourists for instance, and then over-stay, take employment when they don't hold the appropriate permit, or fall foul of bureaucratic procedures.

- Colonial ties linking Italy, Portugal and Spain have underpinned some migration to these countries. That said, newer migration flows lack such strong political-historical structuring factors and have led to a multiplicity of national origins of migrants in southern Europe. An interesting feature of the 2001 Portuguese regularisation was that 33 per cent of the 76,000 people who had regularised their status by July 2001 were from the Ukraine. Portugal and the Ukraine can hardly be characterised as countries with close ties. The perception of Portugal as a country where it is relatively easy to live and work – and the communication and the transmission of such images within migration networks – has played a part in structuring this migration (*Migration News*, September 2001; Baganha, 2000).

- The rapid economic development of southern European countries has created labour market shortages. Moreover, the relatively large informal sector has created spaces for irregular migration.

- Domestic labour market changes have meant that immigrants (employed either formally or informally) are needed to do the jobs that native workers seem no longer willing to do. In Italy there are high levels of unemployment in the south, but southern Italians are less willing either to move north or outside Italy in search of work. High unemployment can co-exist with immigration, which suggests dual labour markets with migrants inserted into those economic activities that native workers are less willing to do.

- A sharp demographic frontier has low-birth rate southern European countries on one side and high-birth rate North African countries on the other.

Economic informality is a key aspect of King's model. Economic informality can be defined as income earning activities that are not regulated by the state in situations where similar activities are regulated (Castells and Portes, 1989). A person can be employed on a building site or as a domestic worker either formally (taxes and social contributions paid) or informally (taxes and social contributions unpaid). Immigration did not cause informality. In the case of Italy, Reyneri (1998) argues that a heritage of informality has been linked to labour market rigidities, high labour costs, strict working regulations, low productivity growth, lax enforcement by public bodies, and low levels of social control, all of which lead to a tolerance of free riders. Mingione and Quassoli (2000: 32) argue that informality is 'an element of continuity in the mode of [Italian] national economic organisation'. Martiniez Viega (1999: 105) makes a similar point in relation to Spain when arguing that 'informal employment' has 'revitalised old traditions'. The irony is that this occurs when immigration could be seen as indicative of Spain's entry into a more advanced stage of capitalist development. Figure 7.1 illustrates the links between the constitutive markets of the economy.

Levels of informality are, of course, difficult to judge although some estimates – or to be more precise, ranges of estimates – can be provided that give an idea of the prevalence of informality as an economic form in southern Europe (see Table 7.1).

The advantages of informality and irregular migration arise from the trade-off between the lower costs for employers who avoid tax and social costs and for the migrants the opportunity to obtain employment and earn more than they would in their country of origin. For states the tolerance of some illegality can be less costly than strict controls and tight social regulation. Moreover, small and medium sized enterprises can have a more precarious cost base, depend on hiring and firing flexibility and thus benefit from the hiring of irregular workers. These can thrive if the

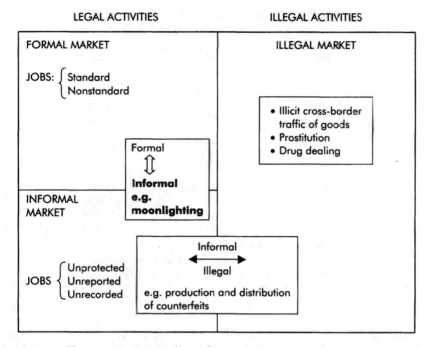

FIGURE 7.1   *The constitutive markets of an economy*
Source: Baganha, 2000: 176

TABLE 7.1   *Estimates of the size of the informal economy in selected European countries*

Country	Range of estimates (% GNP)
UK	7–13
Germany	4–14
Netherlands	5–14
France	4–14
Spain	10–23
Italy	10–26
Greece	29–35

Source: Reyneri, 2001: 22

workplace inspection system is lax. In some economic sectors such as construction, the household economy, agriculture and tourism there are particularly high levels of informality related at least in part to the continued demand for migrant workers and the difficult to regulate nature of these sectors.

TABLE 7.2   *Regularisations in southern*
Europe and the numbers of immigrants
regularised

Greece	1998	c.200,000
Italy	1982	12,000
	1986	118,349
	1990	248,501
	1996	147,900
Portugal	1992	39,166
	1996	35,082
	2001*	90,700
Spain	1985–86	43,800
	1991	109,000
	1996	18,800
	2000	184,249

*Numbers as of August 2001

Sources: Calculated from *Migration News* (various
editions); Solé et al. (1998); Baganha (1999);
Sciortino (1999)

The disadvantages of informality and irregularity can be listed under
five headings (Jahn and Straubhaar, 1999):

- Informal workers are outside of the tax system, but use welfare state
  services.

- Informality can bring the state's regulatory capacity into disrepute.

- Irregular migrants jump the queue ahead of those who go through the
  proper channels. The fact that the regular channels can be a bureaucratic nightmare while there is a demand for migrant workers may
  also help explain irregular migration.

- Irregular migrants are pushed into areas of the economy where they
  are more open to abuse in terms of pay and work conditions.

- Irregular migrants can fall into the hands of traffickers who exploit the
  demand for admission by offering control-busting and risky entry into
  southern European countries.

The most commonly used mechanism to address irregularity has been
regularisations. Table 7.2 provides data on regularisations in Greece, Italy,
Portugal and Spain. Regularisations seek to manage the flow from the
informal to the formal sector. The persistence of a pool of irregular
migrants could encourage employers to switch activities to the informal
sector. At the same time, frequent regularisations can encourage more
irregular migration. To be effective regularisations need to at least have the
impression of being one-off events. If regularisations are like buses – there'll

TABLE 7.3 *Legally resident foreign population in southern Europe*
1990–99 (numbers 'in thousands and percentage of population)

	1990	1991	1992	1993	1994	1995	1996	1997	1998*	1999
Italy	781.1	863.0	925.2	987.4	922.7	991.4	1095.6	1240.7	1250.2	1252.0
	1.4%	1.5%	1.6%	1.7%	1.6%	1.7%	2.0%	2.1%	2.1%	2.2%
Portugal	107.8	114.0	123.6	131.6	157.1	168.3	172.9	175.3	177.8	190.9
	1.1%	1.2%	1.3%	1.3%	1.6%	1.7%	1.7%	1.8%	1.8%	1.9%
Spain	278.7	360.7	393.1	430.4	461.4	499.8	539.0	609.8	719.6	801.3
	0.7%	0.9%	1.0%	1.1%	1.2%	1.3%	1.4%	1.6%	1.8%	2.0%

*Greece was overhauling its statistical system and accurate data were not available.
The estimated foreign population in Greece in 1998 was 309,400, although this did
not include those irregular migrants that had been regularised by the 1998 procedure,
around 200,000 people.
Source: OECD SOPEMI Report, 2001: 282

be another one along soon – then migrants can enter irregularly and
be reasonably confident of regularising their status in the not too
distant future.

Immigration policy

Southern European workers were, of course, an important component of
the 'reserve army' of labour that fuelled post-war economic reconstruction in countries such as Belgium, France, Germany and Switzerland
(Castles and Kosack, 1973). There were also important internal migrations
within southern European countries. Italy stands out in this respect for
the scale of the movement and also because it managed to create the
category of illegal internal migrant. A fascist law of 1939 (repealed in 1961)
sought to curb urbanisation, but meant that many of the hundreds of
thousands of people that moved from the rural south to urban northern
cities in the 1950s fell into the category of illegality. This further weakened
their social and economic position (Ginsborg, 1990: 218–9).

Since the 1980s, southern European countries have become destination
countries for international migrants even though, as Table 7.1 shows, the
legally resident foreign population in these countries remains relatively
small.

Four other issues need to be factored into the analysis. First, figures
such as those above do not show irregular migrants. The numbers of
people who have availed themselves of regularisation programmes gives
some idea of the extent of irregular migration into southern European
countries (see Table 7.2). Second is the diversity of the immigrant population: in 2000, Moroccans were the largest immigrant group in Italy, but
constituted only 11.7 per cent of the legally resident foreign population. It

TABLE 7.4 *Asylum-seekers in southern Europe 1990–2000 (thousands)*

	1991	1992	1993	1994	1995	1996	1997	1998	1999	2000
Greece	2.7	2.0	0.8	1.3	1.4	1.6	4.4	2.6	1.5	3.1
Italy	26.5	6.0	1.6	1.8	1.7	0.7	1.9	11.1	33.4	18.0
Portugal	0.2	0.5	1.7	0.6	0.3	0.2	0.3	0.3	0.3	0.2
Spain	8.1	11.7	12.6	12.0	5.7	4.7	5.0	6.8	8.4	7.2

Source: OECD SOPEMI Report, 2001: 280

TABLE 7.5 *Apprehended clandestine immigrants in Puglia and Calabria by country of origin (January–September 2000)*

Calabria	Albania	Iraqi-Kurds	Kosovars	Turkish-Kurds	Iraq	Turkey	China	Pakistan
	4711	2254	1912	1558	1297	1019	495	208

Puglia	Turkish-Kurds	Iraqi-Kurds	Afghanistan	Iraq	Palestine	Pakistan	Turkey	Morocco
	2058	1668	320	307	178	127	109	52

Source: Pastore 2001: 4

takes 14 different nationalities to arrive at 50 per cent of Italy's foreign population (Caritas Roma, 2001). Third is the gendered character of migration into southern Europe: the labour market participation of male and female migrants differs markedly. Migration by women and their employment in the household economy (house cleaning, elderly care etc.) are important features of migration into southern Europe. Fourth, as Table 7.4 shows, the number of asylum seekers remains low.

One reason for the low number of asylum-seekers (around 28,500 in southern Europe in 2000) is that alternative migration routes are available. Migrants that in a country such as the UK would probably be classed as asylum-seekers are more likely to fall into the category of irregular immigrant in southern Europe. This is illustrated in the case of Italy when the top nine countries of origin of clandestine immigrants apprehended while trying to enter Italy in the southern provinces of Calabria and Puglia are considered. These are countries that don't readily spring to mind when the words 'safe countries of origin' are uttered. It's interesting that Afghanistan, Iraq and Turkey are all in the top-five origin countries for UK asylum-seekers (Home Office, 2001: 3).

The EU's impact

What impact has the EU had on policy development? EU migration policies suggest an external influence on policy development derived from adherence to the requirements of 'Schengenland' and the normative expectation to restrict 'unwanted' immigration that goes with EU membership. Cornelius (1994) argues that immigration policy in Spain arose almost entirely as a result of EU pressures. Pastore (2001: 1) argues that the links between Italian and EU policy are 'systematic and profound'. Freeman (1995) and Baldwin-Edwards (1997) both argue that EU pressures have been a general feature of policy development in all southern European countries. Indeed, Baldwin-Edwards (1999) goes further when arguing that EU practices have been a major source of 'wrong policy' with misfit in both economic terms (migrants are still needed) and political terms (implementation problems). Southern European countries are expected to make the strong EU commitment to restriction a part of their domestic political priorities in line with their Treaty obligations. In the case of Italy, Zincone (1999) contends that the EU's impact has been particularly noticeable on the 'repressive' aspects of policy such as external frontier controls. This was echoed in an interview with an Italian government minister in January 2001 who argued that the new Italian immigration law was needed to make sure that Italy stayed in line with EU requirements (*Corriere della Sera*, 2001).

If EU requirements are generally acknowledged as such a shaping force on policy development then what role does this leave for domestic political factors? Two common linking factors rooted in domestic contexts are economic informality and irregular migration. These in turn touch upon the more general question of state-society relations and suggest a domestic social and political dimension to these discussions. A number of analysts of southern European migration policy have also suggested ways in which domestic contexts also make a difference.

Responses in Italy

Migration by *clandestini* became a hot political issue after the election of Silvio Berlusconi's right-wing coalition in 2001. The coalition contains the 'post-Fascist' *Alleanza Nazionale* and the populist *Lega Nord* that both take a hard-line anti-immigration stance, plus more centrist and Christian Democrat influences. The arrival of more than 900 *clandestini* in Catania in March 2002 prompted the *Lega Nord* leader and minister of institutional reform, Umberto Bossi, to demand their deportation. The President of the Republic, Carlo Azeglio Ciampi called on Italians to remember their own emigration history when considering the arrival of newcomers. The issue demonstrates the capacity of migration to strike at the often fragile Italian party system, to affect Italy's relations with other EU member states, as well as with non-EU member states such as Turkey and the Lebanon that are seen as central to the people smuggling networks that can move Kurds across the Mediterranean to the EU.

Italian governments have adopted the key elements of EU policy and in 1998 joined Schengenland. To its chagrin, Italy was not a founder of Schengen because there were some doubts among the founding five members about Italy's capacity to attain Schengen obligations. Italy became a full member of Schengen in March 1998. During the 1980s,

Italian immigration policy concentrated on legalising and regularising migrant flows rather than reducing them (Pugliese, 1998: 5–28). This laissez faire approach was called into question with the murder in 1989 of an immigrant in the southern region of Calabria, which led to a public outcry and calls that 'something must be done'. The Martelli law of 1990 extended the right to asylum to include people from non-Soviet bloc countries and initiated a new regularisation. Other provisions were more repressive, such as the use of visas to limit migration flows from sending countries, increased emphasis on external frontier controls and provisions for increased deportations. The basic failing of the Martelli Law as identified by Reyneri (1998: 314) was that it failed to tackle irregular immigration – because Zincone (1999: 53) argues, trade unions and pro-migrant NGOs helped shape the law. The result was that the law sent out the message that Italy was relatively open to illegal immigration.

Attempts to manage policy were undermined by the arrival of large numbers of Albanians after 1990 with renewed flows after 1997. It was, however, difficult to legislate between 1992 and 1996 because of the political transition from the first to the second republic following the *mani pulite* (clean hands) corruption scandals of the early 1990s. A 1995 Decree introduced by the technocratic government of Lamberto Dini mainly dealt with expulsions and frontier controls. The Dini decree was renewed either in part or in full five times during 1995 and 1996 but never acquired the parliamentary approval necessary to become law.

The Turco-Napolitano law of 1998 introduced by the centre-left government maintained the repressive elements linked to Italy's EU obligations through reinforced measures dealing with entry, residence and expulsions. Reception centres were introduced for irregular immigrants. The right-wing parties had wanted illegal entry to be classed as a crime. The left resisted this. Reception centres were a compromise and were open to significant regional variation in implementation. The more liberal elements of the Turco-Napolitano Law included provisions for the 'sponsorship' of new immigrants by Italian citizens, legally resident foreigners, regions, local administrations, unions and voluntary organisations. Sponsored migrants would be issued with a temporary permit. Provisions on family reunification were also broadened to include relatives of the 'third degree' such as uncles, aunts and great grandchildren. The law also established provisions for residence permits to be granted to prostitutes prepared to denounce pimps and people traffickers. Italy, Belgium and the Netherlands offer permits to women who denounce their pimps. The Italian authorities issued around 2000 permits on these grounds in 2000 and around 1500 pimps were identified (*Migration News*, September 2001).

The Berlusconi government introduced a new immigration law (Law 795) in 2001. The new law links work and residence permits in the form of a *contratto di soggiorno*. These permits will last only as long as the contract of employment. The new legislation also proposed that sponsorship be abolished. The length of time during which suspected illegal entrants could be detained in reception centres was to be increased from 30 to 60 days. If undocumented migrants were arrested for a second time then they could face between six months and a year in prison. A third arrest could lead to between one and four years behind bars. The provisions on family reunification were also tightened. Only foreigners with work contracts would be able to back family members for admission. Finally, it was proposed that the period for the acquisition of permanent residence be increased from five to six years.

Along with the legislation there were proposals for regularisation of domestic workers because they had become central to the delivery of care to the elderly, for instance, in many Italian families. There was also a counter-mobilisation against the legislation that denounced what it called the racist legislation and capitalised on the fact that the government was fighting on many fronts, as well as having to deal with the management of a diverse coalition of governing parties. In January 2002 an estimated 100,000 people marched in Rome to protest against the legislation.

The main focus of immigration policy measures has been external controls. The Italian government has increased its spending on border controls, collaborated with other states on controls, accessed EU funds to develop schemes to enhance border controls, developed new control technologies, and reorganised its frontier police (Pastore, 2001). This still leaves open the issue of internal controls and what Sciortino (1999) calls the 'Pandora's box' of state-society relations that could be opened if Italian governments attempted to tackle high levels of economic informality that provide the context for the economic incorporation of irregular migrants.

As has already been argued, implementation has an external dimension (external frontier controls and relations with sending states, for instance) and an internal dimension (regulation of society and the labour market, for instance). Jahn and Straubhaar's (1999) analysis of the political economy of illegal immigration focuses on the 'economic market' for migrants and the 'political market' for regulation. If we accept this conceptualisation of the policy process – with some echoes of Freeman's (1995) work – then debates about illegal immigration will centre not so much on the content of legislation, but on the extent to which it will be implemented as a result of balancing the interests of those who call for more migrants and those who call for tighter regulation. If this is the case, then some irregular migration will be tolerated because up to a certain point the costs of control outweigh the costs of illegal immigration. This could be seen as relevant, in the case of Italy, in the sense that well-entrenched informality and a continued demand for migrant workers impinge very directly on the political market for regulation in ways that could hinder the state's ability to tackle economic informality. The internal controls necessary to tackle relatively high levels of informality could be politically costly because they would impinge on the lives of ordinary Italian citizens. As Sciortino (1999: 249) puts it: 'To focus on internal control is to take a political risk'.

This gives us a slightly different take on Hollifield's (2000b) argument that domestic ideas and institutions will constrain the control capacity of states and lead them to prefer external measures such as EU co-operation where these constraints are less pronounced. Hollifield's reference point is France where state penetration of society is far deeper than in Italy. Yet, in Italy too ideas and institutions can inhibit control capacity, albeit as a result of a lower level of state penetration of society creating more space for informality and irregular migration.

Sciortino (1999: 256) also injects a note of healthy caution when considering the 'crisis' of control, which he links to unrealistic expectations and vicarious fears (of immigrant criminality and ensuing moral panic, for instance) rather than a structural feature of the real processes. At the same time, he acknowledges that the problem in Italy (and in other southern European countries too) remains the relatively weak internal controls, which point to the 'special, well-entrenched mode of relationship between the Italian state and Italian society'. This is a theme that recurs when we explore responses in Greece, Portugal and Spain.

Economic informality, irregular migration and strict controls in Greece

Greece combines high levels of economic informality and irregular migration with stringent control legislation. For geographical reasons it is central to many of the people smuggling networks within the EU and on its borders. This is compounded by the sheer scale of Greece's external frontiers that make control in the strict sense of the term well-nigh impossible. These high levels of informality and irregular migration are also coupled with public hostility towards migrants. The survey of attitudes towards minorities by the EU Monitoring Centre on Racism and Xenophobia suggested that Greek respondents had negative attitudes towards minorities that were above the EU average, were less willing to accept refugees, and linked migrants with economic competition and crime (EUMC, 2001: 12). Greek laws have been draconian. The 1991 Immigration Law made illegal immigration an offence punishable by between ten days and five years in jail. Yet, high levels of irregular migration persist. The numbers of irregular migrants were estimated at between 400,000 and 500,000 in the late-1990s, or around 10 per cent of the Greek labour force (Fakiolas, 2000). The large-scale presence of irregular migrants is coupled with a public intolerance of their presence in Greece.

There was some post Cold War 'return migration' by Pontian Greeks from the former USSR. A key issue has been migration from Albania. The militarisation of the Greek-Albanian border is redolent of the 'border games' played on the US-Mexican border – another border of poverty separating relative prosperity from high levels of deprivation (Andreas, 2000; King, Iosifides and Myrivili, 1998). Albanian migrants have been linked to crime and the stereotype of the criminal Albanian immigrant has acquired resonance in social and political debate. It's true that Albanians are more evident in police arrest figures and Albanian gangs have been evident in the smuggling of people, drugs and guns. That said, the high level of arrests of Albanians also reflects police targeting of areas with large Albanian populations and the fact that many Albanians are irregular immigrants and thus breaking Greek law because of this irregular status. In addition to this, there is a spatial concentration of the migrant population, many of whom live in Athens, which has become 'a prototype for the trends towards informalisation of work and the increased social inequality and restructuring of consumption into high-income and very low-income strata' (Iosifides and King, 1998).

For Linos (2002) the 'puzzle' is why Greek governments have continued to tolerate irregular migration when the public are intolerant of this irregularity? She argues that this toleration arises because the Greek 'cartel' party system with dominance by the Greek Socialist Party (PASOK) and some Conservative rule makes it difficult for challengers to break through, consolidates the dominance of the executive branch of government and allows the dominant parties to co-opt state institutions. The outcome is that the dominant parties become less dependent on voters' preferences with the result that it is 'possible to conduct unpopular policy with less fear of electoral loss' (Linos, 2002: 20).

An important issue is whether it is the formally highly restrictive policies that are unpopular or whether the issue is the implementation of policy and the regulation of society. The immigration law introduced into the Greek parliament in 2000 maintained the highly restrictive basis of Greek immigration legislation. The Bill links work and residence in a way that seems destined to maintain high levels of irregularity, particularly because it increases the dependency of migrants on the workings of the Greek bureaucracy, which had major problems coping with the numbers of people who came forward in the first regularisation of 1998. The legislation was also controversial because it limited family reunion and access by irregular migrants and their children to essential public services such as health and education. The legislation failed to tackle many of the issues that arose from the 1998 regularisation. The 1998 regularisation allowed irregular migrants to apply for a temporary 'white card' permit and then for a more permanent 'green card'. The green card process was riddled with bureaucratic obstacles and requirements that many migrants found impossible to fulfil. This led to calls for a second regularisation because of the numbers of people who managed to register with the Greek Organisation for the Employment of Human Resources, but did not manage to submit their application due to the onerous bureaucratic requirements. At the same time, a further regularisation may not improve the situation for those who arrived after the 1998 regularisation or cannot prove the number of years that they have been living in Greece. There is a continued demand for migrants and a large informal sector in which they can find work. Greek policy has, however, been harsh and unprotective and social attitudes hostile (Lazaridis, 1996; Triandafyllidou, 2000). The result has been an inability and/or unwillingness to deal with the major administrative and political issues that concerted attempts at the regulation of economic informality would have for migrants and Greek citizens.

Informality and irregularity in Portugal

Portugal became an immigration country in the 1980s. It has attracted migrants from former colonies, as well as growing numbers from countries with which Portugal does not have strong ties, such as eastern European countries. In some respects, Portugal is an unlikely immigration country: it's relatively poor, has a low qualified work force, and low social security benefits. At the same time, the Portuguese economy is generating labour demands for both skilled and unskilled workers that immigrants meet. What is more, their economic insertion is taking place in both the formal and informal sectors (Baganha, 1998, 2000).

The centre-right coalition elected in March 2002 pledged a tougher line on immigration, but in doing so highlighted implementation issues that are central to southern European migration policy. Portugal is a Schengen state and was quick to put immigration legislation in place in the early 1980s. This was linked to the transition from authoritarian government, administrative modernisation and EU membership rather than to large-scale immigration at that time. Two new laws in 1993 brought Portuguese law into line with Schengen obligations and illustrate the ways in which formal policy developments have been influenced by EU obligations.

Why does Portugal have relatively high levels of informality? Research suggests that it is relatively easy to live and work in Portugal without the necessary permits and that this will continue so long as 'existing government agencies maintain their traditional inefficiency in controlling labour' (Baganha, 1998: 276). There is little stigma attached to informal work and sometimes even the state can be an informal employer. The result is that the informal economy is an integral part of the Portuguese national economy. The economic insertion of migrant workers is also gendered with men tending to work in sectors such as construction and building while the economic participation of female migrants is directed towards sectors of the household economy. Around 65 per cent of the immigrant population live in the metropolitan area of Lisbon.

The formal adherence to EU requirements has also been accompanied by regularisations, which are driven by domestic priorities. In 2001, Portugal launched a new regularisation programme, which by August 2001 had seen 90,700 work permits issued. Around 30 per cent of those regularised were Ukrainians. The numbers of people regularised could cause us to reflect on the idea of 'fortress Europe'. There has been continued large-scale migration into southern Europe despite the introduction of restrictive immigration legislation. But these issues of enforcement and implementation raise other questions that relate to state capacity, as well as to expectations about the role of the state. Baganha (2000) argues that there is less expectation in Portugal that the state will be able to regulate society. State-avoidance can be more common, which suggests a different mode of state-society relations: that the social, economic and political costs of regulation can be high and that they relate more generally to social control.

From low to higher intensity immigration politics in Spain

Spain too became an immigration country in the 1980s and joined the EU in 1986. In a *Financial Times* article in October 2000 it was argued that the Spanish 'melting pot' was beginning to bubble. By this was meant that immigration was becoming a hotter political issue with important implications for what Arango (2000: 247) argues had been a 'low intensity, low tension model of immigration in the 1990s'. Spain had adopted a fairly liberal policy approach. In 1991, for instance, it recognised that it was a country of immigration. This becomes more startling when it is borne in mind that it had barely become one, while other longer-standing countries of immigration such as Germany could not at that time bring themselves to admit this. Spain has followed a similar pattern to other southern European countries, in the sense that it has brought its immigration and asylum legislation into line with that of other EU member states and thus accords with the practical and normative pre-disposition to restrict, which is the hallmark of this policy.

The accordance with EU requirements was seen as the driving force behind immigration policy development (Cornelius, 1994). Arango (2000) also identifies the EU's role on policy development. Yet, as already discussed, the EU frame tends to impinge most directly on external frontier controls rather than to open the 'Pandora's box' of internal controls and state-society relations.

Between 1985 and 2000 the number of immigrants in Spain increased fourfold. The legislative frame was put in place very early. Arango (2000: 267) linked the 1984 Asylum Law to more general administrative modernisation because there were very few asylum-seekers in Spain at that time. The rules of the game for the entry, admission, residence and work of non-EU foreigners was regulated by the 1985 *Ley de Extranjería* (Foreigners Law). As Solé et al. (1998: 339) argue, the effect of the legislation was to create 'the legal category of "immigrant", which in turn created the category of "illegal" immigrant because most immigrants were unable to regularise their situation'.

The 1985 law created three routes into Spain. First, applying for a visa from abroad with evidence of a job offer. The application would be made to the Spanish consulate in the country of origin and then passed to the

Spanish Foreign Ministry. The Foreign Ministry would then forward the application to the Ministry of Labour and Social Security, which would request a report from its office in the province where the migrant proposed to work. For the permit to be issued the investigating authorities would have to be satisfied that there were no Spaniards or EU nationals capable of doing the job. Second, Spain has employed a quota system for new migrants. Third, regularisations ushered irregular migrants from the informal to the formal economy.

Spain has also experienced political mobilisation around the immigration issue both on the pro- and anti-side of the debate. There was, for instance, a strong element of anti-immigration sentiment in the response to the murder of a 26 year old woman in the town of El Ejido by a young man identified by witnesses as being of Maghrebi origin. The monitor of Spanish public opinion provided by the Centre for Sociological Research shows that the immigration issue had acquired increased salience. The number of respondents that included immigration as one of the two or three most important issues in Spain rose from 6.7 per cent in September 2000 to 31.1 per cent in February 2001 before dropping back to 9.9 per cent in December 2001 (CIS Barometro surveys 2001). There were also much-publicised tensions in the summer of 2001 in the small village of Las Pedroneras where 2000 undocumented migrants arrived in a village of 5000 people in pursuit of around 700 garlic picking jobs (*Migration News*, September 2001). At the same time, there has been a pro-migrant counter-mobilisation. Arango (2000: 267) argues that this can be connected with a civic associational culture linked with Spain's transition from authoritarian government to liberal democracy 'characterised by a wide espousal of the universalistic and progressive values associated with democracy' as articulated by trade unions and by NGOs.

Legislation promulgated in early 2000 had been criticised for encouraging illegal immigration because it gave undocumented migrants access to health and education and also to political rights such as union membership. This legislation was approved at the time when the centre-right *Partido Popular* (PP) lacked an absolute majority in Parliament. The result was that the PP relied on the support of other parties such as the Catalan nationalists who heavily influenced the shape of the legislation with the result that the PP ended up with more liberal legislation than it had wanted.

The legislation was then changed in a more restrictive direction when the PP won an absolute majority in the 2000 general election. The subsequent immigration law of August 2000 removed the rights of irregular migrants to union membership, the right to association, to demonstrate and to go on strike. The new law also sought to increase the numbers of expulsions, which directly threatened the 30,000 or so people that had been denied regularisation in 2000. The prospect of deportation led 700 irregular immigrants to go on hunger strike. The left, trade unions and pro-migrants NGOs mobilised in support of the hunger strikers in ways that were redolent of support for the *sans papiers* in France. In August 2001, the Spanish government announced that irregular immigrants who can prove that they have been working in Spain since January 2000 can obtain legal residency. In future it is planned that a quota system based on labour market needs will regulate flows.

Migration and foreign policy

Spain is also interesting because policy developments indicate links between migration and foreign policy. Movement by people from one state to another does, of course, affect politics within and between states. What is new is the changed geo-political configuration, the altered perceptions of security, migration's entry into the realm of 'high politics', and the impact of European integration. Spain has seen its relations with Mediterranean states as a foreign policy opportunity which could allow Spain to 'co-operate as a first division European country, and by doing so, facilitate its eventual ascent into the lead group of EU countries' (Gillespie, 1996: 195). Spain has been a leading player in co-operation organised within the Barcelona Process that involves the 15 EU member states and 12 Mediterranean states. Since 2000 the Barcelona Process has evolved to include Justice and Home Affairs issues. Spain has also negotiated bilateral agreements with north African countries that provide for the return of irregular migrants. The agreement signed with Morocco on July 25 2001 sets an annual quota of between 10,000 and 20,000 immigrants and provides that irregular migrants can be returned within 72 hours. The Spanish government was dissatisfied with the agreement because it applied mainly to labour issues and they had wanted to include policing. By the end of 2001 the agreement had still not been implemented because of a major disagreement between the Spanish and Moroccan governments about the western Sahara. This led the Moroccan ambassador to Spain to be absent from Madrid for much of 2001 (Gillespie, 2002). The problem with regulating the flow is that Spain and Morocco are separated by only 14 km at their nearest point. More than 50,000 Moroccans were returned in the first seven months of 2001 compared to 11,000 in the whole of 2000 (*Migration News*, September 2001).

Spain has not been alone in seeking agreements with sending countries. Italy has negotiated an agreement with Albania (as well as north African and Baltic states). In 1997 the Italian government was even able to send Italian naval vessels into Albanian territorial waters in an effort to prevent boats full of would-be migrants departing for Italy. Italy has also participated in the Central European Initiative through which it co-operates with Austria and 14 central and east European countries on illegal immigration, terrorism and cross-border crime.

Greece too has particular concerns because it is at the hub of people smuggling and trafficking networks. In November 2001, Greece and Turkey signed an agreement that will allow Greece to send back illegal immigrants that entered the country through Turkey within 14 days of their arrival. International migration relations between the two countries had become tense. In September 2000, the Greek authorities arrested 1200 Turks accused of being involved in people smuggling and of charging up to $1000 per person for illegal entry to Greece. On December 3 2001 the Greek authorities forcibly returned 34 of a group of 89 Afghans and Iraqi Kurds to Turkey without allowing them to apply for asylum. Amnesty International expressed the concern that these people could then be forcibly returned to their countries of origin where they might face serious violations of their human rights.

To sum up, southern European countries have all adopted their national legislation to account for EU requirements. This has led to increased emphasis on external frontier control and an increased capacity to control these external frontiers, as well as an increased willingness to expel illegal immigrants (and establish agreements with third countries to facilitate these expulsions). The EU has provided a policy frame that heavily influenced the repressive elements of southern European policy with the accompanying normative disposition to restrict. There is, of course, the lingering counterfactual: would these countries have done these things anyway if it had not been for the EU? The development of immigration and asylum policy could be explained as part of more general administrative modernisation (although here too the impact of EU membership plays a part) or as a response to immigration that would have occurred with or without EU membership (although the EU has provided the frame for adaptation). In formal terms, there is a reasonable 'goodness of fit' between EU objectives and domestic policies and institutions centred on control of external frontiers. If we turn our attention to the issues of economic informality and irregular migration then we see more divergence. A key feature of migration into southern Europe has been the economic insertion of migrant workers in the informal sector. The response to this – regularisations – runs counter to the restrictive objectives of EU policy if they lead to further irregular migration in expectation of the next regularisation. Yet, to tackle informality and irregularity has implications for state-society relations that go far beyond the immigration issue. Indeed, as is shown in the next section, informality and irregularity also have implications for immigrant policies in southern European countries.

Immigrant policies

The typical reference points for debates about immigrant integration tend to be the nation state and national society (Favell, 2001). European countries have conceptualised the integration of immigrants in relation to the distinct institutional settings provided by these nation states. The typical response in older immigration countries has been an attempt to 'nationalise' migrant populations in relation to prevailing institutions and the ideas that animate those institutions. This also assumes the sovereign capacity of these states to realise this 'integration' and the supposition that facilitating institutions such as the welfare state are central to this project.

Catch-up or exceptionalism?

Are southern European countries following the approach adopted in older immigration countries? These nation states and national societies face pressures from European integration and more general pressures arising from the internationalisation of economic and political life. There are also significant regional variations within southern European countries. The EU's impact on immigrant integration was until the late 1990s very limited, although this is likely to change when the June 2000 directives on race equality and on direct and indirect discrimination in the workplace are incorporated into national laws.

There's another issue too, and one that relates to the discussion of economic informality and irregularity discussed above. We have so far taken our point of reference to be European states where the state's penetration of society (in social democratic welfare states, for example, or highly organised societies) is at a fairly high level. What form do debates about immigrant integration take when the state's penetration of society is not at such a high level, where state avoidance, lax enforcement and free-riding are more prevalent, and where expectations of the role of the state and its capacity to 'deliver' benefits for its citizens are not as deeply embedded?

There is a temporal element at work linked to the fact these are relatively new immigration countries. Debates tend to centre on day-to-day issues associated with first generation immigrants, such as housing and employment. There has been less attention paid to cultural rights and identity or on participation in formal political institutions, although these debates do exist and are likely to become more central in years to come as permanent settlement leads to the formation of ethnic minority communities.

As we have already seen, informality and irregularity have played a key role in social responses to migration. Irregular migration has implications for external frontier controls, but also for internal social controls. The irregular status of many immigrants leaves them in a structurally weak position that fundamentally affects their relations with the institutions of receiving societies, mediates their welfare state inclusion and exclusion, and has played an important part, for instance, in the social construction of the 'immigrant criminal' (Quassoli, 2002).

Another key variable that relates closely to the integration of immigrants is the organisation of the welfare state. It has been argued that there is a southern European welfare state model derived from a combination of occuptionalism (a maintenance system) with universalism (health care system) that is not found in other parts of Europe (Ferrera, 1996). Because of relatively low levels of coverage there can be a reliance on non-state institutions such as voluntary organisations, as well as moral obligations within the family that particularly fall on women. For instance, Saraceno. (1994) argues that the Italian 'familialist' welfare system is based on the perception of the family as unit of income and resources with women having a primary responsibility in the provision of care. In addition to this, informality leads to high levels of tax evasion and also to state avoidance strategies. This can lead us to think about the relationship between state and society and the implications for migrants that these types of welfare system and the levels of informality that co-exist alongside them can have.

In her analysis of the social rights of migrants in Portugal Maria Baganha (2000) argues that the problems for migrants are the immediate questions of poor housing, low welfare state protection, high levels of informality, the role played by the Catholic church and voluntary organisations, as well as significant regional variations. But these are not issues that are confined to migrants. They also affect Portuguese citizens and have implications for state-society relations and the perception of citizenship as a process and thus as more than just a formal status. Baganha argues that part of the problem in Portugal is that Portuguese citizens have not 'internalised' their own social rights in the sense that they tend to view the state as unreliable and to take their own social protection measures and engage in state avoidance strategies. Baganha then argues that if Portuguese citizens have not internalised their own social citizenship then there may not be an expectation that similar rights be extended to migrants. Informality thus has implications both for state-society relations and for citizenship as a process of inclusion. It demonstrates that we need to consider the characteristics of the local, regional and national units that mediate inclusion and exclusion and their relationship in southern Europe to irregularity and informality.

In Italy as in other southern European countries there has been a remarkable local divergence because much of the responsibility for dealing with migrants falls on towns and cities that can be more or less well equipped to deal with these issues. In Italy, Zincone (1999) argues that the diversity of the response had the beneficial effect of allowing a thousand flowers to bloom and for some of the better ideas from the periphery to inform practices at the centre. Yet there was little funding to support these plans. The brightest of bright ideas are likely to lose some of their brilliance if there is no money to actually implement them.

The Spanish government published a 'Plan for the social integration of foreigners' in 1994, but this was a statement of good intentions rather than a practical plan of action. There was little political mobilisation around immigration in the 1990s – although there were mobilisations against the August 2000 immigration law – and debate that the most direct struggles concern the day-to-day issues of housing and employment. It's then argued that migrant groups have adopted different responses to Spanish society and institutions:

- Concealment and minimisation of differences.

- A double link based on transnational ties allowing people to survive in the receiving country and be equipped to return home some time in the future.

- The creation of ghettos with limited contacts outside of the family and community of co-nationals.

- Pluralised insertion with mobilisation for equal rights (Solé et al. 1998: 343–4).

Across southern Europe, as in Spain, the main concerns have centred on the immediate issues that face first generation immigrants. Legally resident immigrants are extended rights of denizenship with usually the same formal workplace and welfare state rights as nationals. Irregular migrants are in a more precarious position with regards to the social and political institutions of the receiving society. In Italy the 1995 Dini decree extended access to emergency health care, the treatment of serious accidents and free preventative medicines to irregular migrants. Greece, however, has taken a very tough line in trying to deny access to basic public services to irregular migrants. In Italy, the 1998 Turco-Napolitano law extended the right to free public health care to include the children of irregular migrants. The Turco-Napolitano law also proposed to extend local voting rights to legally resident foreigners, although this was ruled unconstitutional by the Legal Office of the National Assembly and the plans dropped. The January 2000 immigration law in Spain also extended workplace rights to migrants such as the right to join a trade union and strike, although these provisions were removed in the August 2000 legislation.

The role of the Catholic Church has been important in migration into Catholic countries such as Italy, Portugal and Spain. The Catholic Church has acted as a kind of employment agency for Catholic migrants. Many of the women from south and central America and from the Philippines that have found work in the household economy moved within migration networks with a strong Catholic Church influence.

The religious identity of immigrants has been a subject that has caused some concern and became much polemicised in Italy following the September 11 2001 terrorist attacks on New York (most notably in Fallaci, 2001). Loyalty and disloyalty were much debated, as was the position of Islam in Italian society, particularly following the arrests of suspected militants at the Islamic Cultural Centre in Milan. As in other European countries, it has been difficult to find an authentic voice for the diverse community of Muslims in Italy. This has two effects. It makes it more difficult to co-opt. It also means that the most extreme voices can emerge as falsely representative of Muslims.

Immigration and crime

Another key issue has been the issue of 'immigrant criminality', which, in turn, is linked to the 'immigrant-irregular-marginal-criminal' construction (Quassoli, 2001). In Greece, the perception of the Albanian criminal has had a powerful influence on debates about immigration, on perceptions of security/insecurity, and on public hostility to immigrants. Albanians in Greece do figure higher in arrest figures, and the activities of Albanian gangs have caused concern, but the arrest figures are distorted by the targeting of areas where Albanians live and the fact that many Albanians are illegal immigrants, which is an offence in Greece. This is not to say that immigrants don't commit crimes, but that the irregularity and marginality of migrants are closely linked to the construction of immigrant criminality.

In Italy too there are strong perceptions of immigrant criminality. According to the EUMC, 72 per cent of Italian respondents perceive immigrants as being more disposed to criminality than Italians. But what are the components of this social construction of immigrant criminality as a source of insecurity? To answer this requires analysis of the social position of migrants, of which their participation in the informal economy is a key element, and the perception of migrants by the legal and judicial process. In these terms, we account for both the structural weakness of the migrants' position and for the 'cognitive and moral dimensions' that inform the work of the legal and judicial process. These can also become entangled with judgements about migrants' cultural, ethnic or national traits (Quassoli, 2001: 150–1).

Insertion in the informal economy has been seen as contributing in a crucial way to the perception of 'immigrant criminality'. In the Italian courts, a key variable used to explain deviance or normalcy is whether the migrant has a regular job. As Quassoli (2001: 153) argues 'The coupling of normalcy and formal employment plays a key role in the evaluation of the defendant's personality and the circumstances under which the crime took place. Thus their legal status and their integration in the formal and informal labour markets determine the position of migrants *vis-à-vis* the courts'. Similar factors are also at work in other southern European countries because of the high levels of economic informality and the associated structural weaknesses that this can lead to for migrants when engaging with the forces of law and order in the societies in which they live.

Conclusion

This chapter's analysis of southern Europe has demonstrated the importance of examining the categorisation of migrants and the ability of institutions and organisations to shape understandings of migration and migrants. Migration policy issues have centred on both external and internal policy dimensions, but with a particular focus on irregular migrants and economic informality. Informality and irregularity have important implications for immigration and immigrant policies, but these categories are not just synonyms for 'backwardness' in the sense that southern European countries are more open to migration than northern European countries. Southern Europe is proximate to areas from which there are migration pressures, there is demand for migrant workers, while the area is closer to some of the world's trouble spots. The point is that migrants can be viewed differently in southern Europe – as illegals, rather than say as asylum seekers in older immigration countries – and processed in different social and political contexts.

The persistence of irregular migration could be attributed to the absence of effective external controls and a lack of fit with EU policy. In these terms, we could suppose that the EU's impact on law and policy in southern European countries has been limited. This perception would be mistaken. Southern European countries have adapted to the restrictive elements of EU policy, which have focused on external controls, with the result that legislation in southern European countries accords with that in other member states. There is, of course, the point that perhaps southern European countries would have developed such policies anyway irrespective of the EU's influence because of increased immigration since the 1980s, but this is not a particularly convincing argument. The policy frame provided by the EU has had a decisive influence on the 'repressive' elements of policy in these countries. The EU was also a more general pressure for administrative modernisation in Greece, Portugal and Spain. In addition to this, we can also see attempts to externalise these controls and forge closer links between migration and security that are also prevailing features of the EU response.

The adherence to EU policy is, though, only part of the story. These external controls also need to be considered alongside internal controls. It is here that informality and irregularity suggest some divergence with an EU model predicated on external and internal control and in turn, it could be argued, that makes assumptions about the organisation of society and the regulatory capacity of member states. Southern European countries are not as highly organised, the penetration of society by state institutions is at a lower level, while expectations about the state's role differ. Moreover, a key feature of the policy response in southern Europe – the frequent use of regularisations – has been largely governed by domestic responses to economic informality and irregularity than by EU policy.

Irregularity and informality also impinge on the issue of immigrant integration. If we take older immigration countries as a reference when discussing immigrant integration, then we tend to bring with us other elements of the conceptual baggage derived from highly organised societies, coupled with citizens' expectations about state capacity. This implicit reference to older immigration countries doesn't work quite so well in southern European countries where state-society relations are configured differently and where state capacity and, equally importantly, expectations about state capacity can differ. These points are developed more fully in the following chapter which explores responses in central and eastern European countries that are not yet EU members, but whose migration policy development have been largely driven by the obligations of future EU membership.

8

The Europeanisation of Migration Politics in Central and Eastern Europe

Migration was central to the Cold War-ending domino effect of state collapse initiated when the East German/Hungarian border was opened. Migration has also become a key aspect of the move towards EU membership for central and eastern European countries (CEECs).[1] EU accession has also become a live issue in central and eastern European politics. The romantic 'return to Europe' and wave of popular support for the EU that occurred in the wake of the Soviet bloc's collapse has been replaced by a more hard-headed debate about the requirements of membership and whether membership is desirable (Henderson, 1999; Szczerbiak, 2001). This chapter examines the immigration and asylum instruments that are an important part of the relations between the EU and accession states, as well as debates about these measures. The chapter shows that policy in the CEECs has arisen almost entirely as a result of the requirements of EU accession and that EU policy models and ideas about borders, security and insecurity have been exported to CEEC countries, although whether they will work as intended is a different question.

Accession means the adaptation of EU laws and policies. Among the myriad obligations contained within the 80,000 pages of the EU law, the CEECs must adapt to the EU *acquis* on free movement, immigration and asylum as a condition for membership. The CEECs have thus been placed on a steep learning curve and must look towards practices and ideas in EU member states. The free movement *acquis* is the clearest, but EU member states have shown some reluctance to allow CEECs to benefit from it until a transition period of up to seven years has been served. The immigration and asylum *acquis* is much less clear, but it is in this area that adaptational pressures are strongest. Because the goalposts keep shifting there can be technical imprecision coupled with a strong normative expectation about what CEECs have to do. Formal EU links have been supplemented by a web of bilateral and multilateral ties outside of formal EU structures that provide venues for ministers and officials to meet, as well as forums for the diffusion of policy ideas.

At its most basic, the deal between existing member states and applicant states is that EU membership will be accompanied by tight control of the EU's eastern frontiers. This could be seen as contradictory because tightly controlled borders run counter to the free movement framework that is a defining feature of European integration. Yet, as has become clear in earlier chapters, European integration has boundary removing features while also establishing new boundaries. This reflects broader dilemmas raised by the openness of economies to flows of capital and money, but not to people. EU member states seek a balance between closed states and open economies. The incorporation of the CEECs further tests this balance and raises the salience of issues associated with borders, boundaries and frontiers in an integrating Europe. The move by the CEECs towards the EU has also been riddled by a lack of mutual trust between applicant states and the EU with the attendant risk of sub-optimal policy outcomes that impose undesirable or unattainable policies and thereby confound other EU objectives such as democratisation and liberalisation.

The boundary issues with which this chapter is particularly concerned are migration in its various forms and its interaction with the dynamics of European integration. These issues are not exclusively related to central and eastern Europe. The argument is not for central and east European exceptionalism in the same way that there was not an argument for southern European exceptionalism in the previous chapter. The argument is that the politics of migration and immigration in central and eastern Europe shows how international migration relations between European countries have been reconfigured with a key role played by the EU. The migration policy dilemmas in central and eastern Europe are writ large because of the scale of the enlargement, the experience of international migration in its many forms, debate about the meaning and significance of borders, ideas about security and insecurity, the position of minorities within and beyond these countries, new patterns of interdependence and integration to which European integration contributes, and an emerging political debate about the costs and benefits of EU membership.

In light of these considerations, this chapter explores the EU's impact on CEECs as they seek to adapt to the migration policy *acquis* while also drawing attention to issues of institutional compatibility, compliance and implementation, which taken together all have implications for the basis question of whether the EU's migration policy *acquis* can be applied to central and eastern Europe. The chapter continues to broaden this book's focus away from older north-west European countries of immigration to see how both the EU and the migration issue are enlarging.

Immigration policy

The discussion of immigration control in CEECs is directly derived from the obligations of EU membership. Immigration control policies are largely a result of European integration. Perhaps because of this and because of the restrictive emphasis of EU policies, eastwards enlargement of the EU and the development by CEECs of the immigration and asylum *acquis* has helped breathe new life into the term 'fortress Europe'. Indeed, some argue that Europe could be drawing a new iron curtain as it extends its immigration and asylum policies eastwards and installs new hard borders on its eastern frontiers. These types of metaphors are excessive for some reasons that have been touched upon in earlier chapters and others that will be explained during this chapter. Even so, as Heather Grabbe (2002a) notes there can be inherent tensions because: 'Behind the oft-used rhetoric of "not putting up a new iron curtain" lies a complex set of compromises whereby each country has tried to navigate between EU pressures and other policy concerns, both domestic and external'.

Patterns of migration

The backdrop for debates about immigration control were the (unrealised) predictions about the potential scale of east-west migration at the end of the Cold War and fears generated by this expectation. Numbers of up to 25 million potential migrants were mentioned and, even though the total number of migrants in the first half of the 1990s amounted to around 2.5 million people, these claims about large-scale migration helped justify the development by the EU of restrictions on migration from former Soviet bloc countries (Codagnone, 1999). Migrants from CEECs have accounted for around 15 per cent of the EU's total migrants since 1989 (OECD, 2001). These migrants fall into eight main types:

- Temporary labour migrants (there were around 200,000 Polish seasonal workers in Germany in 1999, for instance).

- Intra-regional flows of workers.

- Workers from developing countries.

- Workers from western Europe.

- Return migration.

- Ethnic migration.

- Asylum seekers and refugees.

- Irregular migration with cross-border crimes such as people trafficking a particular cause for concern.

TABLE 8.1   *Legally resident foreign populations in the Czech Republic, Hungary and the Slovak Republic (percentages)*

	1992	1993	1994	1995	1996	1997	1998	1999
Czech Republic	0.4	0.8	1.0	1.5	1.9	2.0	2.1	2.2
Hungary	–	–	1.3	1.4	1.4	1.4	–	1.3
Slovak Republic	–	0.2	0.3	0.4	0.5	0.5	0.5	0.5

Source: **OECD SOPEMI Report 2001: 280**

This picture is superimposed on a 'complex mosaic of relatively short-term movement based on "labour tourism" and petty trading and comprising a highly intensive shuttling back and forth across international borders to make a living' (Iglicka, 2001: 8). As an OECD (2001: 68) report put it, central and eastern Europe is becoming a 'theatre of much more complex movements' than just a straightforward move to the west. Much of this migration is temporary, but since the 1990s there has also been more longer-term migration in CEECs. Figures are patchy, but Table 8.1 shows the foreign population in the Czech and Slovak Republics and Hungary.

Policy challenges

Migration within, from and between CEECs did, of course, occur before the end of the Cold War (on Poland, for instance, see Iglicka, 2001). The relatively rapid development of a migration policy context during the 1990s has however been closely related to the EU and to four potential sources of strain.

- Unpredictable migration pressures could lead to perceptions of loss of control, particularly if the rhetoric of control and the maintenance of 'hard' borders are stoked-up in conditions that are not conducive for attainment of this objective.

- The scale and extent of borders means that policing them is costly. Poland, for instance, has 'green' (i.e. relatively unpopulated) borders of 407 km with Belarus and 526 km with the Ukraine. These costs of control occur, it should be remembered, in relatively poor countries where there are other calls on the public purse.

- The development of new controls at the EU's eastern frontier can confound other objectives such as cross-border migration for trade purposes. The informal nature of much of this activity also means that it can be a source of wealth generation and provide access to consumer goods that would otherwise be difficult to attain. Cutting off this movement can cause domestic social and political pressure. Ease of movement can be a pressure valve.

- State and nation-building in central and eastern Europe illustrate the point that nation and state are rarely co-terminus. States may claim an *ethnos* as their *demos*, but the geo-political map is rarely so straight-forward. Three million Magyars, for instance, live not in Hungary but in neighbouring states. Substantial numbers of Russians live in the Baltic States. Roma are present in most CEECs.

Discussing borders and frontiers in central and eastern Europe makes us think about the nature of these borders and their relation to 'the European project'. The EU itself does not have external frontiers. Its borders are those of its member states. It is the member states that retain responsibility for policing them. The EU's notional external frontiers are not fixed. They 'moved' with four previous enlargements of the EU in 1973, 1981, 1986 and 1995, which brought nine new member states into the Union and will move again in the near future. These borders are also more than just a line on the ground or on a map. Borders have a formal, legal meaning but also represent practices and ideas associated with these lines. According to Anderson (1997), borders involve agreements between neighbouring states, the management of these borders by police and customs authorities, and arrangements between neighbouring states on cross-border co-operation. Within these practices are ideas about the role and purpose of these borders with the effect that policy-makers, border zone inhabitants and the population more generally all have ideas about their meaning and significance. The EU's single market is, of course, centred on a frontier-free EU within which people, services, goods and capital can move freely; but this is also predicated upon control of the single market's external frontiers and ideas, for instance about 'good' movement and 'bad' movement within the European space.

It is at this point that Jan Zielonka (2001) detects a flaw in the exercise of exporting the EU immigration and asylum *acquis* to the CEECs. If such a venture is predicated on attempts to reconstruct 'hard' borders then he argues that this defect will become more apparent as the EU moves east-wards and the divergences within the EU – in socio-economic terms, for instance, grow larger. He argues that 'The very notion of a hard, external border as envisaged by the single market project and the regime of Schengen is basically flawed and unlikely to survive the following enlargement' (p. 508). In these terms, he argues that the EU is less of a 'post-Westphalian state' with hard and fixed external borders, socio-economic homogeneity, a European cultural identity, one type of citizenship and 'absolute sovereignty' regained at European level (if it ever aspires to be). Instead, he argues that the EU is more of a 'neo-medieval empire' with overlapping authorities, divided sovereignty, varied institutional arrange-ments, multiple identities and diversified types of citizenship with differ-ent sets of rights and duties. Zielonka's point is that the future enlargement will magnify, accelerate and hence confirm these trends towards diversity, multiplicity and differentiation. In turn, this implies that the EU must embrace alternatives to absolute sovereignty that involve overlapping authority, multiple cultural identities and flexible institutional arrange-ments in order to promote free movement within and across its borders.

Control defying strategies

It is in the context of the history of cross-border migration and trading patterns within CEECs that Ewa Morawska (2001) develops her analysis of 'control defying strategies' of 'East Central' migrants from Poland, the Czech Republic and Hungary moving mainly to Germany, Austria and Scandinavia and 'East East' (Ukraine, Belarus, Armenia, for instance) migrants moving from ex-Soviet republics to East-Central countries. The control defying strategies of 'East-Central' and 'East-East' migrants take six forms (Morawska, 2001: 174).

1. Migrants profit from 'gaps' in receiving societies because of contra-dictory and multiple interests that may close the door with one hand for security reasons, while leaving it ajar with another for economic reasons. The gaps for irregular migrants in CEECs are fairly substan-tial given that the size of the informal economy has been estimated at between 25 and 60 per cent of economic activity.

2. There is a relatively low level of politicisation of international tourism, which can then take the form of *Arbeitstouristen* (work tourism). These work tourists 'pursue '*homo sovieticus*' strategies of beating the (now liberal democratic) system' (Morawska, 2001: 173).

3. Linked to the previous point, entry visas for short-term visitors from most CEEC states in the queue for EU membership have been eliminated.

4. The development of communications and transport technologies makes travel easier.

5. The social networks that sustain this cross-border *pendel* migration often work on the basis of a level of trust between participants that is not evident in dealings with the state.

6. The informalisation of economic activity creates gaps for the 'inser-tion' of 'East-Central' and 'East-East' migrants.

This complex mosaic of movement has important implications for the conceptualisation of 'integration' in the absence of highly organised states expected to perform integrating roles and in the presence of informalised economies and relatively weak welfare systems. The risk is that informalisation and beat the system mentality sustain the peripheralisation of CEECs and hinder the development of 'economic society' (trusted regulating institutions) that has been seen as central to democratisation (Linz and Stepan, 1996). Moreover, the kinds of questions raised by the European Commission about administrative and judicial capacity relate directly to the protection of minority rights.

In this context, the multiplicity, diversity and differentiation that Zielonka (2001) welcomes in the 'neo-medieval' EU may not be a source of reassurance for minority groups if adequate structures for the protection of their rights are not put firmly in place. Multiplicity, differentiation and diversity could be seen by the inhabitants of border regions as a threat if they bring with them economic uncertainty and undesirable social change. Migrants and minorities could then be scapegoated as the causes of insecurity. In this context some good old-fashioned legal certainty in the shape of effective anti-discrimination laws is important. As we have seen, EU legislation in this area in June 2000 looked to tackle racist, ethnic and religious based discrimination.

The requirements of EU membership

We can now move on to look at the process of accession more carefully. How has the accession process been negotiated? The Copenhagen summit meeting of EU heads of government in 1993 linked the accession of CEECs to 'political conditionality'. The conclusions to the summit meeting stated that 'membership requires that the candidate country has achieved stability of institutions guaranteeing democracy, the rule of law, human rights and the respect of and protection of minorities'. Between 1993 and 1997 measures were particularly focused on bringing the CEECs into line with the single market. Immigration and asylum were relatively late onto the agenda because the member states were not keen to see too much Commission influence in these areas.

Since 1997 the negotiations have intensified. A 'reinforced pre-accession strategy' was launched by the Commission in its 'Agenda 2000' proposals for policy and institutional changes in the light of enlargement. In terms of immigration and asylum, applicant states were to adopt the formal conventions and instruments, informal and non-binding measures, and the agreed elements of draft instruments in negotiation. In addition a June 1998 meeting of EU and accession state interior ministers agreed to put Schengen into effect in applicant states prior to accession.

In its 2001 report on progress towards accession, the Commission shifted its emphasis from transposition of the *acquis* to implementation with more attention on administrative and judicial capacity in candidate countries. It was also reported that the accession to Schengen would occur in a two-step process. First, high levels of border control as a condition for accession followed by the lifting of internal border controls with existing member states at a later stage depending on a separate unanimous decision by the Council.

This transition has been a bone of contention. Germany led calls for a 7-year period during which full free movement rights would not be granted to EU citizens in CEECs. The common negotiating position adopted by EU member states goes with the 7-year idea, but waters it down by adopting a 2+3+2 formula which states that the situation will be reviewed after 2 years and then again after 3. Only in the most exceptional circumstances will the transition extend beyond 5 years. Even so, the Netherlands, Denmark, Sweden and Ireland have already said that they won't apply the restriction while the UK has indicated to the Polish government that it would be unlikely to go beyond the first 2 years of the transition.

Lurking in the background of this discussion is the fear of large-scale migration that could, for instance, undercut the labour market position of member state nationals. According to research for the European Commission, potential migration from CEEC states was estimated at around 300,000 each year after accession then stabilising at around 3.5 per cent of the total EU population after 30 years of membership (OECD, 2001: 72). Whether fears about large-scale movement are justified is not necessarily the point because such fears can influence social and political behaviour. The immigration and asylum pre-conditions of membership remain onerous and the feared large-scale migration from central and eastern Europe drives the exporting of immigration and asylum practices and ideas.

Sandra Lavenex (1999, 2001) tries to cut through this debate with a detailed look at the impact of the EU migration *acquis* on the CEECs. She argues that the EU policy frame is shaped by two 'conflicting paradigms': a liberal frame derived from international human rights standards and a security frame driven largely by fears about migration. She then goes on to explore the development of EU policies in CEECs to argue that European integration appears to validate a state-centred security frame. EU member states, for instance, retain their symbolic commitment to asylum while busily reducing the ability of asylum seekers to enter their state territory.

Policy learning and policy transfer

How can non-EU member states be persuaded to pursue the objectives of EU member states? There is a coercive element because the migration *acquis* is an obligation of membership. In addition to this, Milada

Vachudová (2000: 153) argues that CEECs have also been keen to 'prove their western character' as they bid for EU membership. This has meant demonstrating some resolve to control their external frontiers. The main mechanisms have been the incorporation of the central and eastern European countries into the EU's restrictive policies with the CEECs acting as a kind of 'buffer zone' to absorb some of the migration potential that could otherwise have been directed towards EU member states. Pastore (2001) argues that the effects are not entirely negative by pointing out that European integration can take the heat out of long-standing border disputes and put in place immigration controls, which may well be valued by citizens of CEECs in the same way that they are in other European countries.

The EU – or more particularly those units within the Commission and Council most concerned with enlargement – has sought to externalise responsibility for the management of unwanted migration through the use of bilateral measures, Schengen, 'third pillar' co-operation and the creation of buffer zones for those migrants defined by state policies as unwanted. Developments in central and eastern Europe demonstrate some effects of these policies and the ways in which the EU is more than an external venue to which European countries 'escape' in order to achieve domestic objectives; but also possesses the capacity to affect laws, institutions, policies and collective identities in the member states and beyond.

The EU member states pursued a strategy of 'unilateral incorporation' with the attempt to develop tighter border controls in CEECs, to designate them as safe countries to which rejected asylum applicants could be returned, and to help put in place the legal, administrative and judicial infrastructure necessary to back-up these migration policy competencies. The approach can be traced to the 'informal' co-operation that developed in the SEA's aftermath. The Dublin Convention on asylum and the meeting held between interior ministers in London in 1992 began to develop a policy approach. This was done without reference to the CEEC states that would be central to this approach. CEECs were to be defined as 'safe' countries to which asylum seekers could be returned. Under international law states are obliged to take back their own citizens. It was a novelty that CEECs were asked to take back other country's citizens too without being party to the EU agreements.

Various concepts have been used to explain this process. Ideas about policy learning and policy transfer have obvious resonance. Heather Grabbe (2002a) talks about 'one-way' policy transfer and 'active exporting'. A problem for the CEECs is that it is not always clear what is actually being transferred because the immigration and asylum components of the *acquis* are work in progress while some core aspects are deemed too sensitive to be divulged to the applicant states. Elena Jileva (2002: 75) discusses 'a technical depoliticised process of exporting the Union's *acquis communautaire* to the CEECs'. Indeed, this processing of political issues as technical questions is a typical feature of the EU policy process and one that is not linked exclusively to enlargement. Technical problems imply that some solution to the problem can be found if enough technocrats put their mind to it. Political problems raise thornier issues that might defy technocratic solutions.

The adaptational pressures are strong and there has been little scope of CEECs to influence the migration policy requirements of accession. This can be contrasted with the scope that was provided for prospective member states during previous enlargements (Grabbe, 2001, 2002b). The UK, for instance, received substantial trade concessions based on its relations with Commonwealth countries. The accession of Sweden and Finland was accompanied by the incorporation of Norway and Iceland as Schengen observers in order to sustain Nordic free movement arrangements. No such arrangements have been offered to the Carpathian region even though free movement arrangements can be important for social, family and economic reasons in this part of the world too.

The effect has been that the *acquis* for CEECs is much more rigid with significant negotiating asymmetries. The issue of compliance lurks in the background. The Commission's 2001 report on progress towards accession frequently remarks about administrative capacity in accession states (CEC, 2001c). Zielonka (2001) argues that 'institutional mimicry' can, at least on paper, satisfy the requirements of accession agreements, although the Commission has become very focused on implementation.

In these kinds of terms we can distinguish between three logics that all appear to have some bearing on the adjustments and dynamics of eastwards enlargement as it applies to migration. First, there is the desire of EU member states to *make* the CEECs 'European' in the sense of adopting the EU *acquis*. Second, is the desire on the part of these member states to *become* 'European' and to show that they are ready to assume the responsibilities of membership. Third, there is some pressure to *seem* 'European' in the sense that the burdens of accession are so great and raise significant compliance issues with the result that mimicry rather than more deep-rooted institutional isomorphism could be a more likely outcome. Adaptation to the *acquis* is also difficult because it is a moving target that is being developed and re-developed by member states.

Mechanisms of policy transfer

Four mechanisms for this policy transfer and for the steep international policy learning curve on which the CEECs found themselves can be identified.

1. Unilateral and bilateral processes link the EU with accession states. The Budapest Process is a particularly good example. The Budapest Process developed in the wake of two ministerial conferences on illegal

immigration (1991) and uncontrolled migration (1993). The 1993 meeting established a steering group, the Budapest Group – with representatives of the EU Presidency, Schengen, EFTA and four other states. The Budapest Process has since expanded to include 43 states and 10 intergovernmental organisations and is now looking to extend its focus beyond central and eastern Europe towards Mediterranean countries. The Budapest process focuses on: co-operation on border guards; combating trafficking in human beings; training in the EU/Schengen *acquis*; business input into co-development projects designed to stem migration flows; and the development of asylum and refugee systems. Jileva (2002) argues that for Bulgaria the Budapest Process was an important way for state officials to find out what they were supposed to do.

2. The 'safe third country' rule and readmission agreements provide that asylum applicants could be returned to countries defined as safe. The EU's eastern neighbours were defined as safe with the effect that asylum seekers could be returned to them. The mechanisms by which return was to occur were provided for by a complex web of readmission agreements. The first such agreement was between the Schengen states and Poland in 1991. The reward for Poland is that restrictions on short-term visas for Poles were relaxed while the Polish authorities also received financial assistance to help develop border control and surveillance technologies. The impact of readmission agreements can be seen if we take the agreement with Romania as an example. In 1992 there were 100,000 asylum-seekers from Romania in Germany. A readmission agreement was signed in 1994. In 1995 there were 3500 Romanian asylum-seekers in Germany. Between 1993 and 1995 around 85,000 people were returned to Romania. The CEECs were then encouraged to reach their own readmission agreements with neighbouring states further away from the EU with the effect that responsibility was offloaded to states with less and less capacity to deal with asylum seeking migrants in ways that accord with the principles laid down in international laws.

3. The export of the EU visa policy, which plays an important part in 'moving the borders of Europe' (Guild, 2001). Particular states have their own concerns that are dealt with through bilateral discussions or through groups such as the Budapest Process.

4. The development of asylum systems in CEECs. Lavenex (1999) argues that this was putting the cart before the horse in the sense that the definition of these countries as 'safe' preceded the efforts to develop asylum systems. The implementation of systems has been closely monitored by international organisations such as the UNHCR and the IOM, which have networks of offices in central and eastern European countries and produce regular reports that update the strengths and weaknesses of these developments.

The immigration policy frame adopted by the CEECs has been largely inspired by the requirements of accession to the EU and dominated by security concerns. This also demonstrates the ways in which ideas about security have been redefined since the end of the Cold War to include new 'threats' such as uncontrolled immigration and asylum. Moreover, internal and external security are more closely linked. As we saw in Chapter 6, the pillared approach was always slightly artificial in the way that it separated foreign and security policy from internal security and immigration/asylum from free movement. To invoke Pastore's (2001) Machiavellian allusion, the Prince's 'two arms' are becoming one.

If policy mechanisms are analysed then we can say that there has been a largely one-way process of policy transfer with significant immigration and asylum policy implications. While it's not always clear what is actually being transferred, the requirement to adapt is strong. This has prompted a rapid process of policy learning coupled with efforts to transpose the *acquis* into national laws and practices. However, the distinction introduced earlier between *making, becoming* and *seeming* European is useful in the sense that adapting to the requirement of EU membership can be motivated by external imposition, by a desire to join the EU, and by institutional mimicry in order to accord with the requirements of EU membership. Implementation and compliance questions are writ large as the EU's immigration and asylum *acquis* moves eastwards.

Immigrant and minorities policies

In the introductory chapter to this volume it was argued that debates about integration have tended to take a nation-state and national society centred frame of reference. The chapter on southern Europe showed the continued relevance of these arguments, but also highlighted the importance of probing the forms of state organisation and state-society relations more carefully.

In this section, we take debates about immigrant and minorities policy forward by looking at the characteristics of the response in CEECs. We can discuss two aspects of immigrant policies that are thrown into stark relief in CEECs. First, the existence of sizeable national minorities in CEECs and, second, state-society relations in countries where state structures are not strong and may not be trusted, or at least not seen as entirely reliable. As we saw in southern Europe, the role of the state and expectations held by citizens about this role can differ. The result of this is that expectations about states' capacities to respond to immigration and national minorities can also differ. We are also discussing a situation of rediscovered nationhood following the collapse of the Soviet Union. Post Cold War political turmoil did create a groundswell of support for accession to the EU, but political disintegration also provides fertile ground for the 'reinvention' of ethnic identities and nationalistic politics (Hockenos, 1993; Ignatieff, 1998).

Migrants and minorities in central and eastern Europe

The discussion in CEECs differs from that in north-west and southern Europe in that it is less about the formation of immigrant communities, although it is about this too, than about the position of minorities within CEECs. Kymlicka (1995) argues that national minorities have the right to preserve their culture and that this places obligations on the state regarding legal protection, the provision of services to these national minorities (such as education in their language) and representation.

The definitions of national minorities can be arbitrary. Slovenia, for instance, sets aside two seats in its parliament for minorities with one for the Hungarian minority and one for the Italian minority. There are no seats for the larger Croatian minority because they are defined as an immigrant group (assumed voluntary entrants) rather than a national minority. The Roma too receive no seats in the Slovenian parliament.

The European Commission's annual monitoring of the political conditions attached to EU membership has also focused on the position of Russian minorities in the Baltic states. Non-citizens constitute 28 per cent of the Latvian population and 25 per cent of the Estonian population. Citizenship and nationality have been important issues. After securing independence in 1991, Estonia reinstated its 1938 nationality laws that provided for a minimum 3-year period for naturalisation. This classified the Russian-origin population as immigrants. A 1993 law forbade non-citizens from holding public office. In December 1998, the Estonian Parliament added Estonian-language proficiency requirements to both the election acts even though these violate the Estonian Constitution as well as international obligations regarding non-discrimination and freedom to be elected. Yet, as Stephen Deets (2001) points out, the absence of European citizenship norms means that the Estonians can defend their actions as being in line with practices in other European countries. Why should Estonia treat its Russians as a protected minority with voting rights when Germany has long denied such rights to its Turkish origin population?

A particularly salient issue is the protection of minority rights both within and outside of CEECs because of the view that national and ethnic cultures are tied to personal liberty and that states have certain obligations to preserve them. Indeed, the protection of minority cultures has been tied to EU accession as an aspect of political conditionality. This does raise some thorny issues. It's not always easy to identify these groups and then to respond to changes in group identities. People can be turned into representatives of their supposed national or cultural identity without having chosen this role. State policies can then play an important part in identity construction. Also, which groups are to be protected? There can be accusations of unfairness if some minorities are privileged and others are not.

All of these issues are illustrated by recent developments in Romanian electoral politics where minorities that do not cross the 3 per cent electoral threshold are entitled to a seat in the lower chamber of parliament if they receive more than 5 per cent of the average vote needed to elect one representative. The minority candidates are listed on the ballot with all the other candidates, and everyone is free to vote for them. This means that individual voters do not need to identify themselves as members of a minority. The problem in the 1996 elections was that more people voted for ethnic parties than had claimed these ethnic identities in the census. This led Stephen Deets (2000) to suggest that political entrepreneurs might establish ethnic parties because of the easier route to parliamentary representation it can provide. As he also points out, the number of 'ethnic parties' has risen in each election. The fairness issue also looms large because the Polish party secured a seat in Parliament with just 1,842 votes whereas the 175,000 votes received by the Pensioners Party did not earn a single seat.

There's an external dimension to these issues too. Legislation passed by the Hungarian Parliament in June 2001 extended rights to Hungarians living abroad. There are 3 million Magyars living outside of Hungary. Article 6 of the Hungarian Constitution (revised in 1989) provides that: *'The Republic of Hungary bears a sense of responsibility for the fate of Hungarians living outside its borders and shall promote and foster their relations with Hungary'*. Hungary is not alone in this because the constitutions of many other CEECs including Romania, Slovenia, Macedonia, Croatia, the Ukraine, Poland and the Slovak Republic all provide for ethnic co-belongers living abroad. Minorities account for between 13 and 15 per cent of the Romanian population with 8 per cent of the Romanian population of Hungarian origin (Venice Commission, 2001). A concern is that European integration can consolidate borders between new EU member states and surrounding countries with which there can be strong ties between co-ethnics.

The Roma

Estimates of the Roma population, which is mainly concentrated in Slovakia, Hungary, Romania and Bulgaria, range between 1.5 million and 4 million. The Roma population is difficult to measure because the population is not settled and because of fears about disclosing identity to the census authorities because of the racism and discrimination that could result.

Discrimination against the Roma is one of the most pressing minority rights issues in CEECs. The Roma have no homeland to press their concerns and do not seek a homeland. In terms of the usual models of ethnic politics there have also been problems because Roma are less likely to engage in the kinds of state-oriented terms that are recognisable to students of ethnic mobilisation This means that there have been problems acting coherently as an ethnic bloc in national and EU politics. Even if mobilisation were to occur then there is a risk of a backlash from nationalists, which further reinforces the need for the consolidation of social, administrative, legal and judicial practices founded on principles of non-discrimination. The EU has been keen to highlight these concerns in its annual reports on progress towards accession, but an element of hypocrisy can also be noted because of the ways in which immigration control policies have been exported to CEECs that are designed to ensure that those who are identified as possible victims of discrimination cannot enter EU member states and make claims for asylum. The UK government, for instance, was accused of discriminating against Roma from the Czech Republic through the use of 'pre-clearance immigration controls'. A Czech TV undercover reporter of Roma origin travelling with a non-Roma Czech national was barred from boarding a flight to London while the non-Roma colleague was able to travel. This led to allegations of double standards. The Czech Republic was open to criticism of mistreatment of minorities, but EU member states were reluctant to accept these minorities and were developing 'external' controls to ensure that potential migrants could not enter their state territory.

The 1991 census in the Czech Republic reported that there were 33,489 Roma, although the Council of Nationalities estimated the real figure to be between 200,000 and 250,000, or about 3 per cent of the population. The Council for Nationalities also estimated the unemployment levels of Roma to be between 70 and 90 per cent, while 70 per cent of the children placed in remedial schools were Roma (Roma children are 15 times more likely to be placed in these schools than other Czech children). The European Roma Rights Centre (ERRC) has identified these remedial schools as playing a key role in educational segregation. Roma children are disproportionately in these schools because they under-perform in tasks designed for Czech children and because of racist attitudes towards Roma children. The effects, according to the 1991 census, were clear. Only 1.2 per cent of Roma children completed full secondary education, compared to 80.3 per cent of Czech children. The number of Roma students in universities was too small to measure (ERRC, 1999).

Similar patterns are evident in Slovakia too, where the Minority Rights Group has estimated the Roma population to be between 480,000 and 520,000, or just under 10 per cent of the total population of 5.3 million. Roma mainly live in the southern and eastern parts of Slovakia and face three main problems: official denials that rights violations take place; continued exclusionary administrative and social practices which marginalise Roma; social pressures for Roma to change their lifestyle and conform with Slovakian social norms (ERRC, 1997).

Official figures in Romania also under-estimate the total Roma population. The 1992 census classified 409,111 people as Roma, but estimates by the Minority Rights Group put the figure at between 1.8 million and 2.5 million, around 10 per cent of the population. The Roma were particularly subject to violent persecution in the years after the fall of the Ceaucescu regime with anti-Roma pogroms reported between 1990 and 1993 (Human Rights Watch, 1991; Fonseca, 1995). The EU has been critical of Romanian treatment of its Roma population. In 2000, the Commission reported that 'Roma remain subject to widespread discrimination throughout Romanian society. However, the government's commitment to addressing this situation remains low and there has been little substantial progress in this area since the last report'. The ERRC reported non-prosecution as a norm, a climate of impunity, child homelessness and discrimination in key aspects of social life such as housing and education and in access to goods and services (ERRC, 2001).

In addition to the position of national minorities there is also some evidence of the formation of immigrant groups in CEECs. Labour market organisation and the role of the welfare state play a key role in the integration of newcomers by providing them with a repertoire of social and economic possibilities that can either promote or hinder inclusion. If social citizenship and norms have not been internalised by nationals to the same extent that they have been in highly organised societies such as Sweden, and there is a low level of expectation about state capacity to deliver inclusion, then it is less likely that the state will be expected to deliver the integration of newcomers. The other side of the coin, of course, is that expectations about the ability to control population may be lower too. There are also patterns of trade and trade-related migration that have deep roots in CEECs. Iglicka and Sword's (1999: 164) analysis of the Warsaw bazaar, which is mainly a clothing market with an estimated turnover of around US $500 million a year, found it to be 'the tip of an iceberg of an extensive trading network which spreads out across Poland, but also across the eastern border'.

Accession to the EU brings with it onerous requirements, which can heighten uncertainty in CEECs. Trends towards diversity, multiplicity and differentiation in an enlarged EU also require some legal certainty. In this case, the transposition of the EU's anti-discrimination directives of June 2000 into the national law of the accession states as a condition for their membership could provide a supranational frame for inclusion and anti-discrimination in the face of national legal and judicial processes that have been found wanting on occasions.

Conclusion

This chapter has shown how the obligations of EU membership have directly impacted upon immigration and asylum policy in the CEECs.

The EU sought to externalise its control policies through the definition of safe third countries and safe countries of origin and the development of a complex web of readmission agreements that put in place mechanisms to return asylum seekers to central and east European countries. The adoption of these policies provides us with a good example of the exporting of EU policy based simultaneously on coercion (adoption as a requirement for membership), willingness (to be seen as 'European' in the sense of controlling external frontiers), and mimicry (to satisfy the requirements of membership, at least on paper). The CEECs were not consulted about the content of the immigration and asylum *acquis*. The next EU enlargement will have a strong focus on the borders and boundaries of the new Europe and ideas and practices associated with security and insecurity both within the member states and in surrounding states and regions that are drawn into the EU's web of interdependence.

The EU has exported immigration and asylum policies to outside of the EU that have tended to replicate those of existing EU member states. This has been criticised for trying to recreate 'hard' borders when this is no longer appropriate. Whether or not the pursuit of some kind of post-Westphalian state is the intention, the EU clearly is likely to face difficulties when seeking to implement control policies in CEECs. This is because of the complex forms of movement in central and eastern Europe and the control defying strategies that migrants can pursue. Practical implementation problems can arise because these are relatively new issues for which CEECs are not well-prepared. EU enlargement tends to be processed as a legal, political and administrative exercise. Social and political issues then tend to be also processed as technical concerns in line with the EU's preferred mode of operating. But the issues run deeper than this and relate to perceptions of state capacity to control population and integrate immigrants. If states are weak, not trusted, or not seen as reliable while labour markets are highly informal and welfare systems under-developed then the conceptual foundations of discussions of immigration and immigrant policies that underpinned the discussion of immigration policies in older north-west European countries are misplaced when we examine countries where structures and expectations differ.

This chapter and the chapter on southern Europe that preceded it have argued that we need to go beyond the discussion of the formal transposition of EU law and questions of administrative capacity ('goodness of fit' in a narrower sense, important though these are) to also consider the types of state structures, their capacity, as well as expectations about the role of states, because these have crucial bearing on discussions of immigration policy and immigrant policy and give us an idea about the ways in which the conceptual and geo-political widening of migration has changed relations between European countries with the EU as a forum for policy development and the diffusion of ideas.

Note

1 The 'Luxembourg group' comprising Hungary, Estonia, Slovenia, Poland, and the Czech Republic began negotiations in 1998. The 'Helsinki group' including Slovakia, Lithuania, Latvia, Bulgaria, Romania began negotiations in 2000. In addition to this, the Stability Pact group comprising Albania, Bosnia-Herzegovina, Croatia, the Federal Republic of Yugoslavia and Macedonia, are moving towards closer economic and political relations with the EU although membership remains some way off.

9

Conclusion:
The European Politics of Migration?

This book set itself two tasks. First, to explore the extent to which there are horizontal linkages between European countries of immigration linking them in terms of their responses to immigration. Second, to analyse the extent of a vertical dimension derived from the EU's impact on the European politics of migration and immigration. This allows us to assess the extent to which it makes sense to talk of a *European* politics of migration and immigration influenced in shape, form and content by national level social, economic and political dynamics and by European integration. The book's analysis was developed around the themes of immigration policies, immigrant policies and the development of EU responsibilities in order to facilitate this approach.

There are strong national particularities that can prompt a distinction between European countries in terms of their approach to these issues. There can also be divergence within European countries as well, of course. At the same time, there are similarities between European countries in terms of the ways in which they respond to international migration and the ways in which an emerging EU policy context presents important implications for policy-making within states, relations between states, and for relations between EU states and surrounding states and regions. The book has highlighted elements of convergence and divergence and thus staked out some of the issues that will be central to future debates about national policies and common EU migration policies. The multi-levelness of migration policy and the sharing of responsibility between states and supranational actors within the EU have become a key feature of policy responses since the 1990s.

Two contextual factors were identified out in the introductory chapter. First, it was noted that the intention within this book was to explore the ways in which changes in institutions and organisations in European countries, and changed relations between them, play a key role in generating understandings of the various forms of international migration. Rather than seeking to analyse the ways in which international migration 'challenges' various aspects of institutional and organisational life, the aim has been to probe the links between institutional and organisational change and perceptions at elite and popular levels of international migration in its various forms. This has allowed us to relate debates about international migration to more general pressures on European countries such as labour market changes, welfare state pressures, the changed post-Cold War geo-political configuration and European integration. The advantage of this approach is that it emphasises the ways in which perceptions of international migration in its various forms by economically developed European states play an important part in the categorisation of migrants. The response to migration is then less to do with the personality or character of individual migrants rather than it is with the perspectives on international migration and migrants by institutions and organisations at national and international level.

Second, the book dealt with the conceptual and geo-political widening of migration to include new types of migration, new forms of state and supranational response and new countries of immigration in southern, central and eastern Europe. This conceptual and geo-political widening is particularly associated with the post Cold War 'third wave' of international migration and the growth in asylum seeking migration and migration defined by state policies as illegal. It is insufficient to analyse a few of the 'older' immigration countries of western Europe and then extrapolate to southern, central and eastern Europe as though they are either in some way 'deviant' and exceptional cases or likely to follow a basically similar trajectory to that in older immigration countries, or both. Common analytical tools associated with the assessment of immigration and immigrant policies can be used when exploring policy developments in these countries. At the same time, there are distinguishing factors associated with, for instance, the relative newness of migration issues, higher levels of economic informality, and differently configured state-society relations that present some differences with older immigration countries. These newer immigration countries have also been more directly exposed to the EU's influence on policy development, particularly the CEECs. This suggests some pressure for adaptation and convergence, but as was also seen, the formal commitment made by CEECs to EU membership does not necessarily imply that adaptation can be swiftly or easily attained if basic institutional compatabilities remain. Or, for that, matter, if there is a lack of mutual trust between existing and prospective EU member states that makes adaptation a difficult and fraught process. Not least because it's not always entirely clear to what CEECs are supposed to adapt.

The continuation of migration in 'non-immigration' countries

A puzzle that has preoccupied many scholars of international migration since the 1970s is the continuation of immigration into self-declared non-immigration countries. This is an interesting issue because it tells us something about the constrained control capacity of European immigration countries, but also the ways in which these constraints are often linked to particular types of migration flow. Thus, as was seen, the ending of large-scale recruitment of migrant labour in the early 1970s was not the same as the end of immigration because family migration continued and, more recently, has been supplemented by asylum seeking migration and by migration defined by state policies as illegal.

Much of this migration since the mid-1970s has been linked to migration networks centred on post-colonial connections or on labour recruitment agreements. As such these did not necessarily signify a general constraint on the control capacity of immigration countries, but rather a more specific constraint linked to past migration flows. Moreover, while states have been legally bound at both national and international level to continue to accept certain types of migrants, such as family members, they have made considerable efforts to curtail the possibility of future migration.

More recently, the structuring effects of colonial ties and recruitment agreements have lost some of their resonance. This becomes clear in southern Europe where there are widely diverse countries of origin and often-weaker ties between sending and receiving countries. As mentioned earlier, the fact that approximately one third of the people who availed themselves of the 2001 Portuguese regularisation were from the Ukraine tells us something about the diminished impact of political-historical structuring factors. It also indicates the communication of images and information about migration possibilities between Portugal and the Ukraine and the subsequent development of migration ties between the two countries.

The context within which efforts to regulate international migration occurs has changed in the 1990s as a result of the conceptual and geo-political widening of international migration. To analyse the efforts to regulate international migration it is useful to distinguish between external and internal controls. By doing this, we can also get a better idea about convergence and divergence between European countries. There is substantial convergence in terms of the use of both external measures – with the EU playing a key role here – and the development of internal control techniques, often closely linked to the welfare state.

External measures focus on the control of borders, but also, as Elspeth Guild (2001) has put it, the ways in which European countries are 'moving the borders of Europe'. This moving of the borders of Europe is closely linked to European integration, the building of the single market, and the attempt to recreate hard borders on the EU's southern and eastern flanks. Potential migrants are, therefore, likely to encounter far more stringent control measures in their country of origin before they even begin to make a journey to Europe. For instance, the deployment of British immigration officials to conduct 'pre-entry screening' in sending countries is a good example of this. Moreover, sending countries have been co-opted within the EU's framework of controls through, for instance, the recognition of 'safe countries of origin', 'safe third countries' and the establishment of a web of readmission agreements. For central and eastern European countries the imposition of such measures and the creation of a 'buffer zone' around the EU have been important aspects of the accession process.

James Hollifield (2001) makes an important point when he notes that states will prefer to externalise their controls because this frees them from some of the legislative and judicial constraints that they face at national level. These international agreements and the EU enlargement process have been largely immune from public scrutiny and yet have had major effects on the nature of the immigration control framework in Europe. So, while the types of borders and border regime in the EU are changing this does not signify a loss of control. To return to a point made earlier, the fact that people will place their fate in the hands of criminal gangs and risk their lives on rusty old boats in an attempt to cross the Mediterranean and try to enter a European country does not signify a loss of control. Rather it shows the extent to which tighter restrictions generate new evasions – the growth of people smuggling, in this case – and can then sustain a migration industry, as well as creating new types of 'immigration problem'. In a sense, though, these new problems bring us back to the issue raised at the start of this chapter. These labels tell us less about the personality or character of migrants than they do about the ability of states to categorise migrants into various types of 'wanted' and 'unwanted' category.

There has also been a developing array of internal control measures that are often closely linked to the borders of the national welfare state. These have been most evident in European countries where welfare state pressures and changed welfare state ideologies have had important effects on the perception of migration and migrants. This has been particularly the case in response to asylum-seeking migration where schemes such as dispersal, removal of the right to work, and the replacement of cash paid benefits with vouchers have helped to place asylum seekers outside of the community of legitimate receivers of welfare state benefits. These measures seek to reduce the possibility of settlement – at least while the claim is adjudicated – and ensure that this form of migration, unlike others, can be reversible: the 'guests who didn't come to stay', so to speak.

There's another point here too that relates to the ways in which these new forms of migration are understood as troubling. It has been argued that since the 1990s there has been a downplaying of national semantics. Michael Bommes (2000) makes this point when assessing the treatment of the *Aussiedler* in Germany. Germany is instructive in this respect because it was the main country of destination for most migrants after the end of the Cold War. He argues that there has been a downplaying of national semantics associated with the ideas about a German community of descent understood in ethno-cultural terms and an increased emphasis on membership of the community of GNP contributors. On this basis, Bommes argues that the guestworkers have been included albeit at a lower level than Germans and that since the mid-1990s the *Aussiedler*, along with asylum seekers, have a lower level of welfare state access. This is not particular to Germany. In the UK, Sweden and the Netherlands changes in background institutional conditions – particularly welfare state pressures and changed welfare state ideologies – have had important effects on the responses to migration and the perception of migrants and their descendants within these imagined national communities.

There's another side to this coin. Since the end of the 1990s there have been renewed openings to labour migration because of the demographic changes and skills shortages in some economic sectors. European countries have thus entered the global competition for skilled migrants. European countries are likely to find themselves facing a number of dilemmas associated with this new migration, but these are not necessarily new dilemmas. It may seem like a contradiction that these countries can be open to some forms of migration and try to close the channels for other types (the 'liberal paradox' of open markets and closed states). Actually, though, it bounces us back to the dilemma expressed by Aristide Zolberg, that when we try to explain immigration policies in European countries we must account for the walls that they build and the small doors that they open.

Assessing the European politics of migration

We can now return to the questions raised in this book's introduction. A horizontal analytical dimension was specified that sought to compare responses in European countries. This level of analysis centres on the issues of convergence and divergence. If responses are diverse then we would expect to see debates channelled through national, social and political contexts that give different meaning in both practices and ideas to state responses to international migration. We could end up with a series of competing national exceptionalisms with little scope for comparison. If we seek convergence then we will look for elements of similarity in state responses to international migration. This could focus on the form that immigration politics takes, the institutional venues such as the labour market and welfare state that mediate inclusion, and the impact of shared ideas about membership of the imagined national community.

If we explore the extent to which European immigration politics have been characterised by distinct national responses to international migration then there is evidence to suggest that much of the debate has been channelled through distinct national institutional settings that give particular meaning to immigration and immigrant policies. These are not cast in stone, can change and have changed. Moreover, more general changes in background institutional conditions arising from welfare state pressures or European integration have important effects on the understanding of international migration and migrants.

Where changes in national approaches have arisen they have often been linked to domestic political processes. In both France and Germany there were major debates about immigration in the 1980s and 1990s. The EU's impact was at the margins. In both countries the EU did provide an external venue which allowed the pursuit of restrictive policies: reduced legislative and judicial constraints played little part in these debates, but the driving forces behind policy change were mainly located within national political arenas. In these terms, European integration has been coincidental rather than causal; while states have also shown an ability to redefine their relationship to the international system (asylum standards, for instance) in ways that can facilitate the attainment of state policy objectives. The EU's impact has been more directly evident on southern, central and eastern European countries.

That said, the EU's role in these developments should not be over-stated. A distinction was made between the horizontal and vertical in order to try and distinguish between common factors linking member states and the effects of European integration. Chapter 6 sought to carefully specify the EU's role and to identify the sources of power derived largely from market-making that are central to European integration. The EU defies both a narrow state-centrism but also confounds post-national universalism. It was shown that the EU's impact on immigration debates was quite marginal until the late 1990s. That said, the EU did provide a venue in the late 1980s and early 1990s for the development of new forms of co-operation on immigration control that were not subject to the kinds of domestic legal and political constraints that had been seen as inhibiting control capacity in some EU member states. In this sense, the EU facilitated the attainment of state objectives and was an attempted reassertion rather than a weakening of state authority. Even so, European integration possesses the capacity to feed into domestic contexts, as was evident, for instance, with the posted workers debate in Germany. Moreover, the 'escape to Europe' thesis appears to better reflect the post-Maastricht policy framework with its strong intergovernmental focus. Post-Amsterdam communitarisation has major constraints, but does stake a path towards a more common approach within the main Treaty rather than an intergovernmental 'pillar'.

In order to understand better the multi-levelling of European immigration politics, a distinction was also made between the *institutionalisation of Europe* and the *Europeanisation of institutions*. The shift to European-level co-operation and integration gives us some idea about the EU's partial migration policy with a highly developed free movement framework and a much less developed (albeit developing) immigration and asylum policy framework.

The effects of EU policy on member states – the Europeanisation of institutions - are likely to be uneven across states. This is not to say that older immigration countries have simply exported their approaches to the EU level because they too have been open to the effects of EU migration policy ('posted workers' in Germany and EU anti-discrimination laws in France provide two examples). That said, the effects of European integration have been most pronounced in newer immigration countries in central and eastern Europe where EU policies have been a pronounced source of domestic policy change. Yet, the EU's attempt to replicate the control and command-style policies of older immigration countries can run into problems in southern, central and eastern Europe where attempts to regulate migration encounter economic informality and irregular migration, and thus touch upon state-society relations more generally.

The institutionalisation of Europe has thus been partial and subject to the restraining influence of the member states that have so far kept the upper hand in areas related to immigration and asylum. The Europeanisation of institutions at member state level is subject to some mismatches and institutional incompatibilities. These could make it difficult to enforce the EU migration policy *acquis* particularly if it's based on unrealistic expectations about control capacity. There can also be difficulties if the *acquis* runs counter to other EU objectives, such as democratisation and liberalisation. This in effect brings us back to the liberal paradox already discussed, derived from the articulation between the relative openness towards movement of capital, goods and services and the relative closure as applied to the movement of people.

The spatial and temporal reconstruction of migration and policy challenges

The EU migration framework is neither simply a state-centred device for the attainment of domestic policy objectives nor a form of post-national universalism creating rights that cross borders implying nation state redundancy. While the EU does extend rights to EU citizens (who are nationals of a member state) it does not as things stand, generally extend these rights to third country nationals, while there is also an attempt to develop hard borders between the EU and surrounding states and regions.

These developments can be linked to what can be called the spatial and temporal reconstruction of EU migration policy. The spatial reconstruction refers to the development of the EU migration framework with a relocation of decision-making that is most evident in the supranationalised area of free movement, but also apparent for immigration and asylum. This relocation has led to the establishment of distinct sources of legal, political and symbolic power associated with the EU's core objectives, the Treaty basis and associated legislation. This spatial reconstruction raises border and boundary issues that are generated by the attempt to promote certain forms of openness associated with European integration coupled with the maintenance of closure against those forms of international migration defined as unwanted.

Since the end of the 1990s there has also been an attempted temporal reconstruction of migration, by which is meant an attempt to re-establish at a temporal distance from the guestworker recruitment of the 1960s new labour migration into EU member states to fill skills shortages in some economic sectors. Here too there is a multi-level dimension imparted by the Commission's attempts to stake out a role for itself as the co-ordinator of national migration policies.

This does not mean that there is a common EU migration policy. There is a highly developed free movement framework that is supranationalised and that imposes real constraints on the member states. Co-operation on immigration and asylum are less developed. At the same time, it is worth recalling that co-operation in these areas was only formalised when the Maastricht Treaty came into effect in 1993. So, rather than bemoaning a lack of progress or pondering the insurmountable obstacles to common policies, it might also be worth reflecting on the quite rapid developments that have occurred in less than ten years. In effect, the parameters of a common approach can be detected as a result of post-Amsterdam 'communitarisation' as it applies to both immigration and asylum and, also, to anti-discrimination measures contained in Article 13 and subsequently given legal effect by the two anti-discrimination directives of June 2000.

What issues are likely to arise as EU institutions seek to pursue the mandate laid out for them by the Treaty of Amsterdam and in the conclusions by the heads of government after the Tampere summit meeting of October 1999? A particular difficulty is that the member states have not given themselves the tools to do the job. They have agreed on the outline of a common approach, but are hamstrung by a reliance on unanimity, which reflects the sensitivity of the issues involved. In its biennial 'scoreboard' the European Commisison notes the disjunction between what the member states say that they want to do and what they are then prepared to agree on.

Two other issues also arise, which impinge very directly on the legitimacy of the multi-level political system that links states and the EU. The implications of this spatial and temporal reconstruction and the policy challenges that it raises can be illustrated by using Fritz Scharpf's (2000) distinction between input and output elements that taken together contribute to the perceived legitimacy of political institutions. First, there is the question of the 'input oriented authenticity' of migration policy, which relates to the type of decision-making process associated with this policy area. EU level co-operation and integration have tended to occur in relatively shielded venues that have not been open to wider public debate. This shielding means that decisions made in such arenas could offer scope for progressive outcomes, but can also suffer from a lack of legitimacy that could be bestowed by broader public debate. The effect could be that 'behind closed doors' decision processes could be exploited by anti-immigration and populist political forces as arguments against both European integration and immigration/immigrants. If unpopular institutions assume responsibility for unpopular issues and are seen as doing so in a secretive and unaccountable manner then this can become a real legitimacy problem for the EU.

It's not only the decision-making process that impinges on the perceived legitimacy of political institutions. There is also the question of their capacity to deliver agreed objectives. The formulation and implementation of EU policy depends on a balance between member state interests and the pursuit of common EU objectives by supranational institutions. The management, co-ordination and implementation of EU migration policy will occur within a dual executive within which responsibilities are shared between EU institutions and the member states, which means that there is scope for the fragmentation of responsibility. This leads directly to the issue of output-oriented effectiveness. If the EU lacks the capacity to implement agreed policies then these compliance problems impact very squarely on the perceived legitimacy of the system. Migration policy presents some major policy challenges because of the diversity of state responses and because of the geopolitical and conceptual widening of the migration issue to include new types of migration, new forms of state response with effects on newer immigration countries. It is possible in the post-Amsterdam EU to detect the outline of common EU migration policies, but these teeter on a precarious balance of powers between states and supranational institutions and on state policies and forms of state organisation that, while displaying some aspects of convergence, retain distinct elements.

It is possible to detect a politics of migration and immigration in Europe with both horizontal connections in terms of state responses and vertical linkages derived from the EU. The development of EU migration policy also poses a major challenge for emerging patterns of Europe-wide governance as the EU encroaches on issues of high politics that were once the sovereign preserve of nation states. European countries remain key actors, but are no longer the only actors. They share power with other member states and with EU institutions.

This balance of power between states and supranational institutions in a multi-level Europe impacts upon politics within these states and relations between these states, as well as neighbouring states and regions.

International migration alone does not drive changes within these nation states. It is better understood as one facet of the political sociology of the nation state in an integrating Europe with the capacity to inform us about the territorial, organisational and conceptual borders of these countries. As has been argued, changes within European countries and changed relations between them have had important effects on the perceptions of international migration and migrants. International migration squarely impinges on a range of issues that have been, and are likely to continue to be, central to the developing multi-level European migration policy framework. Welfare state and labour market pressures, security concerns and foreign policy interests all have a bearing on perceptions of international migration and migrants. While the welfare state-related perceptions of migration and migrants will remain strongly national, because welfare states remain national and there is no supranational alternative in view, the understanding of international migration and migrants from the perspective of economically developed European countries has been, is and will continue to be influenced in shape, form and content by European integration.

Bibliography

Ålund, Aleksandra and Carl-Ulrik Schierup (eds) (1993) *Paradoxes of Multiculturalism: Essays on Swedish Society*, Aldershot: Avebury.

Ålund, Olof, Pers-Anders Edin and Peter Fredriken (2001) *Settlement Policies and the Economic Success of Immigrants*, Discussion paper 2730, London: Centre for Economic Policy Research.

Amiraux, Valérie (2000) 'Unexpected Biographies: Deconstructing the National Welfare State', in Michael Bommes and Andrew Geddes (eds) *Immigration and Welfare: Challenging the Borders of the Welfare State*, London: Routledge.

Anderson, Benedict (1983) *Imagined Communities: Reflections on the Origins and Spread of Nationalism*, London: Verso.

Anderson, Malcolm (1997) *Frontiers: Territory and State Formation in the Modern World*, Cambridge: Polity Press.

Andreas, Peter (2000) *Border Games. Policing the US-Mexico Divide*, Ithaca (NY): Cornell University Press.

Arango, Joaquin (2000) 'Becoming a Country of Immigration at the End of the Twentieth Century', in Russell King, Gabriella Lazaridis and Charalambos Tsardanidis (eds) *Eldorado or Fortress? Migration in Southern Europe*, London: Macmillan.

Bade, Klaus (1994) *Das Manifest der 60. Deutschland und die Einwanderung*, Munich.

Baganha, Maria (1998) 'Immigrant Involvement in the Informal Economy: The Portuguese Case, *Journal of Ethnic and Migration Studies*, vol. 24, no. 2.

Baganha, Maria (2000) 'Immigrants Social Citizenship and Labour Market Dynamics in Portugal', in Michael Bommes and Andrew Geddes (eds) *Immigration and Welfare: Challenging the Borders of the Welfare State*, London: Routledge.

Baldwin-Edwards, Martin (1997) 'The Emerging European Union Immigration Regime: Some Reflections on Its Implications for Southern Europe', *Journal of Ethnic and Migration Studies*, vol. 35, no. 4.

Baldwin-Edwards, Martin (1999) 'Where Free Markets Reign: Aliens in the Twilight Zone', *South European Society and Politics*, vol. 3, no. 3.

Bank, Roland (2000) 'Europeanising the Reception of Asylum Seekers: The Opposite of Welfare State Politics' in Michael Bommes and Andrew Geddes (eds) *Immigration and Welfare: Challenging the Borders of the Welfare State*, London: Routledge.

Banton, Michael (2001) 'National Integration in France and Britain', *Journal of Ethnic and Migration Studies*, vol. 27, no. 1.

Barry, Brian (1996) 'Political Theory Old and New', in Robert Goodin and Hans-Dieter Klingemann, *A New Handbook of Political Science*, Oxford: Oxford University Press.

Bastenier, Albert (1994) 'Immigration and the Ethnic Differentiation of Social Relations in Europe', in John Rex and Beatrice Drury (eds) *Ethnic Mobilisation in a Multicultural Europe*, Aldershot: Avebury.

Bhabha, Jacqueline and Sue Shutter (1994) *Women's Movement: Women under Immigration, Nationality, and Refugee Law*, Staffordshire: Trentham Books.

Bigo, Didier (2001) 'Migration and Security', in Virginie Guiraudon and Christian Joppke (eds) *Controlling a New Migration World*, London: Routledge.

Bleich, Erik (2001) *Continuity as the Path to Change: Institutional Innovation in the 1976 British Race Relations Act*, paper presented to the annual meeting of the American Political Science Association, San Francisco, August 30-September 2, 2001.

Böcker, Anita and Tetty Havinga (1998) *Asylum and Migration in the European Union Patterns of Origin and Destination*, Luxembourg: OOPEC.

Bommes, Michael (2000) 'National Welfare State, Biography and Migration: Labour Migrants, Ethnic Germans and the Re-ascription of Welfare State Membership' in Michael Bommes and Andrew Geddes (eds) (2000) *Immigration and Welfare: Challenging the Borders of the Welfare State*, London: Routledge.

Bommes, Michael and Andrew Geddes (eds) (2000) *Immigration and Welfare: Challenging the Borders of the Welfare State*, London: Routledge.

Boswell, Christina (1999) 'The Conflict Between Refugee Rights and National Interests: Background and Policy Strategies', *Refugee Survey Quarterly*, vol. 18, no. 2.

Boswell, Christina (2000) 'European Values and the Asylum Crisis', *International Affairs*, vol. 76, no. 3.

Brochmann, Grete and Tomas Hammar (eds) (1999) *Mechanisms of Immigration Control: A Comparative Analysis of European Regulatory Policies*, Oxford: Berg.

Brubaker, W. Rogers (ed.) (1989) *Immigration and the Politics of Citizenship in Europe and North America*, Lanham (MD): University Press of America.

Brubaker, W. Rogers (1992) *Citizenship and Nationhood in France and Germany*, Cambridge (MA): Harvard University Press.

Brubaker, W. Rogers (1994) 'Commentary: Are Immigration Control Efforts Really Failing?', in Wayne Cornelius, Philip Martin and James Hollifield (eds) *Controlling Immigration: A Global Perspective*, Stanford: Stanford University Press.

Brubaker, W. Rogers (2001) 'The Return of Assimilation: Changing Perspectives on Immigration and its Sequels in France, Germany and the United States, *Ethnic and Racial Studies*, vol. 24, no. 4.

Caporaso, James (1996) 'The European Union and Forms of State: Westphalian, Regulatory or Post-Modern?', *Journal of Common Market Studies*, vol. 34, no. 1.

Caritas Roma (2001) *Dossier Statistico sull' Immigrazione*, Rome: Caritas.

Castells, Manuel and Alejandro Portes (1989) 'World Underneath: The Origin, Effects and Dynamics of the Informal Economy', in Alejandro Portes, Manuel Castells and Lauren Benton (eds) *The Informal Economy: Studies in Advanced and Less Developed Economies*, Baltimore (MD): Johns Hopkins University Press.

Castles, Stephen and Godula Kosack (1973) *Immigrant Workers and Class Structure in Western Europe*, Oxford: Oxford University Press.

Castles, Stephen and Mark Miller (1998) *The Age of Migration*, 2nd edition, London: Macmillan.

CEC (1999) *Action Plan of the Council and the Commission on Implementing the Provisions of the Treaty of Amsterdam on an Area of Freedom, Security and Justice*, Official Journal 1999 C 19/1, Brussels: OOPEC.

CEC (2000a) *Communication from the Commission to the Council and the European Parliament: Towards a Common Asylum Procedure and a Uniform Status, Valid Throughout the Union, for Persons Granted Asylum*, COM(2000) 755 final.

CEC (2001a) *Communication from the Commission to the Council and the European Parliament on an Open Method of Co-ordination for the Community Immigration Policy*, COM (2001) 387 final.

CEC (2000b) *Communication from the Commission to the Council and the European Parliament on a Community Immigration Policy*, COMM (2000) 757 final.

CEC (2001c) *Making a Success of Enlargement. Strategy Paper and Report of the European Commission on the Progress Towards Accession by each of the Candidate Countries*, Brussels: OOPEC.

Centraal Buro voor de Statistiek (1998) *Statistical Yearbook 1998*, Voorburg: The Netherlands.

Chopin, Isabelle and Jan Niessen, Jan (2001) *The Starting Line and the Incorporation of the Racial Equality Directive into the National Laws of the EU Member States and Accession States*, Brussels/London: Migration Policy Group/Commission for Racial Equality.

Codagnone, Cristiano (1999) 'The New Migration in Russia in the 1990s' in Khalid Koser and Helma Lutz (eds) *The New Migration in Europe: Social Constructions and Social Realities*, London: Macmillan.

Collinson, Sarah (2000) 'Migration and Security in the Mediterranean: A Complex Relationship', in Russell King, Gabriella Lazaridis and Charalambos Tsardanidis (eds) *Eldorado or Fortress? Migration in Southern Europe*, London: Macmillan.

Commission of the European Communities (CEC) (1985) *Guidelines for a Community Policy on Migration*, COM(85) 48 final.

Commission Nationale Consultative des Droits de l'Homme (2001) *Le Racisme e la Xénophobie*, Paris: CNCDH.

Cornelius, Wayne (1994) 'Spain: The Uneasy Transition from Labor Exporter to Labor Importer', in Wayne Cornelius, Philip Martin and James Hollifield (eds) *Controlling Immigration: A Global Perspective*, Stanford (CA): Stanford University Press.

Cornelius, Wayne, Philip Martin and James Hollifield (1994) 'Introduction: The Ambivalent Quest for Immigration Control', in Wayne Cornelius, Philip Martin and James Hollifield (eds) *Controlling Immigration: A Global Perspective*, Stanford (CA.): Stanford University Press.

Corriere della Sera (2002) 'Regolarizzare tutti gli immigrati che già lavorano', January 20.

Crossman, Richard (1977) *The Diaries of a Cabinet Minister*, London: Hamilton.

Crowley, John (1993) 'Paradoxes in the Politicisation of Race: A Comparison of Britain and France, *New Community*, vol. 19, no. 4.

Crowley, John (1999) 'The Politics of Belonging: Some Theoretical Considerations', in Andrew Geddes and Adrian Favell (eds) *The Politics of Belonging: Migrants and Minorities in Contemporary Europe*, Aldershot: Ashgate.

Danese, Gaia (1998) 'Transnational Collective Action in Europe: The Case of Migrants in Italy and Spain', *Journal of Ethnic and Migration Studies*, vol. 24, no. 4.

Deakin, Nicholas (1964) *Colour and the British Electorate, 1964: Six Case Studies*, London: Pall Mall Press.

Deets, Stephen (2001) *Europe and the Politics of Minority Rights*, Woodrow Wilson Centre for International Studies, Meeting Report no. 221.

Dobson, Janet, Khalid Koser, Gail McLaughlan and John Salt (2001) *International Migration and the United Kingdom: Recent Patterns and Trends*, Home Office Research, Development and Statistics Directorate, Home Office: London.

Edelman, Murray (1988) *Constructing the Political Spectacle*, Chicago: University of Chicago Press.

Ehlermann, Hans-Dieter (1998) *Differentiation, Flexibility, Closer Co-operation: The New Provisions of the Amsterdam Treaty*, Robert Schuman Centre Working Paper, European University Institute, Florence.

Eichenhofer, Eberhard (ed.) (1997) *Social Security of Migrants in the European Union of Tomorrow*, Osnabrück: Universitätsverslag.

Elman, Amy (2000) 'The Limits of Citizenship: Migration, Sex Discrimination and Same-Sex Partners in EU Law', vol. 38, no. 5.

Entzinger, Han (2001) *The Rise and Fall of Multiculturalism: The Case of the Netherlands*, Manuscript.

Esping Andersen, Gosta (1990) *The Three Worlds of Welfare Capitalism*, Princeton (NJ): Princeton University Press.

Esser, Hartmut and Hermann Korte (1985) 'The Policy of the Federal Republic of Germany' in Tomas Hammar (ed.) *European Immigration Policy: A Comparative Analysis*, Cambridge: Cambridge University Press.

European Council Consultative Committee on Racism and Xenophobia (1995) *Final Report*, Ref. 6906/1/95 Rev 1 Limite RAXEN, Brussels: General Secretariat of the Council of the European Union.

European Parliament (1991) *Report of the Committee of Enquiry on Racism and Xenophobia*, Brussels: OOPEC.

European Parliament (1998) *EU Anti-Discrimination Policy: From Equal Opportunities Between Men and Women to Combating Racism*: Brussels: European Parliament Directorate General for Research Working Document, Public Liberties Series, LIBE 102.

European Roma Rights Center (ERRC) (1997) *Time of the Skinheads: Denial and Exclusion of Roma in Slovakia*, Brussels; ERRC.

ERRC (1999) *A Special Remedy: Roma and Schools for the Mentally Handicapped in the Czech Republic*, Brussels: ERRC.

ERRC (2001) *State of Impunity: Human Rights Abuse of Roma in Romania*, Brussels: ERRC.

European Union Migrants' Forum (1996) *Proposals for a Revision of the Treaty on European Union at the Intergovernmental Conference of 1996*, Brussels: European Union Migrants Forum.

(EUMC) European Union Monitoring Centre on Racism and Xenophobia (2001) *Attitudes Towards Minority Groups in the European Union*, Vienna: European Union Monitoring Centre on Racism and Xenophobia.

Evans, Peter, Dietrich Rueschmeyer and Theda Skocpol (1985) *Bringing the State Back In*, Cambridge: Cambridge University Press.

Everson, Michelle (1995) 'The Legacy of the Market Citizen' in Jo Shaw and Gillian More (eds) *The New Legal Dynamics of the European Union*, Oxford: Clarendon Press.

Faist, Thomas (1994) 'How to Define a Foreigner: The Symbolic Politics of Immigration in German Partisan Discourse', *West European Politics*, vol. 17, no. 2.

Faist, Thomas (2000) *The Volume and Dynamics of International Migration and Transnational Social Spaces*, Oxford: Oxford University Press.

Fakiolas, Rossetos (2000) Migration and Unregistered Labour in the Greek Economy', in Russell King, Gabriella Lazaridis and Charalambos Tsardanidis (eds) *Eldorado or Fortress? Migration in Southern Europe*, London: Macmillan.

Fallaci, Oriana (2001) *La Rabbia e l'Orgoglio*, Milan: Rizzoli.

Favell, Adrian (1998a) 'Multicultural Race Relations in Britain: Problems of Interpretation and Explanation', in Christian Joppke (ed.) *Immigration and the Nation State: Immigration in Western Europe and the United States*, Oxford: Oxford University Press.

Favell, Adrian (1998b) *Philosophies of Integration: Immigration and the Idea of Citizenship in Britain and France*, London: Macmillan.

Favell, Adrian (2001) 'Integration Policy and Integration Research in Europe: A Review and Critique', in T. Alexander Aleinikoff and Douglas Kluesmeyer, *Citizenship Today: Global Perspectives and Practices*, Washington: Carnegie Endowment for International Peace.

Favell, Adrian and Andrew Geddes (2000) 'Immigration and European Integration: New Opportunities for Transnational Political Mobilisation?' in Ruud Koopmans and Paul Statham (eds) *Challenging Immigration and Ethnic Relations Politics: Comparative European Perspectives*, Oxford: Oxford University Press.

Feldblum, Miriam (1993) 'Paradoxes of Ethnic Politics: The Case of Franco-Maghrebis in France', *Ethnic and Racial Studies*, vol. 16, no. 1.

Feldblum, Miriam (1994) 'Reconsidering the "Republican Model"', in Wayne Cornelius, Philip Martin and James Hollifield (eds) *Controlling Immigration: A Global Perspective*, Stanford: Stanford University Press.

Feldblum, Miriam (1999) *Reconstructing Citizenship: The Politics of Nationality and Immigration Reform in Contemporary France*, Albany (NY): State University of New York Press.

Ferrera, Maurizio (1996) 'The Southern Model of Welfare in Social Europe', *Journal of European Social Policy*, vol. 6, no. 1.

Fijalkowski, Jurgen (1995) 'Aggressive Nationalism, Immigration Pressure and Asylum Policy', *International Migration Review*, vol. 27, no. 4.

Financial Times (2002) 'Stoiber Makes Immigration an Election Issue', 25 May.

Fischer, Peter and Thomas Straubhaar (1996) *Migration and Economic Integration in the Nordic Common Labour Market*, Copenhagen: Nordic Council of Ministers.

Fonseca, Isabel (1995) *Bury Me Standing. The Gypsies and Their Journey*, London: Chatto and Windus.

Freeman, Gary (1994) 'Britain: The Deviant Case', in Wayne Cornelius, Philip Martin and James Hollifield, *Controlling Immigration: A Global Perspective*, Stanford: Stanford University Press.

Freeman, Gary (1995) 'Modes of Immigration Politics in Liberal States', *International Migration Review*, vol. 29, no. 3.

Freeman, Gary (1998) 'The Decline of Sovereignty? Politics and Immigration Restriction in Liberal States', in Christian Joppke (ed.) *Challenge to the Nation State: Immigration in Western Europe and the United States*, Oxford: Oxford University Press.

Gallisot, R. (1989) 'Nationalité et Citoyenetté, *APRES-DEMAIN*, no. 286.

Garbaye, Romain (2000) 'Ethnic Minorities, Cities, and Institutions: A Comparison of the Modes of Management of Ethnic Diversity of a French and British City', in Ruud Koopmans and Paul Statham (eds) *Challenging Immigration and Ethnic Relations Politics: Comparative European Perspectives*, Oxford: Oxford University Press.

Garrett, Geoffrey and George Tsebelis (2001) 'The Institutional Foundations of Intergovernmentalism and Supranationalism in the European Union', *International Organisation*, vol. 55, no. 2.

Gaspard, Françoise (1995) *A Small City in France*, Cambridge (MA): Cambridge University Press.

Geddes, Andrew (2000a) *Immigration and European Integration: Towards Fortress Europe?*, Manchester: Manchester University Press.

Geddes, Andrew (2000b) 'Lobbying for Migrant Inclusion in the European Union: New Opportunities for Transnational Advocacy, *Journal of European Public Policy*, vol. 7, no. 4.

Geddes, Andrew (2001a) 'Denying Access: Asylum Seekers and Welfare State Benefits in the UK', in Michael Bommes and Andrew Geddes (eds) *Immigration and Welfare: Challenging the Borders of the Welfare State*, London: Routledge.

Geddes, Andrew (2001b) 'Explaining Ethnic Minority Representation: Contemporary Trends in the Shadow of the Past', in Jon Tonge, David Denver, Lisa Harrison and Lynne Bennie (eds) *The British Elections and Parties Review, Volume 11*, London: Frank Cass.

Geddes, Andrew and Adrian Favell (1999) *The Politics of Belonging: Migrants and Minorities in Contemporary Europe*, Aldershot: Ashgate.

Geddes, Andrew and Virginie Guiraudon (2002) 'The Anti-Discrimination Policy Paradigm in France and the UK: Europeanization and Alternative Explanations for Policy Change', Paper Presented to the Joint Session of Workshops of the European Consortium for Political Research, Turin, Italy, March 2002.

Geddes, Andrew and Paul Statham (2002) *'Explaining British Asylum Politics: A Resilient Nation State at the Border of Schengenland'*, Paper Presented to the 43rd Convention of the International Studies Association, New Orleans, USA, March 2002.

Gillespie, Richard (1996) 'Spain and the Mediterranean: Southern Sensitivity, European Aspirations', *Mediterranean Politics*, vol. 1, no. 2.

Ginsborg, Paul (1990) *A History of Contemporary Italy: Society and Politics 1943–1988*, London: Penguin.

Goodwin-Gill, Guy (1996) *The Refugee in International Law*, Oxford: Clarendon Press.

Grabbe, Heather (2001) 'How Does Europeanisation Affect CEE Governance? Conditionality, Diffusion and Diversity', *Journal of European Public Policy*, vol. 8, no. 4.

Grabbe, Heather (2002a) 'Stabilizing The East While Keeping The Easterners Out: Internal and External Security Logics in Conflict', in Sandra Lavenex and Emek Uçarer, (eds) *Migration and the Externalities of European Integration*, Lanham (MD): Lexington.

Grabbe, Heather (2002b) 'Europeanization Goes East', in Kevin Featherstone and Claudio Radaelli (eds) (2002), *The Politics of Europeanisation*, Oxford: Oxford University Press.

Green Cowles, Maria, James Caporaso and Thomas Risse (eds) (2000) *Transforming Europe: Europeanization and Domestic Change*. Ithaca, NY: Cornell University Press.

Guild, Elspeth (1996) *The Developing Immigration and Asylum Policies of the European Union: Adopted Conventions, Resolutions, Recommendations and Conclusions*, The Hague: Kluwer Law International.

Guild, Elspeth (1998) 'Competence, Discretion and Third Country Nationals: The European Union's Legal Struggle with Migration', *Journal of Ethnic and Migration Studies*, vol. 24, no. 4.

Guild, Elspeth (2001) *Moving the Borders of Europe*, Inaugural lecture, University of Nijmegen, 30 May.

Guiraudon, Virginie (1998) *International Human Rights Norms and their Incorporation: The Protection of Aliens in Europe*, European Forum Working Paper EUF 98/04, Florence: European University Institute.

Guiraudon, Virginie (2000a) *Les Politiques d'Immigration en Europe: Allemagne, France, Pays-Bas*, Paris, L'Harmattan.

Guiraudon, Virginie (2000b) 'The Marshallian Triptych Re-ordered: The Role of Courts and Bureaucracies in Furthering Migrants' Rights', in Michael Bommes and Andrew Geddes (eds) *Immigration and Welfare: Challenging the Borders of the Welfare State*, London: Routledge.

Guiraudon, Virginie and Gallya Lahav (2000) 'A Reappraisal of the State Sovereignty Debate. The Case of Migration Control' *Comparative Political Studies*, vol. 33, no. 2.

Guttmann, Amy (ed.) (1994) *Multiculturalism: Examining the Politics of Recognition*, Princeton: Princeton University Press.

Hailbronner, Kay (1998) 'European Immigration and Asylum Law under the Amsterdam Treaty', *Common Market Law Review*, vol. 35, no. 5.

Halfmann, Jost (2000) 'Welfare State and Territory' in Michael Bommes and Andrew Geddes (eds) *Immigration and Welfare: Challenging the Borders of the Welfare State*, London: Routledge.

Hammar, Tomas (1985) *European Immigration Policy: A Comparative Study*, Cambridge: Cambridge University Press.

Hammar, Tomas (1990) *Democracy and the Nation State: Aliens, Denizens and Citizens in a World of International Migration*, Aldershot: Avebury.

Hammar, Tomas (1999) 'Closing the Doors to the Swedish Welfare State', in Brochmann, Grete and Tomas Hammar *Mechanisms of Immigration Control: A Comparative Analysis of European Regulatory Policies*, Oxford: Berg.

Hammar, Tomas, Grete Brochmann, Kristof Tamas and Tomas Faist (1997) *International Migration, Immobility and Development*, Oxford: Berg.

Handoll, Andrew (1995) *Free Movement of Persons in the EU*, Chichester: Wiley.

Hansen, Randall (2000) *Immigration and Citizenship in Post-War Britain*, Oxford: Oxford University Press.

Hargreaves, Alec (1995) *Immigration, 'Race' and Ethnicity in Contemporary France*, London: Routledge.

Haut Conseil à l'Intégration (1991) *Pour un Modèle Français d'Intégration: Premier Rapport Annuel*, Paris: La Documentation Français.

Henderson, Karen (1999) *Back to Europe: Central and Eastern Europe and the European Union*, London: UCL Press.

Héritier, Adrienne (1997) 'Policy-making by Subterfuge: Interest Accommodation, Innovation and Substitute Democratic Legitimation in Europe: Perspectives from Distinctive Policy Areas, *Journal of European Public Policy*, vol. 4, no. 2.

Hix, Simon (1998) *The Political System of the European Union*, London: Macmillan.

Hix, Simon and Jan Niessen (1996) *Reconsidering European Migration Policies: The 1996 Intergovernmental Conference and Reform of the Maastricht Treaty*, Brussels: Churches Commission for Migrants in Europe.

Hockenos, Paul (1993) *Free to Hate: The Rise of the Right in Post-Communist Eastern Europe*, London: Routledge.

Hoffmann, Stanley (1966) 'Obstinate or Obsolete? The Fate of the Nation State and the Case of Western Europe' *Daedalus*, vol. 95.

Hofstadter, Richard (1955) *Social Darwinism in American Thought*, Boston: Beacon Press.

Hollifield, James (1992) *Immigrants, Markets and States: The Political Economy of Post-War Europe*, Cambridge (MA): Harvard University Press.

Hollifield, James (1994) 'Immigration and Republicanism in France: Searching for the Hidden Consensus', in Wayne Cornelius, Philip Martin and James Hollifield (eds) *Controlling Immigration: A Global Perspective*, Stanford (CA): Stanford University Press.

Hollifield, James (1999) 'Ideas, Institutions and Civil Society: On the Limits of Immigration Control in France' in Grete Brochmann and Tomas Hammar (eds) *Mechanisms of Immigration Control: A Comparative Analysis of European Regulation Policies*, Oxford: Berg.

Hollifield, James (2000a) 'The Politics of International Migration: How Can We Bring the State Back In?', in Caroline Brettel and James Hollifield (eds) *Migration Theory: Talking Across Disciplines*, London: Routledge.

Hollifield, James (2000b) 'Immigration and the Politics of Rights: The French Case in Comparative Perspective', in Michael Bommes and Andrew Geddes (eds) *Immigration and Welfare: Challenging the Borders of the Welfare State*, London: Routledge.

Home Office (2001) *Community Cohesion: A Report of the Independent Review Team*, London: Home Office.

Home Office (2002) *Secure Borders, Safe Haven, Integration with Diversity in Modern Britain*, London: HMSO.

Human Rights Watch (1991) *Destroying Ethnic Identity: The Gypsies of Bulgaria*, New York: Human Rights Watch.

Hunger, Uwe (2000) 'Temporary Transnational Labour Migration in an Integrating Europe and the Challenge to the German Welfare State' in Michael Bommes and Andrew Geddes (eds) *Immigration and Welfare: Challenging the Borders of the Welfare State*, London: Routledge.

Huysmans, Jef (2000) 'The European Union and the Securitization of Migration', *Journal of Common Market Studies*, vol. 38, no. 5.

Iglicka, Krystyna (2001) *Poland's Post-War Dynamic of Migration*, Aldershot: Ashgate.

Iglicka, Krystyna and Keith Sword (1999) *The Challenge of East-West Migration for Poland*, New York: St Martins Press.

Ignatieff, Michael (1998) *The Warriors Honour: Ethnic War and the Modern Conscience*, London: Vintage.

International Organisation for Migration (2000) *World Migration Report*, IOM: Geneva.

Iosifides, Theodoros and Russell King (1998) 'Social Spatial Dynamics and the Exclusion of Three Immigrant Groups in the Athens Conurbation', *South European Society and Politics*, vol. 3, no. 3.

Ireland, Patrick (1994) *The Policy Challenge of Ethnic Diversity: Immigrant Politics in France and Switzerland*, Cambridge (MA): Harvard University Press.

Ireland, Patrick (1995) 'Migration, Free Movement and Immigrant Integration in the EU: A Bifurcated Policy Response', in Stefan Liebfried and Paul Pierson (eds) *European Social Policy: Between Integration and Fragmentation*, Washington DC: Brookings Institution.

Ireland, Patrick (1997) 'Socialism, Unification Policy, and the Rise of Racism in Eastern Germany', *International Migration Review*, vol. 31, no. 3.

Jahn, Andreas and Thomas Straubhaar (1999) 'A Survey of the Economics of Illegal Immigration', *South European Society and Politics*, vol. 3, no. 3.

Jileva, Elena (2002) 'Insiders and Outsiders in Central and Eastern Europe: The Case of Bulgaria', in Sandra Lavenex and Emek Uçarer (eds) *Migration and the Externalities of European Integration*, Lanham (MD): Lexington.

Joly, Danielle (1997) *Refugees in Europe: The Hostile New Agenda,* London: Minority Rights Group.

Joppke, Christian (1997) 'Asylum and State Sovereignty: A Comparison of the United States, Germany and Britain', *Comparative Political Studies,* vol. 30, no. 3.

Joppke, Christian (1998) 'Why Liberal States Accept Unwanted Immigration', *World Politics,* vol. 50, no. 2.

Joppke, Christian (1999) *Immigration and the Nation State: The United States, Germany and Great Britain,* Oxford: Oxford University Press.

Joppke, Christian (2001) 'The Legal-Domestic Sources of Immigrant Rights', *Comparative Political Studies,* vol. 34, no. 4.

Kaye, Ronald (1999) 'Redefining the Refugee: The UK Media Portrayal of Asylum-Seekers' in Khalid Koser and Helma Lutz, *The New Migration in Europe: Social Constructions and Social Realities,* London: Macmillan.

Keck, Margaret and Sikkink, Kathryn (1998) *Activists Beyond Borders: Advocacy Networks in International Politics,* Ithaca NY: Cornell University Press.

Kepel, Gilles (1987) *Les Banlieues de l'Islam,* Paris: Seuil.

King, Russell (2000) 'Southern Europe in the Changing Global Map of Migration, in Russell King, Gabriella Lazaridis and Charalambos Tsardanidis (eds) *Eldorado or Fortress? Migration in Southern Europe,* London: Macmillan.

King, Russell, Theodoros Iosifides and Lenio Myrivili (1998) 'A Migrant's Story: from Albania to Athens', *Journal of Ethnic and Migration Studies,* vol. 24, no. 1.

Kivisto, Peter (2001) 'Theorizing transnational migration: a critical review of current efforts', *Ethnic and Racial Studies,* vol. 24, no. 4.

Kofman, Eleonore (1999) 'Female Birds of Passage a Decade Later', *International Migration Review,* vol. 33, no. 2.

Koslowski, Rey (1998) 'European Migration Regimes: Established and Emergent', in Christian Joppke (ed.) *Challenge to the Nation State: Immigration in Western Europe and the United States,* Oxford: Oxford University Press.

Kymlicka, Will (1995) *Multicultural Citizenship: A Liberal Theory of Minority Rights,* Oxford: Oxford University Press.

Lavenex, Sandra (1999) *Safe Third Countries: Extending the EU Asylum and Immigration Policies to Central and Eastern Europe,* Budapest: Central European University Press.

Lavenex, Sandra (2001) 'Migration and the EU's New Eastern Border: Between Realism and Liberalism', *Journal of European Public Policy,* vol. 8, no. 1.

Lavenex, Sandra and Emek Uçarer (2002) *Migration and the Externalities of European Integration,* Lanham (MD): Lexington.

Layton-Henry, Zig (1992) *The Politics of Immigration,* Oxford: Blackwell.

Layton-Henry, Zig (1994) 'Britain: The Would-Be Zero Immigration Country', in Wayne Cornelius, Philip Martin and James Hollifield (eds) *Controlling Immigration: A Global Perspective,* Stanford (CA): Stanford University Press.

Lazaridis, Gabriella (1996) 'Immigration to Greece: A Critical Evaluation of Greek Policy', *Journal of Ethnic and Migration Studies,* vol. 22, no. 6.

Levy, Daniel (1999) 'Coming Home? Ethnic Germans and the Transformation of National Identity in the Federal Republic of Germany', in Andrew Geddes and Adrian Favell (eds) *The Politics of Belonging: Migrants and Minorities in Contemporary Europe,* Aldershot: Ashgate.

Lijphart, Arend (1975) *The Politics of Accommodation: Pluralism and Democracy in the Netherlands,* Berkeley: University of California Press.

Lindbom, Anders (2001) 'Dismantling the Social Democratic Welfare Model? Has the Swedish Welfare State Lost its Defining Characteristics?', *Scandinavian Political Studies*, vol. 24, no. 3.

Linos, Katerina (2002) 'Understanding Greek Immigration Policy' in Dimitris Keridis (ed.) *New Approaches to Balkan Studies*, Dulles (VA): Brasseys.

Linz, Juan and Alfred Stepan (1996) *Problems of Democratic Transition and Consolidation: Southern Europe, South America and Post-Communist Eastern Europe*, Baltimore: Johns Hopkins University Press.

Lochak, Danielle (1989) 'Les Minorités et le Droit Publique Français: Du Refus des Différences à la Gestion des Différences', in A. Fenet and G. Soulier (eds) *Les Minorités et leurs Droits Depuis 1789*, Paris: L'Harmattan.

Long, Marceau (1988) *Etre Français Aujourd'Hui et Demain: Rapport de la Commission de la Nationalité*, Volumes 1 & 2, Paris: La Documentation Français.

Mann, Michael (1995) 'A Political Theory of Nationalism and its Excesses', in Sukuma Periwal (ed.) *Notions of Nationalism*, Budapest: Central European University Press.

Mann, Michael (1999) 'The Dark Side of Democracy: The Modern Tradition of Ethnic and Political Cleansing', *New Left Review*, 235.

Marshall, Barbara (2000) *The New Germany and Migration in Europe*, Manchester: Manchester University Press.

Marshall, T.H. (1964) *Class, Citizenship and Social Development*, New York: Doubleday.

Martiniez Viega, Ubaldo (1999) 'Immigrants in the Spanish Labour Market', *South European Society and Politics*, vol. 3, no. 3.

Mattli, Walter and Anne-Marie Slaughter (1998) 'Revisiting the European Court of Justice', *International Organisation*, vol. 52, no. 1.

Messina, Anthony (1996) 'The Not So Silent Revolution: Post War Migration to Western Europe', *World Politics*, vol. 49, no. 1.

Migration News, various issues, Davis (CA): University of California. http://migration.ucdavis.edu

Miller, Mark (1981) *Foreign Workers in Europe: An Emerging Political Force*. New York: Praeger.

Mingione, Enzo and Fabio Quassoli (2000) 'The Participation of Immigrants in the Underground Economy in Italy', in Russell King, Gabriella Lazaridis and Charalambos Tsardanidis (eds) *Eldorado or Fortress? Migration in Southern Europe*, London: Macmillan.

Moch, Leslie Page (1992) *Moving Europeans: Migration in Western Europe Since 1650*, Bloomington: Indiana University Press.

Modood, Tariq and Richard Berthoud (1997) *Ethnic Minorities in Britain: Diversity and Disadvantage*, London: Policy Studies Institute.

Monar, Jorg (1994) 'The Evolving Role of Union Institutions in the Framework of the Third Pillar', in Jorg Monar and Roger Morgan (eds) *The Third Pillar of the European Union*, Brussels: Interuniversity Press.

Monar, Jorg (2001) 'The Dynamics of Justice and Home Affairs: Laboratories, Driving Factors and Costs', *Journal of Common Market Studies*, vol. 39, no. 4.

Morawska, Ewa (2001) 'Gappy Immigration Controls, Resourceful Migrants and Pendel Communities: East-West European Travellers', in Virginie Guiraudon and Christian Joppke (eds) *Controlling a New Migration World*, London: Routledge.

Moravcsik, Andrew (1999) 'A New Statecraft? Supranational Entrepreneurs and International Co-operation', *International Organisation*, vol. 53, no. 2.

Moroksavic, Mirjana (1984) 'Birds of Passage are Also Women', *International Migration Review*, vol. 18, no. 4.

Müller-Graf, P-C (1994) 'The Legal Basis of the Third Pillar and its Position in the Union Treaty' in Jorg Monar and Roger Morgan (eds) *The Third Pillar of the European Union*, Brussels: Interuniversity Press.

Noiriel, Gerard (1996) *The French Melting Pot: Immigration, Citizenship and National Identity*, Minneapolis: University of Minnesota Press.

O'Leary, Siofra (1996) *The Evolving Concept of Community Citizenship: From Free Movement of Persons to Union Citizenship*, The Hague: Kluwer Law International.

Organisation for Economic Co-operation and Development (OECD) (2001) *Trends in International Migration: The 2001 SOPEMI Report*, Paris: OECD.

Parekh, Bhikhu (1999) *The Future of Multi-Ethnic Britain: The Parekh Report*, London: Profile Books.

Parekh, Bhikhu (2000) *Rethinking Multiculturalism*, London: Palgrave.

Pastore, Ferruccio (2001a) *Reconciling the Prince's Two Arms. Internal and External Security Policy Co-ordination in the European Union*, Paris: Western European Union, Occasional Paper 30.

Pastore, Ferruccio (2001b) 'La Politica Migratoria', in Mario Caciagli and Alan Zuckerman (eds) *Politica in Italia 2001*, Bologna: Il Mulino.

Paul, Kathleen (1997) *Whitewashing Britain: Race and Citizenship in the Post-War Era*, Ithaca (NY): Cornell University Press.

Peers, Steve (1998) 'Building Fortress Europe: The Development of EU Migration Law', *Common Market Law Review*, vol. 35, no. 6.

Phizacklea, Annie (ed.) (1983) *One Way Ticket: Migration and Female Labour*, London: Routledge.

Pilkington, Edward (1988) *Beyond the Mother Country: West Indians and the Notting Hill White Riots*, London: Tauris.

Piore, Michael (1979) *Birds of Passage: Migrant Labour and Industrial Societies*, Cambridge: Cambridge University Press.

Political and Economic Planning (PEP) (1967) *Racial Discrimination*, London: PEP.

Pollack, Mark (1999) 'Delegation, Agency and Agenda-setting in the Treaty of Amsterdam', *European Integration On-Line Papers*, @http://eiop.or.at/eiop/texte/1999-006a.htm

Portes, Alejandro (1995) 'Economic Sociology and the Sociology of Immigration: A Conceptual Overview', in A. Portes (ed.) *The Economic Sociology of Immigration: Essays on Networks, Ethnicity and entrepreneurship'*, New York: Russell Sage Foundation.

Pugliese, Enrico (1998) *Gli Immigrati in Italia*, 5th edition, Rome: Laterza.

Quassoli, Fabio (2002) *Migrant as Criminal: The Judicial Treatment of Migrants' Criminality*, in Virginie Guiraudon and Christian Joppke (eds) *Controlling a New Migration World*, London: Routledge.

Radtke, Frank-Olaf (1994) 'The Formation of Ethnic Minorities and the Transformation of Social into Ethnic Conflict in a So-called Multicultural Society; The Case of Germany', in John Rex and Beatrice Drury (eds) *Ethnic Mobilisation in a Multicultural Europe*, Aldershot: Avebury.

Rath, Jan (1992) 'The Ideological Representation of Migrant Workers in Europe: A Case of Racialisation?', in John Wrench and John Solomos (eds) *Racism and Migration in Western Europe*, Oxford: Berg.

Rath, Jan (1999) 'The Netherlands. A Dutch Treat for Anti-Social Families and Immigrant Ethnic Minorities', in Mike Cole and Gareth Dale (eds), *The European Union and Migrant Labour*, Oxford: Berg.

Renan, Ernest (1882) *Qu'est ce qu'une Nation*, reprinted in *Qu'est ce qu'une Nation?*, Paris: Presses Pocket (1992).

Reyneri, Emilio (1998) 'The Role of the Underground Economy in Irregular Migration to Italy: Cause or Effect?', *Journal of Ethnic and Migration Studies*, vol. 24, no. 2.

Reyneri, Emilio (2001) *Migrants' Involvement in Irregular Employment in the Mediterranean Countries of the European Union*, Geneva: International Labour Organisation Working Papers.

Rich, Paul (1986) 'Conservative Ideology and Race in Modern British Politics', in Zig Layton-Henry and Paul Rich (eds) *Race, Government and Politics in Britain*, London: Macmillan.

Richard, Gillespie (2002) 'Lidiando con la ambición: La política exterior y de seguridad de España al inicio del nuevo milenio', *Anuario Internacional CIDOB 2001*, Barcelona: Centre d'Informació i Documentació a Barcelona.

Rogers, Rosemarie (1985) *Guests Come to Stay: The Effects of Labour Migration on Sending and Receiving Countries*, Boulder (CO): Westview.

Rothstein, Bo (1998) *Just Institutions Matter*, Cambridge: Cambridge University Press.

Rudolph, Hedwig (1996) 'The New *Gastarbeiter* System in Germany', *New Community*, vol. 22, no. 2.

Ruggie, John (1983) 'International Regimes, Transactions and Change: Embedded Liberalism in the Post-War Economic Order', in Steven Krasner (ed.) *International Regimes*, Ithaca (NY): Cornell University Press.

Safran, William (1985) 'The Mitterrand Regime and its Policies of Ethno-Cultural Accommodation', *Comparative Political Studies*, vol. 18, no. 1.

Saggar, Shamit (1992) *Race and Politics in Britain*, London: Harvester Wheatsheaf.

Saggar, Shamit (2000) *Race and Representation: Electoral Politics and Ethnic Pluralism in Britain*, Manchester: Manchester University Press.

Sandholtz, Wayne and Alec Stone Sweet (1998) *European Integration and Supranational Governance*, Oxford: Oxford University Press.

Saraceno, Chiara (1994) 'The Ambivalent Familism of the Italian Welfare State', *Social Politics*, vol. 1, no. 1.

Sassen, Saskia (1996) *Losing Control? Sovereignty in an Age of Globalisation*, New York: Columbia University Press.

Sassen, Saskia (1998) 'The *de facto* Transnationalizing of Immigration Policy', in Christian Joppke (ed.) *Challenge to the Nation State: Immigration in Western Europe and the United States*, Oxford: Oxford University Press.

Sassen, Saskia (1999) *Guests and Aliens*, New York: The New Press.

Schain, Martin (1999) 'Minorities and Immigrant Incorporation in France: The State and The Dynamics of Multiculturalism', in Christian Joppke and Steven Lukes (eds) *Multicultural Questions*, Oxford: Oxford University Press.

Scharpf, Fritz (2000) *Notes Towards a Theory of Multi-level Governing in Europe*. MPIfG Discussion Paper 00/5, Cologne: Max Planck Institut für Gesellschaftsforschung.

Schmitter, Philippe (1996) 'Examining the Present Euro-polity with the Help of Past Theories' in Gary Marks, Fritz Scharpf, Philippe Schmitter and Wolfgang Streeck (eds) *Governance in the European Union*, London: Sage.

Schmitter-Heisler, Barbara (1986) 'Immigrant Settlement and the Structure of Emergent Immigrant Communities in Western Europe', *The Annals of the American Academy of Political and Social Sciences*, vol. 485.

Schnapper, Dominique (1991) *La France de l'Intégration*, Paris: Gallimard.

Sciortino, Giuseppe (1999) 'Planning in the Dark: The Evolution of Italian Immigration Control', in Grete Brochmann and Tomas Hammar (eds), *Mechanisms of Immigration Control: A Comparative Analysis of European Regulation Policies*, Oxford: Berg.

Sciortino, Giuseppe (2000) 'Towards a Political Sociology of Entry Policies: Conceptual Problems and Theoretical Proposals', *Journal of Ethnic and Migration Studies*, vol. 26, no. 2.

Silverman, Max (1992) *Deconstructing the Nation: Immigration, Racism and Citizenship in Modern France*, London: Routledge.

Soininen, Maritta (1999) 'The "Swedish Model" as an Institutional Framework for Immigrant Membership Rights', *Journal of Ethnic and Migration Studies*, vol. 25, no. 4.

Solé, Carlotta, Natalia Ribas, Valeria Bergali and Sonia Parella (1998) 'Irregular Employment Among Migrants in Spanish Cities', *Journal of Ethnic and Migration Studies*, vol. 24, no. 2.

Solomos, John (1988) *Black Youth, Racism and the State: The Politics of Ideology and Policy*, Cambridge: Cambridge University Press.

Soysal, Yasemin N. (1994) *Limits to Citizenship: Migrants and Post-national Membership in Europe*, Chicago: Chicago University Press.

Statewatch, various issues, Statewatch: London. www.statewatch.org

Statham, Paul (2001) 'Political Opportunities for Altruism? The Role of State Policies in Influencing British Anti-Racist and Pro-Migrant Movements', in Marco Giugni and Florence Passy (eds) *Solidarity Movements in International Perspective*, New York: Rowman and Littlefield.

Stetter, Stephan (2000) 'Regulating Migration: Authority Delegation in Justice and Home Affairs', *Journal of European Public Policy*, vol. 7, no. 1.

Stigler, George (1971) 'The Theory of Economic Regulation', *Bell Journal of Economics and Management Science*, vol. 2, no. 2.

Stone Sweet, Alec and Wayne Sandholtz (1997) 'European Integration and Supranational Governance', *Journal of European Public Policy*, vol. 4, no. 3.

Studlar, Donley (1974) 'British Public Opinion, Colour Issues and Enoch Powell: A Longitudinal Analysis, *British Journal of Political Science*, vol. 4, no. 3.

Swedish Migration Board (2001) *Population Statistics 2001*, Stockholm: Swedish Migration Board.

Szczerbiak, Aleks (2001) 'Polish Public Opinion: Explaining Declining Support for EU Membership' *Journal of Common Market Studies*, vol. 39, no. 1.

Taguieff, Pierre-André (1991) *Face au Racisme*, Paris: La Découverte.

Tapinos, Georges (1994) 'Commentary: Questioning the Hidden Consensus' in Wayne Cornelius, Philip Martin and James Hollifield (eds) *Controlling Immigration: A Global Perspective*, Stanford (CA.): Stanford University Press.

Taylor, Charles (1992) *Multiculturalism and the Politics of Recognition*, Princeton (NJ): Princeton University Press.

Thränhardt, Dietrich (1999) 'Germany's Immigration Policies and Politics', in Grete Brochmann and Tomas Hammar (eds) *Mechanisms of Immigration Control: A Comparative Analysis of European Regulation Policies*, Oxford: Berg.

Thränhradt, Dietrich (2000) 'Conflict, Consensus and Policy Outcomes: Immigration and Integration in Germany and the Netherlands' in Ruud Koopmans and Paul Statham (eds) *Challenging Immigration and Ethnic Relations Politics: Comparative European Perspectives*, Oxford: Oxford University Press.

Time Magazine (1987) 'Unnatural Selection', vol. 50, no. 12, 22 September.

Triandafyllidou, Anna (2000) 'Racists? Us? Are you Joking? The Discourse of Social Exclusion of Immigrants in Greece and Italy', in Russell King, Gabriella Lazaridis and Charalambos Tsardanidis (eds) *Eldorado or Fortress? Migration in Southern Europe*, Macmillan: London

Tribalat, Michele (1995) *Faire France: Une Grande Enquete sur les Immigrés et leurs Enfants*, Paris: La Decouverte.

Tyson, Adam (2001) 'The Negotiation of the European Community Directive on Racial Discrimination', *European Journal of Migration and Law*, vol. 3, no. 2.

Uçarer, Emek (2001) 'From the Sidelines to Center Stage: Sidekick no More? The European Commission in Justice and Home Affairs', *European Integration On-Line Papers*, http://eiop.or.at/eiop/texte/2001-005a.htm

United Nations High Commission for Refugees (UNHCR) (2000) *The State of the Worlds Refugees*, Oxford: Oxford University Press.

Vachudová, Milada (2000) 'Eastern Europe as Gatekeeper: The Immigration and Asylum Policies of an Enlarging European Union', in Peter Andreas and Timothy Snyder (eds) *The Wall Around the West: State Borders and Immigration Control in Europe and North America*, Lanham (MD): Rowman and Littlefield.

Van Amersfoort, Hans (1982) *Immigration and the Formation of Minority Groups: The Dutch Experience 1945–75*, Cambridge: Cambridge University Press.

Van Amersfoort, Hans (1999) 'Migration Control and Migration Policy: The Case of the Netherlands' in Grete Brochmann and Tomas Hammar (1999) *Mechanisms of Immigration Control: A Comparative Analysis of European Regulatory Policies*, Oxford: Berg.

Van Selm, Joanne (2002) 'Comprehensive immigration policy as foreign policy?', in Sandra Lavenex and Emek Uçarer, (eds) *Migration and the Externalities of European Integration*, Lanham (MD): Lexington.

Venice Commission (2001) *Report on the Preferential Treatment of National Minorities by their Kin-state*, adopted by the Venice Commission at its 48th Plenary Meeting, Venice, October 19–20, 2001.

Vertovec, Steven (1999) 'Conceiving and Researching Transnationalism', *Ethnic and Racial Studies*, vol. 22, no. 2.

Vink, Maarten (2001a) 'The Limited Europeanization of Domestic Asylum Policy: EU Governments and Two-Level Games', Paper presented to the First YEN Research Meeting on Europeanization, University of Siena, Italy, November 2–3, 2001.

Vink, Maarten (2001b) 'The Limited Europeanization of Domestic Citizenship Policy: Evidence from the Netherlands', *Journal of Common Market Studies*, vol. 39, no. 5.

Wayland, Sarah (1993) 'Mobilizing to Defend Nationality Law in France', *New Community*, vol. 20, no. 1.

Weil, Patrick (1991) *La France et ses étrangers: L'aventure d'une Politique de l'Immigration 1938–1991*, Paris: Calmann-Levy.

Weil, Patrick (1994) 'Commentary: From Hidden Consensus to Hidden Divergence', in Wayne Cornelius, Philip Martin and James Hollifield (eds) *Controlling Immigration: A Global Perspective*, Stanford (CA.): Stanford University Press.

Weil, Patrick (1997) *Mission d'études des legislations de la nationalité et de l'immigration*, Paris: La Documentation Français.

Weil, Patrick and John Crowley (1994) 'Integration in Theory and Practice: A Comparison of France and Britain', *West European Politics*, vol. 17, no. 2.

Wieviorka, Michel (1992) *La France Raciste*, Paris: Fayard.

Wihtol de Wenden, Catherine (1988) *Les Immigrés et La Politique*, Paris: Presse de la Fondation Nationale des Sciences Politiques.

Wihtol de Wenden, Catherine (1994) 'The French response to the Asylum-Seeker Influx' *The Annals of the American Academy of Social and Political Sciences*, Special Edition, Mark Miller (ed.) Strategies for Immigration Control in Liberal Societies, vol. 534, July.

Wilpert, Czarina (1993) 'Ideological and Institutional Foundations of Racism in the Federal Republic of Germany', in John Wrench and John Solomos (eds) *Racism and Migration in Western Europe*, Oxford: Berg.

Wilson, James Q. (1981) *The Politics of Regulation*, New York: Basic Books.

Wrench, John and John Solomos (1992) *Racism and Migration in Western Europe*, Oxford: Berg.

Zielonka, Jan (2001) 'How New Enlarged Borders Will Reshape the European Union', *Journal of Common Market Studies*, vol. 39, no. 3.

Zincone, Giovanna (1999) 'Illegality, Enlightenment and Ambiguity: A Hot Italian Recipe', *South European Society and Politics*, vol. 3, no. 3.

Zincone, Giovanna (ed.) (2000) *Primo Rapporto sull'Integrazione degli Immigrati in Italia*, Commissione per le Politiche di Integrazione degli Immigrati, Bologna: il Mulino.

Zincone, Giovanna (ed.) (2001) *Secondo Rapporto sull'Integrazione degli Immigrati in Italia*, Commissione per le Politiche di Integrazione degli Immigrati, Bologna: il Mulino.

Zolberg, Aristide (1989) 'The Next Waves: Migration Theory for a Changing World', *International Migration Review*, vol. 23, no. 3.

Zolberg, Aristide, Astri Suhrkre and Sergio Aguayo (1989) *Escape from Violence: Conflict and the Refugee Crisis in the Developing World*, New York: Oxford University Press.

Index

Lightning Source UK Ltd.
Milton Keynes UK
UKOW04f0103311014

240763UK00001B/44/P